STUDYING JOHN

STUDYING JOHN

Approaches to the Fourth Gospel

John Ashton

CLARENDON PRESS · OXFORD
1994

Oxford University Press, Great Clarendon Street, Oxford OX2 6DP

Oxford New York
Athens Auckland Bangkok Bogota Bombay
Buenos Aires Calcutta Cape Town Dar es Salaam
Delhi Florence Hong Kong Istanbul Karachi
Kuala Lumpur Madras Madrid Melbourne
Mexico City Nairobi Paris Singapore
Taipei Tokyo Toronto Warsaw
and associated companies in
Berlin Ibadan

Oxford is a trade mark of Oxford University Press

Published in the United States by
Oxford University Press Inc., New York

British Library Cataloguing in Publication Data
Data available

Library of Congress Cataloging in Publication Data
Studying John : approaches to the fourth Gospel.
John Ashton.
Includes bibliographical references and index.
1. Bible. N.T. John—Criticism, interpretation, etc.   I. Title.
BS2615.2.A73 1994   226.5'06—dc20   94-16379
ISBN 0-19-826355-4

3 5 7 9 10 8 6 4 2

Printed in Great Britain
on acid-free paper by
Antony Rowe Ltd.,
Chippenham

For Bob and Prue

ACKNOWLEDGEMENTS

I wish to thank the many friends who have helped me during the writing of this book, especially those who have taken the trouble to comment upon one or more of its chapters—without always expressing agreement. I need to say a special word about Chapter 3, which is a drastically revised version of a lecture delivered successively, during the winter semester of 1991, in the Memorial University, St John's, Newfoundland; Holy Cross College, Worcester, Mass.; and Loyola University, Chicago; and subsequently, the following summer, in Oxford, to the New Testament Seminar. I wish to express my thanks to James Bradley, Frederick Murphy, David Aune, and Christopher Rowland for their friendly invitations and generally helpful comments; also to the staff and students of the Weston School of Theology at Cambridge for their hospitality in the winter and spring of 1991. To these names must be added those of Robert Carroll, Peter Coxon, John Day, John Hyman, Stephen Moore, Robert Morgan, Emer O'Beirne, John Penney, and Douglas Templeton. I am grateful to the staff of the Theology Faculty Centre, now led by Anita Holmes, for their ready assistance, and to Jacqueline Dean and Richard Lindo, at the desk of Bodley's Lower Reading Room, for their helpfulness and patience. The sharp and attentive eyes of Heather Watson, a matchless copy-editor, spotted numerous errors in the draft manuscript, and I am greatly indebted to her, as well as to her colleagues at OUP who have helped to see the book through the various and varied stages of the publishing process. When my ageing printer spluttered to a halt at the very last moment, Mark Goodacre generously came to my assistance. Lastly, I have to thank Cambridge University Press and E. J. Brill, Leiden, respectively, for permission to reprint what are now Chapters 1 and 2.

CONTENTS

ABBREVIATIONS

Anth. Graec.		Anthologia Graeca
Apoc. Abr.		Apocalypse of Abraham
Bib.		Biblica
BZ		Biblische Zeitschrift
CBQ		Catholic Biblical Quarterly
CII		Corpus Inscriptionum Iudaicarum
DB Sup.		Dictionnaire de la Bible, Supplément
ET		English translation
EvT		Evangelische Theologie
Exp.		Expositor
ExpT		Expository Times
IGRR		Inscriptiones Graecae ad Res Romanas Pertinentes, ed. R. Gagrat *et al.*
Int.		Interpretation
JAC		Jahrbuch für Antike und Christentum
JAOS		Journal of the American Oriental Society
JBL		Journal of Biblical Literature
JJS		Journal of Jewish Studies
Josephus,	*AJ*	Antiquitates Judaicae
	Ap.	Contra Apionem
	BJ	De Bello Judaico
JQR		Jewish Quarterly Review
JSNT		Journal for the Study of the New Testament
JTS		Journal of Theological Studies
NT		Novum Testamentum
NTS		New Testament Studies
Odes Sol.		Odes of Solomon
ST		Studia Theologica
T. Asher		Testament of Asher
T. Mos.		Testament of Moses
TRu.		Theologische Rundschau
Vig. Chr.		Vigiliae Christianae
ZNW		Zeitschrift für die neutestamentliche Wissenschaft
ZTK		Zeitschrift für Theologie und Kirche

INTRODUCTION

'That's good,' said a colleague of mine a couple of years ago, when I told him that I was writing another book on John and was thinking of calling it *Studying the Fourth Gospel*, 'First *Understanding*, then *Studying*; maybe you'll follow that up with a book called *Reading the Fourth Gospel*.' Such is not my intention; but of course many scholars have written even more extensively on what has been rightly called 'this perennially fascinating Gospel'. The present collection of essays rides into the arena on the back of my earlier book, *Understanding the Fourth Gospel*; but, having arrived, it is meant to stand on its own feet without further shielding or support.

The eight chapters of this book appear here in the order in which they were written, and are linked only loosely and incidentally. The first two were written and published during the composition of *Understanding*, which incorporates their central theses in a compressed form. The arguments needed to establish these were too intricate to fit comfortably in what was already turning out to be a very long book. Apart from a few minor corrections they are printed here as they first appeared, except that I have translated a few lines here and there to make them accessible to readers with no German and little Greek. Both seem to me to be worth republishing, although Chapter 1 would undoubtedly have been written differently had I been acquainted at the time with Jarl Fossum's proposal that the Logos in the Prologue is a veiled (or maybe not-so-veiled) reference to the Name of God.[1] I think he makes a persuasive case for this thesis. He himself regards it as incompatible with the theory, already advanced by numerous scholars, that there is a conscious allusion to the wisdom tradition in the Prologue; but perhaps he is wrong about this.

Chapter 2 should be now read in the light of a pair of articles by Peter J. Tomson,[2] whose work supplements my own by including

---

[1] In an unpublished paper, 'The Background of the Johannine Logos Doctrine', given to an Oxford New Testament Seminar in 1992. See too his book, *Name of God*.

[2] 'Jonson' in the bibliography of the first two printings of *Understanding*.

many more references to sources in Hebrew and Aramaic; but I remain unconvinced by his interpretation of the Ἰουδαῖοι in John.

The remaining six chapters were composed between January 1991 and September 1993. The most important of these, in my view, is the first: Chapter 3.[3] It fills in what I had come to recognize, even before the publication of *Understanding*, as a serious gap. How did the community move from the low christology of the messianic signs-source to the high christology that was to determine its departure from the synagogue? Such answer as I was able to give in *Understanding* was contained in chapter 9, 'The Son of Man'. But it will not do, if only because that title nowhere figures in the major series of altercations between Jesus and 'the Jews' which, as I had argued in an earlier chapter, testify both to the eventual rupture between the two parties in the synagogue (one conservative, followers of Moses; the other radical, followers of Jesus) and to the *causes* of that rupture. The title at the heart of these altercations is not 'Son of Man' but 'Son of God'. Jan-Adolf Bühner had already shown that the former title is nowhere associated in the Gospel with the theme of mission: the emissary and agent is not the Son of Man but the Son of God.[4] At a certain point in *Understanding* (which I can now locate with some precision as pp. 351–2), I had come within reach of what now seems to me the obvious answer; but in the space of a page or two I had veered away from it again.[5] I hope then that Chapter 3 of the present book will help to fill the gap and redress the balance.

Chapter 4 was to have been a review-article of Robert Fortna's second important book on the signs-source theory, but it rapidly

---

[3] This chapter is a drastically revised version of a lecture delivered successively, in the winter semester of 1991, in the Memorial University, St John's, Newfoundland; Holy Cross College, Worcester, Mass.; and Loyola University, Chicago. A year later I read a slightly adapted version to a study-group under the auspices of the University of Exeter, and again the following year to Christopher Rowland's New Testament Seminar in Oxford. I wish to express my thanks to James Bradley, Frederick Murphy, David Aune, and David Catchpole for their friendly invitations, and also to the staff and students of the Weston School of Theology at Cambridge for their hospitality in 1991. I am grateful to all those named above, and also to Peter Coxon, John Day, and Robert Morgan for their helpful comments on earlier drafts of this paper.

[4] *Gesandte*, 406–7.

[5] See too the conclusion of chapter 8: 'the themes I have discussed in this chapter, origins, mission, agency, sonship, do not, even in combination, account for the whole of the Gospel's high christology or explain how it was actually generated.'

got out of hand. Major theories of this kind should be re-examined and re-evaluated from time to time, particularly when, as in this case, scholars on the two sides of the divide appear to have ceased to be able to communicate with one another. I am conscious, however, that my own attempt to arbitrate between the various positions is rather dry and technical. Had the chapter figured in *Understanding* it would have been relegated to an excursus: anyone deterred by this remark would be well advised to skip it altogether.

Chapter 5 was provoked by a collection of articles on the shepherd discourse which I had been sent for review.[6] This raised, but failed to tackle, the question of the reciprocal relations between diachronic and synchronic approaches of this passage; and I decided to try my hand at this difficult exercise. At the same time I was interested in examining a passage from what, following Barnabas Lindars, I take to be the second edition of the Gospel. In *Understanding* I had deliberately focused on the first edition and said little about any of the numerous passages (not only 10: 1–18, but also chapters 6, 11, 15–16, 17, not to mention 21), which all seem to me to stem from a later period in the history of the Johannine community. But the passage is complex and my discussion tentative.

Chapter 6 was written in fulfilment of a promise to return to the topic of literary approaches.[7]

Chapter 7 is related, though in different ways, to two of the preceding chapters. Most obviously to Chapter 1, for it takes up the wisdom theme prominent in the Prologue but unobtrusive elsewhere in the Gospel. I suggest that under the surface it continues to play a key role. At the same time this chapter may be seen as the positive panel of a diptych whose negative side is on view in Chapter 6. Cannot something be made of the narrative approach after all?

Chapter 8, the concluding chapter, which gives the book its title, is largely a defence of the aims and methods of what is generally known as historical criticism. Most scholars of a traditional bent might be surprised at the suggestion that any such defence should be necessary: historical critics may not be actively supported by the advocates of the new methods, but they are usually left in

---

[6] J. Beutler and R. T. Fortna (eds.), *The Shepherd Discourse of John 10 and its Context.*

[7] *Understanding*, 114 n. 1.

peace to do their own thing. The rather polemical tone of this chapter will be more comprehensible if it is seen as a response to a critical review of *Understanding* which appeared in the spring of 1993.[8] Doubts were cast on my unquestioning acceptance of the assumptions of historical criticism; convinced that I had dismissed far too lightly the contributions of the more recent critical methods, 'from narratology to reader response to deconstruction', the reviewer charged me with a lack of theoretical acumen. It will be evident, I hope, that my previous neglect of the new methods was not unreflecting but deliberate.

The essays in this book represent only a few of the many possible approaches that might be fruitfully adopted in studying the Gospel. Others have been left aside because they seem to me to be dead-ends, and yet others (such as the attempt to trace direct links between this Gospel and the other three) largely because I have nothing new to contribute to them. As for what is here— 'habent sua fata libelli': small books must fend for themselves.

---

[8] *JBL* 112 (1993), 154–6.

I

The Transformation of Wisdom

There are two fundamental questions concerning the Prologue of John's Gospel, one literary, the other historical. The literary question was raised by Bultmann in his seminal article for the Gunkel Festschrift of 1923: 'Up to what point is the pre-existent Logos the subject of the passage, and at what point is he succeeded by the historical Jesus?'[1] The commentators, remarks Bultmann, disagree on the answer to this question, and this disagreement has persisted. For Bultmann the main difficulty arises from the fact that although v. 14 offers the first *explicit* statement of the Incarnation, the Christian reader cannot but take vv. 10f. as an allusion to the life of Jesus, and consequently also v. 5 (which is parallel to it) and probably v. 4 also. Bultmann's solution was to see the Prologue as a pre-Christian Gnostic hymn, stemming from Baptist circles and subsequently taken over by the evangelist and adapted to form the opening of the Gospel. There have been many different answers since.[2]

The second question belongs to the history of religions. Bultmann expressed it in terms of myth, specifically the origin and function of the myth of pre-existence. This formulation was consistent with his belief that the origin of the Prologue was pre-Christian. I prefer to ask directly what a study of the Jewish wisdom tradition can tell us about the meaning of the Prologue.

These two questions are interdependent, and it might be thought best to begin, as Bultmann did, by offering a tentative solution to the literary question. I adopt the alternative course, in the belief that there is still something fresh to be learned from the wisdom literature about the way the Prologue is to be read. First, though, I think it advisable to summarize my own methodological assumptions:

[1] 'Background', p. 19.
[2] Cf. R. A. Culpepper, 'Pivot', who remarks that 'recent commentators are fairly evenly divided on the question of whether the work of the Word in vv. 9–12 is *asarkos* or *ensarkos*' (p. 13). And he adds a long note summarizing the various positions.

1. Behind the Prologue there was a written text or *Vorlage*. This is commonly called a 'hymn', a term which I adopt without committing myself to any form-critical position it may suggest. This text was adapted to serve as the introduction of what we now know as the Fourth Gospel.

2. The adaptation was made by inserting vv. 6–8 and v. 15 into the text, and possibly making further additions and/or alterations as well. I make no assumptions about these; but I shall argue that v. 14 did belong to the *Vorlage*.

3. Any exegesis that depends upon a precisely accurate reconstruction of the *Vorlage* is open to suspicion. This is not because such a reconstruction would be unhelpful, but because it is virtually unattainable. Not one of the many different versions that have been proposed compels assent, and few are immune from the charge of special pleading.[3] In general most of the purely stylistic arguments advanced in favour of one version or other of the hymn are too subjective to command a wide following.

4. The first place to look for the source of any particular element in the Fourth Gospel is in the Jewish Christianity where the Gospel took its rise. In this case the Jewish wisdom tradition that has long been acknowledged to have influenced, directly or indirectly, the author of the hymn, is still the best place to start.[4]

5. I do *not* assume that the hymn was composed before the body of the Gospel. Rather I think it likely that it was written at a time when the composition of the Gospel was well under way. But I shall not be arguing this point here.

I. THE HISTORY-OF-RELIGIONS QUESTION

We do not need to ask from what source the author of the hymn derived his ideas, for both the general theme and the specific

---

[3] See e.g. W. Schmithals, 'Prolog'. Of his own highly speculative and disputable reconstruction he makes the astonishing assertion: 'There can be no doubt about the correctness of the restored hymn and the reconstruction' (p. 33).

[4] The publication of the so-called Trimorphic Protennoia in 1974 has revived speculation about possible Gnostic sources of the Prologue. Like all the other suggested Gnostic sources it is too late to have been a direct influence, and in spite of certain verbal resemblances is too far away in spirit to be regarded as anything but a thin rivulet whose origins are perhaps to be sought in the same broad stream of wisdom speculation from which the Prologue also took its rise. Cf. C. Colpe, 'Überlieferung'.

details are abundantly illustrated in the wisdom tradition.[5] Rather we have to ask what there was in the tradition which could have stimulated his own imaginative response: what precisely did he take from it? (There is a further question that may be asked, in the wake of Martyn[6] and Meeks,[7] concerning the relevance of the tradition to the life of the Johannine community: this may be deferred till later.)

For our purposes the most important general feature of the tradition is the combination of two initially distinct types of wisdom, which I shall call the accessible and the remote. Bultmann saw in the Prologue a contradiction between what he called 'the Logos as an immanent cognitive power and as the bearer of revelation',[8] adding that so far from being confined to the Prologue, this contradiction is a presupposition of all Jewish wisdom literature. I am suspicious of the notion of wisdom as an immanent force, and feel that 'tension' is a more appropriate term than 'contradiction'. But that there is a constant tension or at least a contrast between the accessible and the remote seems beyond question.

It is unnecessary here to venture into the tangled thicket surrounding the question of the distant origins of Israel's wisdom tradition. Traces of the early association of חכמה with skills and crafts persist as late as Ben Sira, who says of the farmer as well as of the engraver, the smith, and the potter: ἕκαστος ἐν τῷ ἔργῳ αὐτοῦ σοφίζεται: 'each of them is skilled in his own craft' (38: 31). If one were to take *1 Enoch* seriously even the skills of the smith and the beautician (not just sorcery and astronomy) would have to be numbered among 'the eternal secrets which were made in heaven' (9: 6); but at least in the canonical books the contrast between the available and the remote forms of wisdom is quite

---

[5] As far as I am aware this debt has not actually been questioned since Rendel Harris's series of articles in the *Expositor* of 1916. This began and ended with a version of the Prologue substituting the word *Sophia* for the word *Logos*, which was backed up with an array of texts from the Jewish wisdom literature that have been cited regularly ever since. In a book of the same title published the following year, Harris expanded his thesis, though he failed to add Baruch 3 to his list of references. Beside Bultmann's 'Background', Harris's treatment seems oddly superficial.

[6] J. L. Martyn, *History and Theology; The Gospel of John*. Martyn has promised an extended study of the Prologue based on the literary seam Käsemann claimed to have discerned after v. 13; cf. 'Source Criticism'.

[7] W. A. Meeks, 'Man from Heaven'.

[8] 'Background', 30.

plain. Typical of available wisdom are the sensible observations of
Prov. 25–9, a collection which opens by making the very point I
wish to establish here: 'it is the glory of God to conceal things,
but the glory of kings is to search things out' (Prov. 25: 2). The
maxims that follow are no doubt to be seen as typical examples of
the results of the king's (in the case, Solomon's) researches, the
first of which, piquantly, concerns his own inscrutability.

The most outstanding account of remote wisdom comes in Job
28, a profound poem on the essential mysteriousness and inaccessibility of חכמה\בינה conceived somehow as immanent in creation.
Its conclusion is surprising: 'Behold, the fear of the Lord, that
is wisdom; and to depart from evil is understanding' (v. 28).
Commentators are surely right to see this final verse as a later
addition: what was utterly beyond man's reach is suddenly transformed into something not just available but commendable, not
just possible but necessary. There is, however, no real attempt here
to reconcile the two conceptions: the poem is left untouched, with
its mystery undiminished by the rather crude counter-assertion
added at the end.

This assertion is certainly the orthodox answer to the question
how to set about acquiring wisdom. This may be why an alternative (and no doubt earlier) answer is omitted by the LXX
translator: 'The beginning of wisdom is this: Get (קְנֵה) wisdom; and
whatever you get, get understanding' (Prov. 4: 7).[9] But in both
cases wisdom/understanding is portrayed as accessible, directly
available to anyone who sets about obtaining it in the right way.

In one respect Job 28, with its unexpected ending, is typical of
much of the literature as it has been transmitted; for the contrast
between the accessible and the remote appears quite frequently,
occasionally underlined, yet usually presented in such a way as
to leave the resolution open. It occurs for instance even more
startlingly in a passage in Proverbs where the same pair of terms,
חכמה\תבונה is used on the one hand to proclaim, 'Happy the man
who finds wisdom, and the man who gets understanding (3: 13),

---

[9] I do not agree with W. McKane, *Proverbs*, 305, that this is 'a weaker sense'
than the alternative: 'Wisdom comes first, [therefore] get wisdom.' On the contrary, it suggests to me a profound understanding of the hermeneutical circle, not
too far from Horace's dictum (part of which Kant adopted as his motto); 'dimidium
facti qui coepit habet: sapere aude: Incipe.' McKane now thinks, he informs me,
that in the second half of Prov. 4: 7 בכל קִנְיָנְךָ is best seen as a *beth pretii*: 'sell all
your possessions to get בינה'.

and on the other to assert that 'the Lord by wisdom founded the earth; by understanding he established the heavens' (3: 19).[10]

In the last two chapters of the same collection (Prov. 8-9), wisdom/understanding is personified in two strangely contrasting ways. First, we recognize the brash, importunate teacher, first met in Prov. 1: 29ff., who takes her stand on the heights beside the way and at the entrance of the gates (Prov. 8: 1-21), and then, without warning, as if the two figures were identical, we are confronted with the favourite of Yahweh,[11] whom he acquired or engendered[12] at the beginning of his dominion. The LXX translator shows his awareness of the abrupt switch by inserting a transitional verse of his own at this point: ἐὰν ἀναγγείλω ὑμῖν τὰ καθ᾽ ἡμέραν γινόμενα, μνημονεύσω τὰ ἐξ αἰῶνος ἀριθμῆσαι: 'If I explain everyday things to you, I will (also) remind you to reckon the things of eternity' (8: 21a). The contrast between the quotidian and the eternal is equally a contrast between the accessible and the remote. One might observe that there is an eternal or at least a timeless quality about the quotidian as well: 'there is nothing new under the sun' (Qoh. 1: 9). Wisdom literature delves into the inexhaustible fund of human experience.

Prov. 8: 22-31 is the earliest passage in the Bible to show a real affinity with the Johannine Prologue. But apart from the shared reference to 'the beginning' of Genesis, the affinity is easier to spot than to define. The poem is put in the mouth of Wisdom, a feminine presence never actually named. She begins by asserting, ambiguously, her close relationship with Yahweh, who has made her peculiarly his own. She has come into existence (begotten, not made?) before the world, witnesses its ordered making, and then, chosen by Yahweh as his regular companion (even playmate), concludes by expressing her delight in the human race. She resembles Puck, ready to 'put a girdle round about the earth', or Ariel, dancing attendance upon Prospero, and the commentators rarely do justice to her elusive gaiety. Does she actually descend to

---

[10] Cf. G. von Rad, *Wisdom in Israel*, 151 n. 4.

[11] The interpretation favoured by the Rabbis, 'master-workman' (foreperson?), reading אָמוֹן, does not really fit the context.

[12] The LXX rendering (ἔκτισεν), which caused such trouble to subsequent Christian commentators, may simply be wrong. Bruce Vawter has argued that 'in no single instance in the OT or in relevant cognate literature are we compelled by the evidence to ascribe to the verb קנה in any of its forms the sense "create"': *JBL* 99 (1980), 205-16.

earth, to play in God's world? Or does v. 31 refer, as McKane thinks, to 'the delightful confidences and reminiscences which Wisdom can share with Yahweh, just because she saw the world coming into existence'?[13] It is hard to be sure. Certainly the יֹם יֹם and בְּכָל־עֵת of v. 30 forbid us to pinpoint her activity. There is something quotidian as well as eternal about her. Her role is to illuminate the creative work of Yahweh, to tell the men to whom she speaks, subtly and indirectly, of *his* attitudes; she reveals a mystery, but says no more *about* it than what is known already. To borrow a phrase of Bultmann, she reveals no more than that she is the revealer.

What is missing from all early personifications of wisdom is any sense of history. Neither the quotidian nor the eternal has a *career*, which is why it is probably a mistake to speak of the personified wisdom of Proverbs 8 in terms of myth. And as long as the two kinds of wisdom, accessible and remote, remain simply contiguous, the contrast between them felt but not discussed and not resolved, there will be no history. History belongs, though in different ways, not to wisdom but to the law and the prophets. How is the remote made accessible, and what happens when it is?

To answer this question it is helpful to put the contrast in a different way. Available wisdom, while it may be taught, is essentially a matter of *experience*. Remote wisdom, if it is to be brought within man's grasp, has to be *revealed*.

In post-exilic Judah the prevailing orthodoxy, that of the deuteronomists, which was to persist into Judaism, insisted that *the* object of revelation was the law, the Torah. Alternative revelations, like the one reprimanded (but none the less described) in the first section of 1 *Enoch*, were unacceptable to this school, which may be why there is so little reference to them in the canonical books. A practical wisdom is of course admissible. Solomon prays for a receptive mind (לֵב שֹׁמֵעַ) 'to discern between good and evil' (a tiny essay in demythologization); and his prayer is granted by the bestowal of a wise and understanding mind (לֵב חָכָם וְנָבוֹן) (1 Kings 3: 9, 12). But there is no mystery here.

The threat to orthodoxy, as one may fairly put it, was felt to come from a remote wisdom irreducible to the kind of practical φρόνησις exhibited by Solomon. It is illustrated in a passage from Proverbs which opens with a verse of such obscurity that it has

[13] *Proverbs*, 358.

left the commentators baffled ('hardly a glimmer of light', says McKane).[14] There has clearly been some tinkering with the text here, which continues, 'I have not learned wisdom, nor have I knowledge of the Holy Ones.'[15] There follows a sardonic riddle:

> Who has ascended to heaven and come down?
> Who has gathered the wind in his fists?
> Who has wrapped up the waters in a garment?
> Who has established all the ends of the earth?
> What is his name, and what is his son's name?
> Surely you know!

> (Prov. 30: 1-4)

'Surely you know' implies 'of course you don't know', for here are mysteries beyond human ken, mysteries which exert a fascination that Deuteronomy, in what appears to be a subsequent insertion into an already late text, is anxious to dispel: 'For this commandment which I command you this day is not too hard for you, neither is it far off. It is not in heaven, that you should say, "Who will go up for us to heaven, and bring it to us, that we may hear it and do it?" Neither is it beyond the sea, that you should say, "Who will go over the sea for us, and bring it to us, that we may hear it and do it?" But the word is very near you; it is in your mouth and in your heart, so that you can do it' (Deut. 30: 11-14).

The remote and inaccessible wisdom (though not named as such) is thus swallowed up by the law, rendered harmless by proximity, a procedure which nicely coheres with the direct identification (in Deut. 4: 6, another late passage) of 'your' wisdom with the law, and clearly foreshadows Baruch and Ben Sira.[16]

---

[14] Ibid. 644.

[15] Margaret Barker, in an unpublished paper to which I am greatly indebted, challenges the widespread assumption that קדשׁים is to be read as a *pluralis maiestatis*. Why should it not have a plural reference (as it must in Job 5: 2; Zech. 14: 5; Ps. 89: 6, 8)? Barker believes that there was a 'deliberate process of mystification here', and compares the textual confusion surrounding Deut. 32: 8. (Perhaps קדשׁים was allowed to stand because it *can* have a singular reference, as in Hos. 12: 1, if the text is right.) Prov. 9: 10 is more doubtful.

[16] 'Keep them and do them [statutes and ordinances]; for that will be your wisdom and understanding in the sight of the peoples.' Barker sees in this passage an acknowledgement on the writer's part that wisdom is too important and traditional a category for him to exclude altogether (though no doubt he would dearly have liked to have done so). In subsuming wisdom under the law he was adopting the next best solution by harnessing this wayward and unpredictable animal to his own wagon. See also Deut. 29: 28, where 'the secret things' (הַנִּסְתָּרֹת) are declared

Baruch, in a profound poem (3: 9–4: 4) with an obvious indebtedness to Job 28, goes a long way towards restoring the sense of mystery banished in Deuteronomy. He is deeply aware of the elusiveness of wisdom (φρόνησις, used in synonymous parallelism with σοφία, σύνεσις, and ἐπιστήμη): 'Who has gone up to heaven, and taken her, and brought her down from the clouds? Who has gone over the sea, and found her, and will buy her for pure gold? No one knows the way to her or has given thought to her path' (3: 29–31). Only God, who knows the entire universe (τὰ πάντα), is said to have found her by his understanding (τῇ συνέσει αὐτοῦ, v. 32) and again: ἐξεῦρεν πᾶσαν ὁδὸν ἐπιστήμης (v. 36). Yet Israel at least had no need to set out on this search, having already been reproached for deserting 'the fountain of wisdom' (3: 12). Had she only walked in the way of God she could have dwelt in peace for ever (3: 13) Thus wisdom is at once mysterious and ready to hand. The author appears to chide Israel for failing to recognize the gift that was hers alone: for God 'gave her to Jacob his servant and to Israel whom he loved—afterward she appeared upon earth and lived among men' (3: 36f.). Then comes the explicit identification: αὕτη ἡ βίβλος τῶν προσταγμάτων τοῦ θεοῦ καὶ ὁ νόμος ὁ ὑπάρχων εἰς αἰῶνα: 'she is the book of the commandments of God, and the law that endures for ever' (4: 1). Wisdom now has a history, but she has also invested the law with her own eternity.

At the beginning of the poem wisdom (φρόνησις) is identified with the ἐντολαὶ ζωῆς; and this theme now reappears: all those who hold fast to her will live (4: 1), and Jacob is urged to 'walk towards the shining of the light' (4: 2).

Ben Sira opens his work with a phrase that strikingly anticipates the Prologue: 'All wisdom comes from Yahweh, and has been with him from all eternity' (1: 1).[17] But in spite of his recognition that there are still unanswerable mysteries in the universe his book is full of a sense of the *availability* of wisdom. The mystery has been drained of all its challenge: man's inability to plumb the depths of wisdom no longer matters, since somehow or other wisdom, through the munificence of the creator, pervades the created

be God's exclusive preserve: 'the revealed things' (הַנִּגְלֹת), which belong to Israel, consist simply of 'all the words of this law'. Also Ezra 7: 11–26 (the letter of commission), where the law (v. 14), whatever its precise content, is clearly the same as wisdom (v. 25).

[17] R. Smend is surely right to prefer the Syriac ܚܟܡܬܐ to the Greek at this point: *Weisheit*, 6.

universe and in some unspecified way is made available to 'all flesh' (1: 10), but particularly to those who show due reverence and respect for their (and her) creator. The author asks, in the riddling manner of earlier sages, 'the root of wisdom, to whom has it been revealed?' (1: 6), but his own answer is all too easy: 'The root of wisdom is to fear the Lord' (1: 20). Indeed the fear of the Lord is not just the beginning of wisdom (1: 14) as it used to be, but its full measure (1: 16) and its crown (1: 18). If you want wisdom you must keep the commandments, 'and the Lord will supply it to you' (1: 26). From being a spontaneous outpouring (1: 9), the gift of wisdom comes to be seen as conditional upon right behaviour. There is nothing here a deuteronomist could quarrel with: 'For the fear of the Lord is wisdom and instruction, and he delights in fidelity and meekness' (1: 27). Furthermore, the unsearchable Wisdom of the opening paragraph is now pictured as owning (or perhaps simply identified with) a store of wise sayings ($\pi\alpha\rho\alpha\beta\text{o}\lambda\alpha\grave{\iota}$ $\grave{\epsilon}\pi\iota\sigma\tau\acute{\eta}\mu\eta\varsigma$: 1: 25), presumably of a kind familiar to any student of the law (cf. 39: 3). As Sira remarks later, 'Hidden wisdom and unseen treasure, what advantage is there in either of them?' (20: 30).

Of the two figures of wisdom, the mysterious and the available, it is then the latter who dominates this work (cf. 4: 11–19; 6: 18–31; 14: 20–15: 8).[18] The former, the companion of God, vanishes after the first few verses, not to reappear until the great hymn of ch. 24, undoubtedly the high point of the book. Even so, the central figure of this grand poem, which owes much to Proverbs 8, is only a distant relative of Yahweh's playful darling. She speaks of her search for a resting-place on earth, wondering 'in whose territory ($\kappa\lambda\eta\rho\text{o}\nu\text{o}\mu\acute{\iota}\alpha$) I might lodge' (v. 7). (Smend thinks that $\alpha\grave{\upsilon}\lambda\acute{\iota}\zeta\epsilon\sigma\theta\alpha\iota$ possibly reflects an original Hebrew שׁכן.) Then 'my creator assigned a place for my tent ($\sigma\kappa\eta\nu\acute{\eta}$) and said, "Make your dwelling ($\kappa\alpha\tau\alpha\sigma\kappa\acute{\eta}\nu\omega\sigma\text{o}\nu$) in Jacob"' (v. 8). The next stanza opens with a reference to the portion ($\mu\acute{\epsilon}\rho\text{o}\varsigma$) and inheritance ($\kappa\lambda\eta\rho\text{o}\nu\text{o}\mu\acute{\iota}\alpha$) of God,[19] which is when wisdom 'took root' (v. 12); and the fifth stanza, which is parallel to the third,[20] establishes the identity of 'all

---

[18] I cannot agree with von Rad, who discusses such texts as these under the general rubric 'Die Selbstoffenbarung der Schöpfung', *Weisheit*, 189–228. It is doubtful if this expression is strictly applicable even to such passages as Job 28 and Sirach 24.   [19] Alluding to LXX Deut. 32: 9, where both terms occur.
[20] Following Smend's division of the poem into 6 stanzas, beginning respectively vv. 1, 7, 12, 16, 23, 30.

these things' (i.e. the fruits of the tree of wisdom) with 'the book of the covenant of the Most High God, the law which Moses commanded us as an inheritance (κληρονομία) for the congregations of Jacob' (v. 23). The author is speaking in his own voice here, but though he reaffirms the unsearchability of wisdom, he is really talking about the law.[21] For all the profundity of the thought and the beauty of the imagery it is hard to rid oneself of the impression that wisdom has been domesticated in this poem.

The Book of Wisdom, in which all the main themes of the tradition coalesce in a remarkable way, falls into two parts, 1: 1–11: 1 and 11: 2–19: 22, of which the second takes up and extends the midrashic section with which the first part closes (10: 1–11: 1).

In the first half of ch. 6 the author is clearly appealing to the old tradition of Proverbs 1–9 whereby Wisdom goes out of her way to make herself accessible: 'She hastens to make herself known to those who desire her. He who rises early to seek her will have no difficulty, for he will find her sitting at his gates (πάρεδρον τῶν πυλῶν αὐτοῦ) . . . because she goes about seeking those who are worthy of her and she graciously appears to them in their paths, and meets them in every thought' (6: 13–16).

With another conscious reference to an old tradition, the author continues by speaking of the beginning of wisdom: 'For the beginning of wisdom (ἀρχὴ γὰρ αὐτῆς) is the most genuine desire for instruction, and concern for instruction is love of her' (6: 17; cf. Prov. 4: 7).

But then comes the strange promise: 'I will tell you what wisdom is and how she came to be (πῶς ἐγένετο), and I will hide no secrets (μυστήρια) from you, but will trace her course from the beginning of creation (ἀπ' ἀρχῆς γενέσεως). Here we have to do with a very different beginning and, one might think, with a very different kind of wisdom. [The author plays upon the term ἀρχὴ γενέσεως a little further on to refer to human conception and birth: 'no king has had a different ἀρχὴ γενέσεως' (from that of the rest of mankind): 7: 5.]

Having thus announced his intention to recount the genesis of wisdom, Greek Solomon tells instead how understanding and the

---

[21] Cf. *4 Ezra* 13: 54 f., which adapts a phrase from Prov. 7: 4 alluding to wisdom and understanding, and applies it to the study of the law.

spirit of wisdom were bestowed upon him personally in answer to a prayer—but his version of the prayer (cf. 1 Kings 3: 6-9) is held over until ch. 9. Throughout these chapters, in fact, supplication alternates with description. No biblical writer comes as close as this author to seeing wisdom as divine: 'she is a breath of the power of God, and a pure emanation of the glory of the almighty' (7: 25). Yet we are never allowed to forget that she is in God's gift: 'give me the wisdom that sits by thy throne (τῶν σῶν θρόνων πάρεδρον)' (9: 4). Nor can we any longer distinguish the intimate of God from the teacher of men. Seated by the throne of God or by the city gates (πάρεδρος is used in both cases) she is equally at home. The two figures of Proverbs 8 at last merge into one: 'With thee is wisdom, who knows thy works and was present when thou didst make the world . . . Send her forth from the holy heavens . . . that she may be with me and toil, and that I may learn what is pleasing to thee' (9: 9-10).

Nevertheless Greek Solomon's most significant and original contribution to the concept of wisdom, from our point of view, lies in the succinct comment with which he concludes his prayer: 'men were taught what pleases thee, *and were saved by wisdom*' (9: 18). The following chapter is a series of brilliant vignettes wherein wisdom is shown to have watched over the great men of Genesis, from Adam to Joseph, and to have planned and executed the crossing of the Red Sea.

With this portrayal of wisdom as the active agent in salvation history (here if anywhere that overworked term receives a proper application), the stage is finally set for her transformation into the Johannine Logos.

There is, however, one more passage demanding consideration, one which seems to mirror the career of the Logos particularly closely: 'Wisdom went out in order to dwell among the sons of men, but did not find a dwelling; wisdom returned to her place and took her seat in the midst of the angels' (1 *Enoch* 42: 1-2).

Coming as it does bereft of any contextual clues in a part of the book (the Parables) that has been suspected of Christian interference, this passage is not easy to handle. It looks like a deliberate contradiction of Baruch and Sirach: it was not wisdom but iniquity, so the passage continues, who on leaving her chambers 'found those whom she did not seek . . . and dwelt among them . . . like dew on parched ground' (42: 3). In the preceding section

Enoch has offered a view of wisdom as a revelation of mysteries *outside the law*, indeed a revelation in which wisdom herself could be virtually identified with iniquity, since in so far as they were transmitted by heavenly beings in revolt against God, these secrets were themselves the cause of human corruption: 'See then what Azazel has done, how he has taught all iniquity on the earth and revealed the eternal secrets which were made in heaven' (9: 6). The true, pure wisdom, contrary to the official teaching of orthodox writers like Ben Sira, did *not* find a home among men, and remained in heaven 'in the midst of the angels': wisdom 'does not turn away *from your throne*, nor from your presence' (84: 3).

This fact is not without significance, for it indicates that the milieu in which the Prologue took its rise cannot be identified *tout court* with the scribal school of thought represented most ably by Ben Sira but foreshadowed as early as Deuteronomy and the spurious conclusion to Job's great hymn. There were alternative (and opposing) views about wisdom held by at least some Jewish thinkers, and these are closer in certain respects to the spirit of the Prologue which, while using terminology highly reminiscent of Ben Sira, resists any suggestion that the wisdom who finally found a home on earth was to be identified with the Torah. Even if *1 Enoch* 42 were to prove to be a late reflection upon the Enochic tradition, it is the same *kind* of summary development that we find in the Prologue, where the Logos is not just a masculine surrogate of the feminine Wisdom but a conscious rival of the Law in his claim to be the unique vehicle of revelation and salvation. The writer of the Prologue, to be sure, unlike Enoch, takes a positive view of this alternative revelation: to disclose 'the eternal secrets which were made in heaven', far from being the work of a malign demon, was the proper function of Jesus Christ. What he disclosed or rather expounded (ἐξηγήσατο) was God himself, something which he could not have done unless he had been not just πρὸς τὸν θεόν but actually identified with God in a way left undefined.

This means that although in some respects, as Rendel Harris argued, the Prologue is the natural successor of the wisdom tradition, it stems from a part of that tradition which exhibits no tendency to domesticate Wisdom and attenuate her mystery. Moreover, if the Logos *did* find a home among men, it was not where he might naturally have been expected to settle ('his own received him not'), and his eventual tabernacling is recorded by the writer with some amazement. How the expression of this amazement is prepared and articulated will be discussed in the second part of this chapter.

This conclusion well accords with the dissociation between Christ and Torah at the end of the Prologue.[22] Whether or not v. 17 was part of the original *Vorlage*, it seems likely that this dissociation marks a polemical attitude on the writer's part (though of course the Torah continues to be seen itself a χάρις, a gift of God, and there is no hint of the kind of aggressiveness prominent in the third chapter of Galatians). If John has any real connection with *Enoch* (and how could this be shown?), he takes a stand against the pessimistic view of *1 Enoch* 42 that it was only iniquity who found a dwelling-place on earth. Paradoxically, in spite of his opposition to deuteronomistic orthodoxy, the author of the Prologue is confident that the mysterious wisdom of the old tradition *did* become accessible to men, and that the mystery was revealed—but not encapsulated in a written law, and not remaining on earth for ever in a directly tangible form.

2. THE LITERARY QUESTION

Turning back to the literary problem, the *meaning* of the text, we find that once again, as so often, Bultmann has put his finger on the key question. At what point does the hymn begin to refer to Jesus? The striking differences of opinion among the commentators[23] reflect, I suggest, a fundamental ambiguity *in the text itself*, and I therefore propose to approach Bultmann's question by testing two hypotheses:

(a) In the Prologue, at least as far as v. 14 we are faced with nothing more or less than a late example, almost certainly Christian, of the traditional Jewish speculation on the theme of Wisdom. The Prologue originated, in other words, as a hymn in praise of Wisdom.

(b) The theme as well as the treatment is specifically Christian. From start to finish the Prologue is a hymn to the Incarnate

---

[22] Whether the expression ἡ χάρις καὶ ἡ ἀλήθεια is a deliberate allusion to Exod. 34: 6 is another matter, and need not be settled here. Many commentators (e.g. Brown, Lindars) simply assume that it is. They may well be right, but it is hard to be sure because חסד is regularly translated by ἔλεος in the LXX.

[23] Cf. n. 2.

Word, properly and accurately summed up as 'the Word was made flesh'.

On the first hypothesis v. 14 represents a fresh and quite remarkable insight; on the second it is simply the final variant of the theme.

This approach has been anticipated to some extent by C. H. Dodd, who also attempts a double analysis, first from the perspective of what he calls 'the cosmical Logos', and secondly from that of 'the Logos incarnate'.[24] He carries this programme through with characteristic care and insight, but he leans too heavily on Hellenistic parallels and his solution ultimately fails to convince. Nevertheless, it scarcely deserves the high-handed treatment it receives at the hands of Käsemann, who dismisses it summarily and without argument as 'extremely dialectical'.[25] Barnabas Lindars follows Dodd in seeing in the paragraph leading up to the statement of the Incarnation 'two levels of meaning running along parallel lines'.[26] But he fails to pursue the implications of this view.

(a) A Wisdom hymn?

Clearly the hypothesis that we are dealing with a Wisdom hymn depends upon the excision, or rather bracketing, of vv. 6–8. For there can be no doubt that with these verses included the Prologue is dealing with the Incarnate Word at least from v. 9 on. But provided that all reference to the Baptist is excluded, and the difficult ἐρχόμενον εἰς τὸν κόσμον of v. 9 either regarded as an editorial insertion or else taken with ἄνθρωπον,[27] then there is nothing which does not fit in admirably with the hypothesis that the hymn is a Christian version of a traditional Wisdom theme.

Here we must briefly consider an important passage in the Dead

---

[24] *Interpretation*, 263–85. See also 'Prologue', 9–22.

[25] 'Structure', 144.

[26] *Gospel*, 78. A similar idea had already occurred to R. H. Lightfoot, *Gospel*, 81.

[27] This is how it is taken by all the ancient versions, with the possible exception of the Sahidic Coptic, which is ambiguous. Dodd, who is attracted by the suggestion that we have to do with an original Hebrew or Aramaic circumlocution for 'man', is also inclined to this rendering, as is E. Haenchen, *Johannesevangelium*, 126. But the majority of modern commentators agree that the versions are wrong at this point, and take ἐρχόμενον with φῶς. Nevertheless, the Greek is cumbersome and the order difficult. If the verse was composed *d'un seul jet*, which I doubt, then A. Feuillet has what appears to me the neatest solution: 'le Logos était la vraie lumière, qui illumine tout homme en venant dans le monde', 'Prologue', col. 633.

Sea Scrolls (1QS 11: 11) whose significance is generally overlooked. Cited by Bultmann without comment as a parallel to John
1: 3,[28] it is frequently quoted but seldom fruitfully. The first to
draw attention to what I believe to be its real significance was T. E.
Pollard,[29] who has been followed by P. Lamarche[30] and I. de la
Potterie.[31] Because of the importance of their suggestions I propose
to summarize their strongest arguments here and to add one or
two of my own.

Vermes translates the passage in question as follows:

> All things came to pass (נהיה) by His knowledge,
> He establishes all things by His design
> And without Him nothing is done (יעשה).[32]

As Pollard points out, the context of this passage in *The Manual of
Discipline* 'has no reference to creation, but rather to the doctrine
prominent in the Scrolls, that God is in control of everything, and
particularly of human destiny'.[33] Raymond Brown quotes the
passage, but glosses the final 'is done' with 'is made' in order to
bring it in line with the traditional interpretation.[34] But at least the
niph'al of היה, as Pollard points out, is not naturally rendered by a
verb expressing creation, an idea which in any case is foreign to
the context.

More significantly, the verb γίνεσθαι, without contextual support
such as it finds in Genesis 1, does not naturally refer to creation
either. Used regularly in the sense of 'happen' or 'come to pass', it
is a verb that corresponds well to the niph'al of היה, which, as
Pollard notes, is the form used by Delitzsch in his Hebrew translation of the Prologue. It is worth adding too that this is how the

But the text is very overloaded: surely a glossator has been at work! The likeliest
solution is that most of v. 9 was, as Brown suggests, composed by the editor
responsible for inserting the preceding three verses, with a view to facilitating the
transition to v. 10. Either ἄνθρωπον or its Semitic equivalent ἐρχόμενον εἰς τὸν κόσμον
will have been the original reading, with the synonym added later as a gloss.
Bultmann, followed by Schnackenburg, opted for the former solution in his early
article ('Background', 35 n. 34), but changed his mind in his commentary *Gospel*,
52 n. 2.

[28] Cf. *Gospel*, 37 n. 5.
[29] 'Cosmology.'
[30] 'Prologue.'
[31] *Vérité*, 162-6.
[32] *Dead Sea Scrolls*, 93.
[33] 'Cosmology', 152. The hymns are particularly redolent of this doctrine. See
1QH 1: 6-24; 4: 13; 10: 1, 9; 12: 10.
[34] *Gospel*, 6.

early Syriac translators understood it.[35] Lamarche also refers to a passage from the Gospel of Truth: 'Nothing happens without him (viz. the Logos), nor does anything happen without the Father's will' (37: 21). In this passage the Coptic is variously rendered 'happens' or 'comes into being', but the majority of translators opt for the former alternative, which, it must be said, is favoured by the context.[36] The latter rendering has clearly been influenced by the standard interpretations of the Prologue, itself the starting-point of the Gnostic commentary.

What about πάντα? De la Potterie argues that in New Testament times the regular expression for the created universe was τὰ πάντα. This is true, not just of the NT, but also, overwhelmingly, of the LXX.[37] The anarthrous form is common in the Johannine writings,

---

[35] The Sinaitic MS is defective at this point; the Curetonian reads ܒܗ ܗܘܐ ܟܠܡܕܡ ܘܒܠܥܕܘܗܝ. The pᵉ'al of ܗܘܐ is as generally unfitted as γίνεσθαι to express the sense of 'being created'. Burkitt's translation of the Curetonian version of Jn. 1: 3 reads: 'Everything came to pass in Him, and apart from Him not even one thing came to pass in Him': *Evangelion Da-Mepharreshe*, 423. This is also the sense required in *4 Ezra* 6: 6, where the Syriac reads ܗܘܐ and the Latin *facta sunt*. For an equivalent use of the niph'al of היה, see 1Q 27 1. i. 3-4: . . . ולוא ידעו רז נהיה לוא מלטו רז נהיה where the niph'al participle has a future meaning (Milik: *le mystère futur*; Sjöberg: *das zu verwirklichende Geheimnis*). Cf. 1Q 26 1: 1. I. Rabinowitz ('a mystery to be') compares CD 2. 10; 13. 8; 1QS 3: 15; 10: 5; 11: 3-4, 18; *JBL* 71 (1952), 19-32.

[36] Contrast 18: 34: 'the one who made the all'; cf. 19: 7.

[37] The form τὰ πάντα does not occur in the Pentateuch except for two highly significant instances in Genesis: Gen. 1: 31 ('God saw everything that he had made'), and Gen. 9: 3, where in making God give τὰ πάντα to Noah and his sons the translator is no doubt deliberately echoing the conclusion of chapter 1: after chaos, in the form of the flood, has been reconquered, the restored universe is handed back to mankind in the person of Noah. Apart from 3 Macc. 2: 3 (ὁ κτίσας τὰ πάντα), the few instances in the historical books (LXX 2 Kings 19: 30; 24: 23; 3 Kings 14: 26; 2 Macc. 10: 23) scarcely count. Nor do the relatively numerous instances in Ecclesiastes, since it is clear that we have to do here with an idiosyncratic translator (Aquila?) oblivious to the solemn overtones of the term discernible elsewhere in the wisdom literature: Job 8: 3; 11: 10; 28: 25 (?); Wisd. 1: 7, 14; 7: 27; 8: 1, 5; 9: 1; 11: 24; 12: 15; 18: 14, 16; Ecclus. 18: 1; 23: 20. To these may be added LXX Jer. 10: 16; 28: 19. (Wisd. 7: 27, where πάντα and τὰ πάντα occur in close proximity, constitutes in itself a strong argument for a felt difference between the two uses: wisdom is omnipotent—πάντα δύναται—and she renews the whole universe—τὰ πάντα καινίζει.) Against this formidable list there are only two instances in the wisdom literature (not counting Ecclesiastes) where τὰ πάντα refers to something other than the created universe: Job 13: 9 and Wisd. 1: 1. Bar. 3: 32, where the phrase ὁ εἰδὼς τὰ πάντα is balanced by ὁ κατασκευάσας τὴν γῆν, is not, I would contend, a counter-example. For further instances see e.g. *T. Asher* 5. 2; Josephus, *Contra Ap.* 2. 190 (τὰ σύμπαντα); Justin, *Dial.* 56. 11; *Did.* 10. 3.

On the other side, among the innumerable instances of the plain πάντα in LXX there are only 6 which might be interpreted as referring to the universe. Elsewhere, especially in the Stoic tradition studied by E. Norden, *Agnostos Theos*, 240-50, there

but there is no parallel in the sense required by the traditional view. All of which suggests that the phrase from Col. 1: 16, ὅτι ἐν αὐτῷ ἐκτίσθη τὰ πάντα ('because the universe was created in him'), far from being a genuine parallel, has probably contributed towards a continuing misinterpretation.

To these arguments should be added the extraordinary difficulty, not to say impossibility, of finding a satisfactory sense for the following verse without resorting to the desperate expedient of putting the stop after ὃ γέγονεν, a punctuation which is grammatically very awkward and is attested by none of the early witnesses.[38] For if we read ὃ γέγονεν ἐν αὐτῷ ζωὴ ἦν, taking ὃ γέγονεν to refer to the created world, and ἐν αὐτῷ, as it surely must on this reading, to the Logos, then, as Schnackenburg so pertinently enquires, 'what kind of life is that?'[39] The following sentence locates ζωή firmly in the realm of spiritual revelation (it is identified with φῶς); but v. 3 then remains utterly obscure. Bultmann's solution is certainly too Procrustean to be satisfactory.[40] Schnackenburg himself, like many of the earliest commentators, abandons the struggle and opts, somewhat gingerly, for the alternative punctuation.

For all these reasons it is necessary to reassess the role of the

---

is less uniformity, as is illustrated by a hymn to Selene (cited p. 250): ἐκ σέο γὰρ πάντ᾽ ἐστὶ καὶ εἰς σὲ τὰ πάντα τελευτᾷ. We should leave out of account examples with πάντων (Wisd. 8: 3; Ecclus. 1: 4; 2 Macc 1: 24) and ἀπάντων (Ecclus. 24: 8), since the genitive plural is always found in the anarthrous form in the LXX (though not elsewhere, as is shown by a number of examples cited by Norden, ibid. 164f.; 245; 247). In Ecclus. 39: 21 the Greek reads πάντα γὰρ εἰς χρείας αὐτῶν ἔκτισται. But here the πάντα has a distributive rather than an inclusive force. In Judith 8: 14 the reading is uncertain, as it is in Isa. 44: 24. This leaves only 3 clear counter-examples: Ps. 8: 17; 103: 24; Ecclus. 43: 33. Of these the first is particularly interesting, since it is actually *corrected* into τὰ πάντα when quoted in the New Testament (Heb. 2: 8 and 1 Cor. 15: 27).

The NT parallels cited by Bultmann (*Gospel*, 37 n. 1) all have τὰ πάντα. Bultmann (p. 19) is aware of the difference, but attempts to explain it away. H. Thyen, referring to John 1: 3 in another context, actually misquotes it, arguing that 'τὰ πάντα [sic!] should not simply be identified with "mankind"' ('Heil', 171 n. 35).

[38] The evidence is most fully set out by K. Aland, 'Untersuchung'. Aland's conclusions are contested by E. Haenchen, who argues: 'One misconstrues the facts when one connects ὃ γέγονεν to verse 4 by invoking the oldest manuscripts, to say nothing of the fact that one does not thereby achieve a meaningful text' (*Johannesevangelium*, 122). But this is precisely one of the strengths of Lamarche's case, with which Haenchen was evidently unacquainted.

[39] 'Was ist das für eine ζωή?', *Johannesevangelium*, i. 216.

[40] 'What has come to be—in him (the Logos) was the life (for it)'; or: 'What has come to be—in it he (the Logos) was the life' (*Gospel*, 39).

Logos in the Prologue, possibly in the direction already indicated in
the *Manual of Discipline*. As Lamarche says, 'in this sentence—so
close to John 1: 3—what takes the place of the Johannine Logos is
the divine plan' (מחשבה)'.[41] Lamarche cites numerous examples of
מחשבות in the sense of 'the thoughts' or 'the plans' of God.[42] And he
argues that they furnish us with a very close conceptual parallel to
the idea of the Logos that pervades the Prologue. For although the
word itself occurs only three times, the whole passage is filled with
the sense of the divine plan—which is in point of fact one of the
meanings of the Hebrew דבר. And this is a meaning rendered more
naturally by λόγος than by σοφία.

More important than any of the passages cited by Lamarche is
the famous epilogue to the prophecy of Second Isaiah:

> For as the heavens are higher than the earth
> so are my ways higher than your ways
> and my thoughts (מחשבותי) than your thoughts
>
> (Isa. 55: 8-9)

which is directly followed by the declaration concerning 'every
word (דברי) that goes forth from my mouth', a declaration that
harks back to the same author's prologue: 'the word of the Lord
abides for ever' (Isa. 40: 8). The whole of the prophet's message is
bracketed by these two statements concerning the word of God,[43]
which may fairly be said therefore to signify the divine plan Second
Isaiah is anxious to promulgate, a plan which involves the super-
imposition of creation upon history.

Much later, in Wisdom 18, the role of Sophia is taken over by the
Logos. In this extended meditation upon the episode of the slay-
ing of the first-born in Egypt, God's instrument is, instead of Sophia,
his 'all-powerful word', which 'leaped from the royal throne into
the midst of the land which was doomed' (Wisd. 18: 15).

All this supports the contention that λόγος in the Prologue is
more than utterance (λόγος προφορικός) and more than thought
(λόγος ἐνδιάθετος): it is the plan of God, in a meaning closely
related to, if not identical with Col. 1: 25, where τὸν λόγον τοῦ θεοῦ
stands in apposition to τὸ μυστήριον τὸ ἀποκεκρυμμένον ἀπὸ τῶν
αἰώνων καὶ ἀπὸ τῶν γενεῶν ('the mystery hidden for ages and
generations').

How then are the opening verses of the Prologue to be inter-

---

[41] 'Prologue', 42   [42] Jer. 29: 11; 51: 29; Mic. 4: 12; Ps. 33: 10f.
[43] Cf. C. Westermann, *Das Buch Jesaja: Kapitel 40-66* (Göttingen, 1966), 38.

preted? From the very beginning God has his plan close to him, and his plan was a facet of his divinity. All human history, every single thing that has ever happened, took place through the mediation of the Logos, but what has come to pass *in* him (i.e. the special events of God's intervention on behalf of his people), this was life, a special life that was God's prerogative to bestow, a life that was also light—illumination and revelation. The contrast here is similar to that lying behind Sir. 1: 10: 'She (wisdom) dwells with all flesh according to his gift, and he supplied her to those who love him.' On this interpretation v. 4 alludes to the tradition most fully represented in Wisdom 10, which describes Wisdom's share in all the main events of Israel's history from Adam to the Exodus. The living history of this small nation, the history, that is, in which the Logos is most immediately involved (ἐν αὐτῷ), is at the same time a revelation for all mankind (cf. Isa. 49: 6). The Logos, guiding and controlling the destiny of Israel (this is after all God's true design) is present not just as its life but as the bearer of God's light. There is still something mysterious about the passage. Although the images are Johannine, they are articulated in a non-Johannine way. In the Gospel life is the reward and the consequence of welcoming the light. Here it is the other way round: life comes first and is identified with light. As Strack-Billerbeck observes, this is also the reverse of the regular rabbinical view that 'the light is the life of humankind'.[44]

The following verse (5) speaks of the light of men that shines in all the God-directed events of history right up to the new dawn of Christianity. But here for the first time a choice is involved: human beings do not have to welcome the shining. For the most part, as Israel's history shows, they do not, and so there is a darkness, a night (σκοτία), and although the darkness does not succeed in mastering or overcoming the light, neither is the darkness entirely dispelled.

As the hymn continues, the σκοτία is defined more closely. (Bultmann and Käsemann both rightly insist upon the parallelism between v. 5 and vv. 10–11.) It is first of all identified as ὁ κόσμος and then, even more precisely, as τὰ ἴδια. There is no question of temporal succession here: the Greek is quite plain: ἦν ἐν τῷ κόσμῳ

---

[44] *Kommentar*, ii. 358. There is perhaps some light to be shed on this passage, as M. McNamara suggests, from the Palestinian Targum on Exod. 12: 42: *Targum*, 103–4.

—the Logos does not enter the world at this point, it is already there. The movement is one of greater precision, sharper focus.

But what is meant by δι' αὐτοῦ ἐγένετο (v. 10)? At first sight it may seem perverse to deny that here at any rate there is a direct reference to creation. But κόσμος in the Gospel (unless exceptionally in ch. 17) does not mean the cosmos, it means the world of men, and often enough of those men who, confronted with the light, stubbornly keep their eyes shut. Käsemann's insistence upon the cosmological slant at this point[45] (which he also reads into the Gospel as a whole) is supported by neither argument nor evidence. Lamarche suggests that the verse is treating 'of the world of men which has come about in history',[46] or even, adds de la Potterie, 'the group of men which has received the light of revelation through him'.[47] On the other hand, there is no justification for Baldensperger's view (in which he is followed by Lamarche) that ὁ κόσμος represents the Greek world, τὰ ἴδια the Jewish. The evangelist nowhere makes this distinction (indeed in ch. 15 at least, ὁ κόσμος must refer primarily to the Jews) and there is no need to assume that it is drawn here. Rather we have a typical example of Hebrew poetic parallelism. In its first two occurrences in v. 10, κόσμος clearly corresponds to τὰ ἴδια: it is the world as the realm of the revealing Word; in its third occurrence it corresponds to οἱ ἴδιοι: it is the world of those men who, in their sullen hebetude, refuse to see the light. It is important to recognize that τὰ ἴδια (the home of the Logos) is not outside the κόσμος but within it (Judaea, Jerusalem, or even the Temple).

Up to this point, although the material of the hymn is human history, the perspective adopted has been atemporal, or almost so. Thus ὃ γέγονεν ἐν αὐτῷ certainly marks an advance upon πάντα δι' αὐτοῦ; but the advance is one of greater intensity and closer definition, like a camera zooming in on a relatively restricted section of the large scene it has hitherto been surveying from afar. The

---

[45] 'Structure', 144. John 17: 5, 24 are the only instances in which κόσμος bears the meaning Käsemann assigns to it. Even where Jesus is spoken of as entering or leaving the world it is the world of men that is meant.

[46] 'Prologue', 40.

[47] *Vérité*, 164. The idea is certainly present in the *Testament of Moses*, though the corrupt state of the text impedes a clear vision: 'omnes gentes quae sunt in orbe terrarum deus creavit ut [et?] nos [,] praevidit illos et nos ab initio creaturae ad exitum saeculi, et nihil est ab eo neglectum usque ad pusillum, sed omnia praevidit et provovit cum eis [promovit cuncta?]' (12: 4–5). Cf. 1QH 1: 14 f., etc.; 4 Ezra 6: 6; Apoc. Abr. 22; Odes Sol. 16: 9: 'the worlds are by his word'.

present tense of φαίνειν in v. 5 shows that the revelatory role of the Logos in human history involves one continuous uninterrupted activity. Similarly, if vv. 10–11 do not actually carry the action further, there is no need on that account to reject them (as W. Schmithals does)[48] as repetitious and redundant. For they too move in the direction of greater precision and intensity.

There is nothing that has been said of the Logos up to this point which could not equally have been asserted of Wisdom, even if, as I have tried to show, some of the overtones of the hymn are most suitably carried by the term λόγος. And this is equally true of the two following verses (12–13), for the grim record of Israel's rejection of the light is offset by the persistent tradition of the Remnant. Dodd has demonstrated how the 'children of God' theme of v. 12 can be matched in the Old Testament.[49]

No doubt the language here echoes the thought-world of the Gospel. This is best explained if the author of the original hymn was a member of the Johannine community and familiar with the themes of light, life, world, child of God, and so on. But it is illuminating to regard his composition first of all from the perspective of Jewish wisdom.

Raymond Brown objects at this point: 'It seems incredible that in a hymn coming out of Johannine circles the ability to become a child of God would have been explained in another way than in terms of having been begotten from above by the Spirit of Jesus.'[50] But surely the real entrance to life in the Fourth Gospel is the acceptance of revelation in faith, which is precisely the point being made in v. 13. Moreover, if we understand the central theme of the hymn to be *revelation* and accept that it emanated from Johannine circles, then the revelation of Jesus must have been seen as the last and definitive manifestation of the shining of the light, a shining which has no end. Such a vision implies that the life and teaching of Jesus are the climax of the divine plan, but it does not yet identify the person of Jesus with the plan: in theory he could be no more than the last of the prophets sent out by Wisdom (cf. Luke

---

[48] 'Prolog', 23–6.

[49] *Interpretation*, 281 f. Bultmann ('Background', 28) points out the parallel with Luke 7: 35: καὶ ἐδικαιώθη ἡ σοφία ἀπὸ τῶν τέκνων αὐτῆς. R. A. Culpepper, in what seems to me the most valuable section of his article ('Pivot'), gives a very full discussion of the background to the term τέκνα θεοῦ in the Johannine writings. It is hard to be sure whether these verses (12–13) belonged to the original hymn or not. Either way, it makes little difference to my own argument.   [50] *Gospel*, 29.

11: 49),[51] a representative of Wisdom in the same simple sense as all the prophets who had preceded him. Upon those who, unlike the majority, welcomed his message, God bestowed the right to become his children.

One can see how on this view v. 14 expresses an altogether novel insight, splendid in its implications: the plan of God has actually taken flesh and Wisdom has pitched her tent among men. Far from being a pale variant upon an already established theme, as Käsemann suggests, the καὶ ὁ λόγος σὰρξ ἐγένετο, on this interpretation, rings out as a marvellously cogent conclusion to the hymn.

Nevertheless the objections against this hypothesis, if it is taken in isolation, are formidable. It is not just that the language is redolent of the preoccupations of the Johannine community: φῶς, σκοτία, ζωή, κόσμος, πιστεύειν, τέκνα θεοῦ. The theme too, the opposition of darkness and light seen in terms of the failure of the Logos (or the light) to receive a welcome from his own people—this theme is present throughout the whole Gospel. And surely no one from the Johannine circle, even someone coming across the hymn for the first time, would fail to make the identification, very early on, between the Logos that is light and the Christ that is truth. So we are led to a consideration of the alternative hypothesis, not however as an alternative, but as a dialectical enrichment.

(b) A hymn to the Incarnate Word?

The view of the Prologue as a hymn to the *incarnate* Word is most fully and effectively sustained by Lamarche. Taking both occurrences of γίνεσθαι in v. 3 as reference to history rather than to creation, he easily evades the kind of difficulty which, as we have seen, forced Schnackenburg to adopt the alternative punctuation. 'The word of God,' writes Lamarche, 'before being the revelation of the mystery was actually an inner word, hidden mystery, divine plan.'[52] So he is able to take ὃ γέγονεν ἐν αὐτῷ as 'what came about in him', and to find in these words an allusion to all that has been accomplished in Jesus: 'his whole earthly life, especially his death, resurrection, and glorification'. The contrast between δι' αὐτοῦ and ἐν αὐτῷ is fully explained: 'Everything that has taken place

---

[51] ἡ σοφία τοῦ θεοῦ εἶπεν· ἀποστελῶ εἰς αὐτοὺς προφήτας καὶ ἀποστόλους. Matt. 23: 34 puts this saying into the mouth of Jesus, and transposes the Wisdom who sends into sages who are sent; cf. Sir. 24: 33 f.

[52] 'Prologue', 42.

through his mediation (δι' αὐτοῦ) has played its part in the realization of the divine plan, but it is only by the events that have taken place directly through and in him (ἐν αὐτῷ), that is to say in Jesus Christ, that the plan of salvation has been accomplished.'[53]

For Lamarche (and it is difficult to deny the attractiveness or indeed the cogency of this interpretation) the whole hymn is concerned with revelation rather than with cosmology. The light specifically mentioned in v. 4 is already implied in what precedes, and the darkness that follows is easily and directly recognized as a symbol of the blindness of mankind to the light which, properly and rightfully, is their enlightenment. The rejection of the proffered revelation by the world in general (v. 10) and the Jews in particular (v. 11) is too well attested elsewhere to require further comment. Only the favoured few, those who by according their faith have received the right to become children of God, have slipped away out of the sinister domain John calls ἡ σκοτία. And so vv. 12–13 form an effective conclusion to the story.

But how, on this hypothesis, are we to account for v. 14? Lamarche, who proposes a chiastic structure of the Prologue somewhat resembling that of Boismard,[54] displaces this verse from the centre: it corresponds, he believes, to v. 9, which is another way of expressing the Incarnation (taking ἐρχόμενον with φῶς). But Lamarche's view depends upon an untenable exegesis of vv. 11–12,[55] and so we are obliged to confront the difficulties raised by this interpretation more directly.

In his 1923 article, Bultmann raised the question whether v. 14 belonged to the original version of the Prologue. Could it not, with what follows, have been added on later either by the evangelist himself or by an editor or redactor? Since he had already argued that the *Vorlage* was pre-Christian one might have expected him to ascribe v. 14, or at least the very Christian-sounding ὁ λόγος σάρξ ἐγένετο to a later hand. On the contrary, it is precisely this phrase that he wishes to retain since, on his view, the group from which the original composition emanated certainly had 'the conception of the historical embodiment of the revealing deity in his emissary'.[56]

---

[53] Ibid. 48.

[54] 'Prologue', 37.

[55] Namely, the distinction between Israel and 'the pagan world'. Lamarche offers no argument for this view, but contents himself with the assertion that the Prologue is written from the same perspective as the Letter to the Ephesians ('Prologue', 47).   [56] 'Background', 32.

Once Bultmann's hypothetical source had been abandoned, this question was bound to be raised again; raised it was by Ernst Käsemann, and subsequently many scholars have followed him in excising this verse from the postulated original.

According to Käsemann, 14a adds nothing to what precedes: is 14a, he asks, 'anything more than the mere taking over of what has already been said in the hymn, a phrase of connection and transition which allows the evangelist to come now to what is really important to himself and to declare the purpose of quoting the hymn?'[57] Since Käsemann holds that 'There is absolutely no convincing argument for the view that vv. 5-13 ever referred to anything save the historical manifestation of the Revealer',[58] he fails to see how the following verse, or at least its opening phrase, could be said to add anything substantial to what has gone before. What is singular in Käsemann's view, apart from its blindness to the plausibility of the Wisdom-hymn hypothesis, is his conviction that the expression ὁ λόγος σὰρξ ἐγένετο in which many commentators have detected a markedly anti-docetic ring, remains in perfect accord with the picture of Christ which he himself discovered elsewhere in the Gospel—a divine being sojourning on earth ('der über die Erde schreitende Gott'). Georg Richter has argued that this interpretation cannot be sustained, on the grounds that γίνεσθαι followed by a predicative noun always implies a real change of state or status.[59] Whether this is so or not (and Klaus Berger has adduced some strong arguments against Richter's position),[60] the chief reasons for refusing to accept Käsemann's position are not properly speaking philological at all. The case rests primarily upon the clear identification of the pre-existent Logos with the Jesus of the Gospel, whose humanity, though seldom stressed, is consistently taken for granted.

It must be acknowledged, however, that such arguments do nothing to establish the *originality* of the verse in question. Richter himself in fact agrees on this point with Käsemann: 'the incarnation is to be understood as real, but the sentence does not come from the evangelist: it is secondary'.[61] Specifically, he ascribes it to

---

[57] 'Structure', 155.
[58] Ibid. 150.
[59] 'Fleischwerdung', 87-8.
[60] 'Zu "Das Wort ward Fleisch".'
[61] 'Fleischwerdung', 92.

the anti-docetic redactor who was also responsible, he thinks, for other insertions of a similar tendency (especially 6: 51b–58; 13: 12–17; chs. 15–16; 5: 28f.).[62]

It must be conceded, I think, that Käsemann and Richter are right to argue that the Gospel is more concerned to proclaim the divinity of Jesus than his humanity (though surely this is not so much denied as taken for granted). Moreover, the hushed reverence we associate with the *incarnatus est* of the Mass, the glad amazement that God has *condescended* to take on a human form, both belong to a later age. Bultmann may be guilty of some over-interpretation here: 'the Revealer is nothing but a man . . . It is in his sheer humanity that he is the Revealer.'[63] (There is something paradoxical about Bultmann's own position here; for having laboriously pared down the humanity of Jesus to the ultimate essence of the Word, he is left with a man who is actually no more human than Käsemann's 'über die Erde schreitender Gott'.)

But of course the fact that the Gospel places no stress upon incarnation as such is no reason for not ascribing v. 14 to the *Vorlage* of the Prologue. This argument would work only if Gospel and Prologue were shown to have been conceived with the same end in view. And this is precisely the point at issue.

The hymn, resonating as it does upon two registers, is asserting throughout, but subtly and implicitly, the identity of the Logos and the Revealer. But until v. 14 there is no explicit statement to that effect. It is of course true, as Richter points out, that

---

[62] To maintain this, Richter has to show that there is nothing in the remainder of the verse either which would imply divinity; for an 'anti-docetic' redactor would naturally be anxious to guard against misunderstanding at this point. Accordingly he argues (1) that σκηνοῦν means simply 'dwell' ('seinen (dauernden) Wohnsitz nehmen'); (2) that in the context it is no more than a synonym for incarnation; (3) that it is best understood from Paul's use of σκῆνος in 2 Cor. 5: 1, 4 and from the use of σκήνωμα in 2 Pet. 1: 13f. Against this, it must be said that (1) though Richter refers to Moulton-Milligan, he omits to mention a papyrus cited there (*Syll.* 177) in which 'the thought of temporary dwelling is well brought out', *The Vocabulary of the Greek Testament* (London, 1930), s.v. 578; (2) he ignores what, in the context, is a scarcely mistakable allusion to Sir. 24: 8, 10; (3) the word δόξα itself, even without σκηνοῦν, would be enough to suggest a divine epiphany, and is certainly a highly unlikely term for the so-called anti-docetic redactor to pick on.

Richter suggests three different ways of understanding v. 14a: (*a*) 'die Fleischwerdung ist nicht real zu verstehen'; (*b*) 'die Fleischwerdung ist zwar real zu verstehen, aber der Ton liegt nicht auf sarx, sondern auf Logos'; (*c*) 'die Fleischwerdung ist real zu verstehen, und der Hauptakzent liegt auf sarx' (p. 86). But the verse maintains the *identity* of λόγος and σάρξ; so it is a fatal mistake to follow Bultmann and Käsemann in looking for a *Hauptakzent* in the first place.

[63] *Gospel*, 62–3.

Christian hymns do exist which contain no direct mention of the Incarnation. But the Prologue is surely incomplete without such a reference. That a Jewish Christian, reflecting on the history of God's revelation as expressed in the wisdom tradition, should have composed a hymn seeing the life and work of Jesus as the final triumphant expression of this revelation—this is conceivable. But to have composed the hymn in such a way that it could also be read as referring *directly* to the Incarnate Word who came into the world and was rejected by his own people, without including any explicit affirmation of the identity of these two figures—this is a suggestion which places too great a strain upon our credulity.

Again, while the σὰρξ ἐγένετο, taken in isolation, might conceivably be thought to be protesting against a docetic interpretation of the Gospel, much in the manner of the opening of 1 John, it is hard to deny that the second half of the verse rounds off the Wisdom theme with a deliberate allusion (in the use of σκηνοῦν) to Sirach 24.

There is a further reason for continuing to see v. 14 as part of the original hymn. This reason, involving an appeal to literary sensitivity, is certainly more subjective than the first two and will carry more weight with some than with others. Bultmann's comparison with the *incarnatus est* of the Mass, rejected so scornfully by Käsemann, touches the truth, it seems to me, in one important respect. For it acknowledges the sudden change of mood, the climactic coda, where the ultimate destiny of the Logos is announced, glowingly, for the first time. Shorn of this climax, the hymn is very much a case of Hamlet without the Prince. And the remainder of the verse ('and dwelt amongst us, and we have seen his glory . . .'), which focuses attention for the first time upon the community who are the recipients of the revelation, fits in admirably with all that precedes. I have compared the movement of the hymn to that of a camera, gradually zooming in upon the focus of interest; this is now defined even more closely as the revelation—in the flesh—to the group itself: ἐν ἡμῖν, ἐθεασάμεθα.

Richter emphasizes how different the perspective of v. 14 is from that of the Gospel as a whole, which tends to ignore the properly incarnational aspect of the coming of Jesus. But the difficulty is more apparent than real. The reason for the author's excitement here is that the divine plan he has been outlining, God's revelation to mankind, has actually been embodied in the very man who

founded the community to which he himself belongs and is proclaimed by it as the Son sent by the Father: 'and we have seen his
glory'. This is the natural outcome of the hymn, not a later
insertion. If it does not put the stress exactly where the Gospel puts
it, this is not because there is any conflict between the two but
because their starting-points are different. The meditation of the
Prologue begins in heaven with the Logos at the side of God; that
of the Gospel begins with Jesus. They reach the same point from
opposite ends. It is *because* they reach the same point that the
evangelist (or, if Lindars is right, whoever was responsible for the
second edition) is prepared to incorporate the hymn into his work.
Had it been felt as incompatible he could easily have omitted it
altogether. In short there is every reason for asserting that v. 14
formed the climax of the original hymn.

In my view there can be no satisfactory interpretation of the
Prologue that fails to recognize the author's double interest: it is a
meditation on wisdom offering a variation on a traditional theme;
it is also a hymn to the Incarnate Word. And the juxtaposition or
rather intermingling of these themes prepares the way for the
climactic utterance of v. 14. The writer's central insight is summed
up here—the identification of Jesus Christ, revered and worshipped
by Christians alone, with the figure of Wisdom. This stems from the
realization, expressed throughout the hymn, that the history of
Wisdom has been re-enacted by Christ: the divine plan seen at work
throughout the history of Israel has actually taken flesh in him.

The commentator who approaches closest to this view is C. H.
Dodd. But he is mistaken, I believe, in envisaging 'a reader in the
Hellenistic world for whom this Prologue is the first introduction to
the Christian faith'.[64] Such a reader, thinks Dodd, would naturally
take the passage to refer to the pre-Incarnate Logos, a concept
readily intelligible to him because of his background in Hellenistic
Judaism. Only the Christian reader, already acquainted with the
Incarnate Logos, could grasp the whole message. But the double
register on which the Prologue plays is not to be explained simply
on the hypothesis of a double readership. Rather it is the key to the
whole understanding of the passage, justifying its movement and
opening the way to the climactic affirmation, 'the Word was made
flesh'.

[64] *Interpretation*, 283.

3. MYTH, HISTORY, OR THEOLOGY?

Most of the problems concerning the meaning of the Prologue are
to be resolved, explicitly or implicitly, by formal exegesis. But what
is possibly the most crucial question of all is the hardest to answer
with any assurance. It is this: what exactly is being affirmed in the
opening of v. 14: ὁ λόγος σὰρξ ἐγένετο? Later theology would have
few doubts about the nature of this claim: with the Word identified
with the Son as one of the three partners in the stately dance of
the Trinity, the ontological force of the affirmation is as unmistakable as it is mysterious. And given the clear affirmations of pre-
existence in the body of the Gospel (one of them inserted into the
Prologue itself: v. 15), the question might appear superfluous. But
of a Prologue detached from the Gospel and its own later accretion
it still makes sense to ask how strong an identity is being asserted
between the λόγος and the σάρξ, between Wisdom and Jesus Christ.

The verb γίνεσθαι, as I have argued, is properly used of an event
or happening. But there is no possibility of viewing incarnation
(or resurrection for that matter) as an event like any other, in
principle observable and open to the scrutiny of the historian. Are
we dealing with a metaphor, of the kind Paul used when he spoke
of the Church as the 'body' of Christ? This seems too weak a
category to cover the claim that is being made here. So if neither
history nor metaphor really fit, what of myth? Is this familiar term
too vague to be counted any more satisfactory than the other two?
It is certainly elusive and probably misleading, unless buttressed by
argument and explanation.

Conscious then of the rather slippery nature of the word
'myth' Elisabeth Schüssler Fiorenza, following a hint of Hans
Conzelmann,[65] has suggested as an alternative the term 'reflective
mythology'. This, as she understands it, 'is not a living myth but
is rather a form of theology appropriating mythical language,
material, and patterns from different myths, and it uses these
patterns, motifs and configurations for its own theological
concerns. Such a theology is not interested in reproducing the
myth itself or the mythic materials as they stand, but rather in
taking up and adapting the various mythical elements to its own
theological goal and theoretical concerns.'[66]

---

[65] 'The Mother of Wisdom', 230-43.   [66] 'Wisdom Mythology', 29.

In so far as it draws attention to the ambiguity of the term 'myth', often employed emotively as well as vaguely, this is a useful suggestion. But the expression 'reflective mythology' (like 'theology') seems to imply a deliberate distancing from the religious experience, and however appropriate to Philo—or Plato— it fails to do justice to the properly religious involvement of the Prologue or the other christological hymns to which Fiorenza wishes to apply it. I believe that the term 'myth', provided it be carefully enough defined, still gives us the right category of understanding.

'Myth', then, I take to mean the expression in story-form of a deeply held *religious* conviction concerning man's relation to the deity, the cosmos (or part of it), or human institutions. (In this sense the narrative of the Fall in Genesis 2–3 is a myth, but the account of creation in Genesis 1 is not: it is rather an anti-myth, the rejection of a Babylonian-type cosmogony.) The myth offers an explanation of how some feature of human life arose, and at the same time furnishes a model, frequently ritualistic, of human behaviour. In general it helps human beings to locate themselves, to know where they belong *vis-à-vis* God, the universe, and their fellow human beings. It operates symbolically rather than literally and in so far as it speaks of the divine this is unavoidable. Any rigorous programme of demythologization, if designed to eliminate symbolic thinking altogether, must end in silence. (Even theology, however far removed it may be from myth, is ultimately rooted in symbol or metaphor.)

Now the place of myth in a historically based religion like Judaism or Christianity is often hard to determine, since history and myth are alternative modes of explanation which cannot be held together with any comfort. But historical events, or alleged historical events, may either be partly mythologized (like the crossing of the Sea of Reeds in Exodus 14) or made to function as myths by being drawn in to explain the origin of a particular custom or institution. However, in such cases the need to maintain some historical plausibility limits the possibilities to a degree which will vary from one culture to another. There are unlikely, for instance, to be any talking animals in such narratives, whereas in pure myth these abound.

What distinguishes Christianity from all other religions is that specifically Christian myths are all constructed round the person of

Christ or some aspect of his achievement or experience, which is believed to be somehow reproduced or re-enacted by the faithful. Thus they make sense of *their* experience by appealing to his. Paul's most astonishing speculative feat was his existentialization, as it were, of the events of the first Easter. More simply, in the Synoptic Gospels, one can see how the Christian community justified and explained its own experience of persecution by seeing it as endured in Christ's name and for his sake.

Nowhere is this kind of explanation stronger than in the Fourth Gospel, one of whose aims, quite clearly, is to try and make sense of the community's rejection by the Jews. An all-pervasive theme in the body of the Gospel, it also helps us to understand the attraction of the tradition of personified wisdom for the author of the Prologue, especially the version according to which Wisdom failed to find a home among her own people. For this was also the experience of Jesus *and of the community*. Once the two communities, Jewish and Jewish–Christian, had parted, the conviction that the history of revelation had been re-enacted by Christ must have helped to sustain the Christians' sense that they too were reliving the rejection undergone by the Revealer. Here is a good example of what Wayne Meeks calls the 'continual, harmonic reinforcement between social experience and ideology'.[67]

The theme of Wisdom in her role as God's agent in revelation is thus taken over, adapted, and made to function as a myth. The author is much more interested in the revelational aspect of this tradition than in the cosmological, for he belongs to a community that sees its founder as the Revealer and is proud of its own mission to further his revelation. The story element of the ancient tradition, though compressed and refined, remains recognizable, and still involves the career of a heavenly being determining the fate of mankind. What is more, it enables the members of the circle from which it emanates to locate themselves *vis-à-vis* the world as a whole and the Jewish community (which in some respects they identified with 'the world') in particular. But the myth is now purely Christian. The identification of the heavenly figure with a historical individual marks the triumphant outcome of a long and complex midrashic development. The Jewish ancestry of the Prologue is evident, and it shares with Judaism the characteristic

---

[67] 'Man from Heaven', 164.

which singles out both religions and distinguishes them from all others, including Gnosticism, that make no claim to a contingently historical revelation.

2

The Jews in John

In 1976 and 1981 there appeared in the pages of *Novum Testamentum* two important articles by Malcolm Lowe on the identity of οἱ Ἰουδαῖοι in early Christian literature.[1] It is the first of these, focused primarily on the Fourth Gospel, that furnished the starting-point of the following reflections.

There are in fact three questions that arise in connection with the Johannine Ἰουδαῖοι; two belong to exegesis, the third to history. The first asks who they are, the second what role or function they fulfil, the third why the evangelist regards them with such hostility. Always a puzzle, this third question has become even more teasingly problematic in recent years, as scholars have come to recognize the fundamental Jewishness of the Johannine group.[2] The three questions are obviously closely linked, and in spite of the fact that the third takes us out of the realm of textual understanding into that of historical explanation, it hangs upon the answers to the other two because it cannot be correctly formulated without them. This chapter is written in the first place as an exegetical study in the belief that there are still some strands left to be unravelled in this densely woven skein. But in disentangling the first two questions I hope to expose the third more clearly.

If the Gospel were indeed the seamless garment Strauss thought it to be, this programme could be carried through quite straightforwardly. Here I assume that Strauss was wrong; and I shall be arguing that certain passages of particular difficulty are best explained as the result of a process of redaction. (Which means utilizing some arguments of a historical kind to help in elucidating

---

[1] 'Who were the Ἰουδαῖοι?'; 'Ἰουδαῖοι of the Apocrypha'.

[2] Hence the prima-facie absurdity of any theory that sees the Gospel as a *Missionsschrift* written with the aim of gaining Jewish converts. So W. C. van Unnik, 'Purpose'; J. A. T. Robinson, 'Destination'. K. Bornhäuser some years earlier had provided a better basis of discussion by distinguishing six possible references of Ἰουδαῖοι, five of which he detected in the Gospel: *Missionsschrift*. As the most widely appropriate rendering of the term, Bornhäuser proposed 'die Fanatiker der Tora' (p. 140).

what are essentially exegetical questions.) This can be illustrated
from the very first occurrence of Ἰουδαῖοι in the Gospel, at John 1:
19, which is an example of a relatively late editorial insertion.[3]
From the interpreter's point of view this instance is not very
important: the most that can be said is that the introduction of the
Ἰουδαῖοι thus early bestows a somewhat hostile flavouring on the
interrogation of John by the priests and Levites. Other passages
present more problems.

I. IDENTITY

Lowe sets out to tackle the first of our questions, concerning the
identity of the Ἰουδαῖοι. His answer, shorn of frills, is that they were
inhabitants of the province of Judaea, not Jews, but Judaeans.

This solution has on the whole been poorly received by professional New Testament scholars. Hartwig Thyen's verdict is
milder than some others. He concedes that 'By and large Lowe's
judgement that οἱ Ἰουδαῖοι is almost always to be translated as "the
Judaeans" rather than "the Jews" is quite accurate'. But then he
adds, unsurprisingly, that 'for John Judaea is not a particular geographical region. As the "own home" (*Eigentum*) of God and his
emissary, Judaea is above all a theological region.'[4] In fact Lowe
himself acknowledges this possibility, or something like it, in an
anticipatory summary of his conclusions with a curiously self-
contradictory ring to it: 'We shall see that the everyday meanings
suffice, so that there is no need to see in John's Gospel some
fantastic allegorical meaning of the word (though its author may
have intended to convey an allegorical meaning too).'[5] Since it is
the 'allegorical meaning' that most interpreters of the Gospel,
Bultmann above all, regard as the most important (the Jews standing as a living symbol of human obduracy and incomprehension
when confronted by the revelation of Jesus), one can readily
understand why Lowe's discussion has not been accorded the close
attention it deserves. But if what Thyen admits to be his 'generally
very pertinent' observations are allowed, why should not future
translators adopt his suggestion and substitute 'Judaeans' for

---

[3] See R. T. Fortna, *Gospel of Signs*, 170.
[4] 'Heil'.
[5] 'Who were the Ἰουδαῖοι?', 110.

'Jews' in all except possibly the four instances in which, according to Lowe's own admission, this rendering does not quite work?[6] Since the negative charge attached to the term Ἰουδαῖοι within the Gospel is conferred *by the Gospel itself*, why should it not be carried by 'Judaeans' just as well as by 'Jews'? Of course the modern reader would have to readjust his ideas and realign his responses, but this is surely Lowe's central point: if the evangelist was in fact referring to the inhabitants of Judaea (and their official leaders or representatives) and not to Jews in general, then it is wrong to continue to use a totally misleading rendering in versions that are consequently bound to be misinterpreted. (And who can say that, given the power of suggestion over the human mind, the repeated association of 'Jews' with animosity towards Jesus does not continue to instil a certain anti-Semitism in many less sophisticated readers despite all the determined disavowals by leading Christian churchmen?)

This is Thyen's answer, in his own words:

All the signs are that 'the Jews' of John's Gospel are the representatives of that 'Jewry' which revived after the catastrophe of the Jewish War under the leadership of the school of Yavneh, and gained legislative power in the measure that the moral standing of the latter was gradually enhanced by the acquisition of more and more judicial authority. And because this revival (almost unbelievable in view of the devastations of the war) took place under Jewish-pharisaical leadership, the erroneous rendering 'the Jews' is, in the last analysis, the only right one.[7]

So to Lowe's conclusion, which I have suggested contains an inner contradiction, Thyen responds with a paradox: the 'erroneous' translation is actually the only correct one!

In this case contradiction and paradox are both the offspring of confusion. Thyen bundles the three questions I have distinguished into the same bag. One must first separate out the question concerning the identity of the Ἰουδαῖοι (which belongs to the straightforward *story* level)[8] from that concerning the role and function of the Ἰουδαῖοι within the Gospel conceived as a complex web of meaning (which belongs on the level of allegory or theology). Alternatively, and perhaps more simply, one could say that whereas Lowe is interested in reference, Thyen is more preoccupied with

---

[6] John 4: 9 (*bis*), 22; and possibly 18: 20.

[7] 'Heil', 180.

[8] This is what J. Louis Martyn called the *einmalig* level, *History*, 9.

sense.⁹ For the moment, following Lowe, we may stick with the first question.

The root difficulty is obvious enough: in translating Ἰουδαῖοι into a modern language like English or German one is forced to choose between alternative renderings. The English word 'Jews' suggests race and/or religion, but not nationality, for which we now have the word 'Israelis'. 'Judaeans', on the other hand, can only refer to natives or inhabitants of Judaea. In the original Greek both references are equally possible, and in Josephus (the contemporary author whose usage is most relevant to this issue) equally common. So here is a case where, as happens not infrequently, *any* translation involves a falsification. In three instances in the Fourth Gospel, 7: 1, 11: 7, and 11: 54 (the last not picked up by Lowe) the rendering 'Judaeans' is more immediately appropriate because in all three the Ἰουδαῖοι in question are directly linked with Judaea. (Even the RSV hesitates over the first of them.) But it would seem odd to reserve the rendering 'Judaeans' for these three instances alone, when the Gospel employs the same word throughout. So what are we to say to Lowe's rather sweeping proposals?

(a) Rites and festivals

Because of the sheerly linguistic difficulty there may be no completely satisfactory answer to this question; nevertheless a number of points may be made. In the first place we may turn to a consideration of the 'neutral' passages, from which the hostile overtones typical of the Fourth Gospel are missing, starting from those in which the term τῶν Ἰουδαίων is used to qualify a feast. These are 2: 13; 6: 4; 11: 55 (Passover); 5: 1 (unspecified, but possibly also Passover); 7: 2 (Tabernacles); and 19: 42 (Preparation). To these must be added 2: 6 (κατὰ τὸν καθαρισμὸν τῶν Ἰουδαίων). In these cases, says Lowe, the various Greek terms should be rendered 'Judean feast/Passover/rites of purification/day of Preparation.'¹⁰ Earlier, in a note, he had made a more modest claim for the last two passages, saying simply, '*It is conceivable* that ὁ καθαρισμὸς τῶν Ἰουδαίων (John 2: 6) and ἡ παρασκευὴ τῶν

---

⁹ From the opening paragraph of his article Lowe uses the words 'meaning' and 'reference' indiscriminately, as if they had the same meaning. The relevance and importance of the Fregean distinction will be defended below.

¹⁰ 'Who were the Ἰουδαῖοι?', 129.

Ἰουδαίων (John 19: 42) have similar connotations (and should thus be rendered analogously)';[11] and he would presumably say the same of John 19: 40, a remark upon burial customs. Now the trouble with John 2: 6 is that it alludes to an episode in Cana in Galilee; so by including this Lowe has exposed himself to an easy rejoinder. Klaus Wengst for one pounces upon this phrase and tosses it back at Lowe with this rather dismissive comment: 'Whatever plausibility Lowe may discover elsewhere for his rather unconvincing thesis, in the case of 2: 6 his view is simply untenable.'[12]

Now Lowe's arguments, it seems to me, are not to be so lightly brushed aside. The point he is making is that in the Graeco-Roman world in which John is writing religious customs and beliefs were associated with the regions and nations from which they originated. (I leave aside his intriguing suggestion that the reason for adding τῶν Ἰουδαίων when mentioning the feasts is 'to explain why people are faced with a journey to Judea':[13] for John 2: 6 at any rate this will not work.) Lowe thinks that at the period when they originated, 'when Judaism was merely the religion of Judea in the strict sense', such phrases would have meant 'feast/Passover of the Judeans'. And 'it is conceivable that such phrases continued somewhat inaccurately to have the same meaning at least long enough for the main author of John's Gospel to have understood them in this way'.[14]

Lowe offers rather weak support for his suggestion that John knew these phrases, or something like them, from the LXX—ἐν πάσαις ταῖς ἑορταῖς οἴκου Ἰσραήλ (Ezek. 45: 17) is the nearest parallel he can find; but this does not invalidate his central contention that when Judaea was still a country with a national identity the primary reference of ἑορτὴ τῶν Ἰουδαίων will have been to a feast of the Judaeans. Wayne Meeks, commenting on an earlier proposal[15] that since the term Ἰουδαῖοι in the Fourth Gospel is primarily geographical it should be translated 'Judaeans' rather than 'Jews', observes that 'no choice may be necessary, for ancient authors in the age of syncretism tend to identify a cultic community either by its principal deity . . . or by its place of origin . . .

---

[11] Ibid. 117–18 n. 54 (my italics).
[12] *Bedrängte Gemeinde*, 39.
[13] 'Who were the Ἰουδαῖοι?', 116.
[14] Ibid. 117.
[15] By C. J. Cuming, 'The Jews'.

When pagan authors speak of *Ioudaioi*, as they usually do when referring to the people we call Jews, the term denotes the visible, recognizable group with their more or less well-known customs, who have their origin in Judea but preserve what we would call their "ethnic identity" in the diaspora.[16] This is an interesting and valuable observation, although the identification of a cultic community by its place of origin is not confined to 'the age of syncretism'. When in England people refer to a religious custom of Poles or Pakistanis they are implying that the custom in question originated in Poland or Pakistan. In fact one could often substitute 'as is done in Poland' or 'as the custom is in Pakistan' without changing the sense. Of course we are once again confronted with the awkward fact that 'Judaeans' has a much more restricted denotation than Ἰουδαῖοι. And at least in the context of a wedding-feast in Galilee it would certainly seem odd to speak of *Judaean* rites of purification. But this oddity derives from the limitation of the English word and does not affect the Greek. In the innumerable instances in which Josephus, by a variety of expressions, refers to the traditions, laws, or customs of his own people, one would often be hard put to it to specify whether the primary reference is to Jews (of the diaspora) or Judaeans.[17] In such cases it is a grave mistake to attempt to adjudicate, as it were, between two conflicting claims, because the claims do not in fact conflict. The whole point of continuing to identify the customs of a particular group of immigrants or their descendants by the name of their nation of origin (whether one uses the adjective 'Polish' or the noun 'Poland') is that their practices have not changed: however long the group may have lived in their host country they can still be singled out by the customs which they share with 'the folks back home'—the Poles of Poland or the Pakistanis of Pakistan. Only if Poland or Pakistan ceased to exist would this natural association become problematic. This is of course what happened to Judaea, but *not until after the Bar Kokhba rebellion*, that is to say well after the publication of the Fourth

---

[16] 'Am I a Jew?', 182.

[17] In *AJ* 13. 397, for instance, the primary reference of τὰ πάτρια τῶν Ἰουδαίων ἔθη might be to Judaeans (cf. 18. 196), but in general Josephus was deeply conscious that the customs of which he was so proud, grounded in the law, were practised by Jews everywhere: ταῦτα πράττομεν οὐ μόνον ἐπ' αὐτῆς Ἰουδαίας, ἀλλ' ὅπου ποτὲ σύστημα τοῦ γένους ἐστὶν ἡμῶν (*Ap*. 1. 32. Cf. *Ap*. 2. 277; *AJ* 14. 65f.; 15. 50, etc.).

Gospel.[18] We should therefore be on our guard against reading into the text of the Gospel a dissociation which did not exist at the time it was composed.

The foregoing discussion, focused as it is upon a handful of passages in the Gospel that are really on the periphery of our concerns (all involving the so-called 'neutral' usage of Ἰουδαῖοι) may seem inordinately long. But this is a case in which it is easier to accept the premisses than the conclusion: even in the isolated instance of purification rites practised in Galilee but identified as a custom τῶν Ἰουδαίων (John 2: 6), there is no reason to deny that an implicit allusion to *Judaea* is part of the meaning. But what is true is that the translator is put in an impossible position. Meeks's observation that 'no choice may be necessary' does not apply to him, since he cannot avoid the anachronistic dissociation between the racial and religious meaning of 'Jews' and the national and regional meaning of 'Judaeans'. So while there is some reason for dissatisfaction with Lowe's proposed rendering of these passages ('Judaean feast' etc.) this stems from the inadequacy of the English language rather than from any real weakness in his arguments.

(b) King of the Ἰουδαῖοι

The next phrase I want to discuss, ὁ βασιλεὺς τῶν Ἰουδαίων, poses similar problems for the translator, but takes us closer to the heart of the Gospel. In the Fourth Gospel Jesus is addressed as βασιλεὺς τοῦ Ἰσραήλ on two occasions, first by Nathanael (1: 49), secondly by the crowd as he enters Jerusalem (12: 13). This is an honorific title, appropriately put on the lips of people acknowledging Jesus' Messiahship. Βασιλεὺς τῶν Ἰουδαίων has a different ring and is not a natural way of speaking for native Jews. Lowe concludes that it would mean King of Judaea in the strict sense for Palestinian Jews, but that Pilate, whose province included Idumaea and Samaria, might have had a larger area in mind. Obviously the real question is not what *Pilate* meant (how could we know?) but what the phrase means in the context of the passion narrative. This cannot be determined without a full exegesis. Here I simply want to argue

[18] One of the last contemporary examples of the local reference might be the expression οἵ ποτε Ἰουδαῖοι that occurs in a 2nd-century inscription from Smyrna (*IGRR* iv. 1431. 29 = *CII* 742). This is probably an allusion to Judaean émigrés rather than (as used to be thought) to Anatolian converts from Judaism. Cf. A. J. Kraabel in *JJS* 33 (1982), 455. (I owe this reference to Dr Peter Hayman.)

that Lowe's suggested rendering, 'King of Judea', does convey at least part of the meaning.

In a brief section headed, like this one, 'King of the Ἰουδαῖοι', Lowe cites among others Diodorus (who calls Aristobulus ὁ τῶν Ἰουδαίων βασιλεύς in *Lib. Hist.* 40. 2), but not, surprisingly, Josephus. This author employs a number of different expressions when speaking of the kings of Israel or Judah. In the section of the *Antiquities* in which he needs to distinguish between the two kingdoms (Books 8–9) he never qualifies βασιλεύς by τῶν Ἰουδαίων but always by Ἰεροσολύμων or τῶν Ἰεροσολυμιτῶν[19] as opposed to τῶν Ἰσραηλιτῶν. In Book 7 his terminology fluctuates: David is called King of the Israelites and of the Hebrews, but also ὁ τῶν Ἰουδαίων βασιλεύς and βασιλεὺς τῆς Ἰουδαίας.[20] In the second half of the work Josephus speaks of an inscription in the temple of Jupiter Capitolinus in Rome reading 'From Alexander, the King of the Ἰουδαῖοι',[21] and later of course the same title is given to Herod.[22]

In general it must be said that Josephus' usage does not bear out Lowe's contention that one possible reference of Ἰουδαῖοι is to Judaeans *as opposed to* other Jews. Nothing in his account of the history of the two kingdoms gives any backing to the idea that Ἰουδαῖοι could be an appropriate term for distinguishing the inhabitants of the southern kingdom from those of the north. In the case of the royal title, only when the danger of ambiguity is past is Josephus prepared to call Herod King of the Ἰουδαῖοι.[23] Of course there is no question of Herod's sovereignty extending beyond the confines of his own kingdom (Judaea, in whatever extension is envisaged by the context); so it could still be argued that at least the primary reference of the term is to the citizens of Judaea. And on the *story* level at which Lowe conducts his inquiry there is an even stronger case for saying that the people crying out for Jesus to be crucified can only be those natives of Judaea to whose compassion and sense of nationhood Pilate appeals

[19] Or occasionally ὁ τῶν δύο φυλῶν βασιλεύς: 8. 246, 298; cf. 8. 274; 9. 4, 142. From Amaziah (9. 186) the two tribes merge into one (Judah).

[20] Israelites: 7. 76, 120 (cf. 6. 368 (Saul)); Hebrews: 7. 105, 128, 131; τῶν Ἰουδαίων: 7. 72 (cf. *BJ* 6. 438); τῆς Ἰουδαίας: 7. 101.

[21] 14. 36. There is some dispute about the name, but not about the title.

[22] 15. 409; 16. 291, 311; cf. 14. 280.

[23] Once, in a rhetorical appeal to the noble example of Jehoiachin, Josephus calls him βασιλεὺς Ἰουδαίων (*BJ* 6. 203). But this is an instance of an exception that proves the rule.

unavailingly when he asks them, 'Shall I crucify your king?' (John 19: 15).

(c) 'Salvation is from the Ἰουδαῖοι'

Most of the preceding discussion has been conducted on the small but relatively open and uncluttered terrain shared by philologists and exegetes—a piece of common ground free from bogs and hidden hollows. What follows is more contentious, not just in the sense that views diverge more sharply, but in the sense that arguments concerning the prehistory of the Gospel text often have the appearance of taking place in separate rooms, or perhaps in a single private den, reserved for exegetes and filled with the smoke of theological *parti pris*, where as in a game of stud poker one's most important cards are concealed from the eyes of the other players. If, like Bultmann, you put all your cards on the table, you risk having them swept aside by your opponent with scarcely a glance, so calmly confident is he of the superiority of his own hand.

In an article of a scope as restricted as this one there can be no question of a detailed defence of all the positions on which it is based. Here I assume not only that the Gospel as we have it was not composed *d'un seul jet* (the proofs of this leap to the eye) but that the attempt to discern different layers is both legitimate and fruitful. As Wellhausen sagely remarked long ago, the difficulty of the enterprise does not remove the reasons that made it necessary to embark on it in the first place.[24] I believe it can be shown (and of course there is nothing novel in such a contention) that the majority of the passages in which the term Ἰουδαῖοι has the meaning most characteristic of the evangelist (that of a hostile group unable and unwilling to accept the revelation of Jesus) belong to a relatively late stratum, dating at the very earliest from the period immediately preceding the expulsion of the Johannine Christians from the synagogue.

If this is so then Jesus' uncompromising assertion, to the Samaritan woman, that 'Salvation is from the Ἰουδαῖοι' (John 4: 22)—incidentally one of the passages Lowe finds hardest to fit in

---

[24] 'If it [sc. the attempt to distinguish different strata in the Gospel] is not very successful, this is no argument against the presence of the data that made it necessary' (*Evangelium*, 7).

with his own thesis—constitutes a challenge as well as a crux. In fact there can be few phrases in the Gospel more capable of laying bare an exegete's basic presuppositions than this one: it sends the commentators flying in all directions. Some of course ignore the difficulty,[25] others evade it. Bultmann, characteristically, dismisses it as a gloss ('for 1. 11 already made it clear that the evangelist does not regard the Jews as God's chosen and saved people'[26]—though surely this is not what is implied by the expression ἐκ τῶν Ἰουδαίων!). Bauer sees it as an example of a source somehow holding its own against the evangelist's general intention.[27] Thyen, who adopts the phrase for the title of his article, attempts, unsuccessfully in my view, a harmonizing exegesis along salvation-historical lines. Of these three different ways of tackling the problem Bauer's seems to me the most promising, but it requires some modification because it is a priori unlikely (and certainly not to be assumed) that an intelligent author will incorporate into his own finished work a dictum with whose general tenor he is in radical disagreement. Nevertheless even Birger Olsson, who is more insistent than most upon the principle of integral interpretation, admits that the passage 'has a pre-history' and that 'the author who gave the narrative its present form had at his disposal different kinds of material, each with its own "history"'.[28]

The positive attitude towards the Ἰουδαῖοι implied in the saying under discussion is not, *pace* Thyen, easily reconcilable with the hostility displayed by the evangelist elsewhere. Even the single appellation Ἰουδαῖος applied unequivocally to Jesus in John 4: 9 gathers *ipso facto* favourable associations which accord ill with the negative overtones it acquires later.[29]

[25] e.g. Bernard, who blandly remarks: 'The evangelist is not forgetful of the debt which Christianity owes to Judaism' (i. 148).

[26] p. 189 n. 6. Thyen ('Heil', 169 n. 30) cites the even harsher dismissal of J. Kreyenbühl: 'Among the most distasteful and impossible glosses that have ever distorted a text and even changed it to mean its exact opposite'.

[27] Rejecting the idea of a glossator operating under the influence of Paul, he says, 'It is easier to believe that the original form of a story reworked by John to suit his own argument is breaking through the surface here to show Jesus taking the Jewish line in his discussion with the Samaritan woman' (ad loc.). In alluding to his opinion of Bauer, Thyen contents himself with no other comment than an exclamation mark!

[28] *Structure and Meaning*, 119.

[29] Colin Hickling argues that in the first four chapters, in material taken over from the tradition, the Gospel displays 'a generally affirmative attitude towards Judaism'; whereas 'a different stance prevails in much of the remainder of the

On examining the episode of Jesus' encounter with the Samaritan woman for itself one can see that it is not an original unity; the profound discussion of the significance of living water has been superimposed upon an earlier, simpler story, whose main focus of interest is the relationship between Samaritans and *Ἰουδαῖοι*. This story (4: 4-10, 16-19) is continued in 4: 20-6; 'where the motif of vv. 5-9 is repeated on a higher level.'[30] This transposition on to a higher level is surely to be attributed to the evangelist or someone close to him: in particular the conjunction of spirit and truth (4: 23) is typical of a work in which spirit is rarely named without some reference to word. So probably the best solution is that of Klaus Haacker,[31] who argues that the salvation phrase, far from being spatchcocked between repetitions of the theme of worship, was an integral element of the source. This he reconstructs as follows:

[19] The woman said to him, 'Sir, I perceive that you are a prophet. [20] Our fathers worshipped on this mountain; and you say that Jerusalem is the place where men ought to worship.' [21] Jesus said to her, . . . [22] 'You worship what you do not know; we worship what we know, for salvation is from the Jews.' . . . [25] The woman said to him, 'I know that Messiah is coming (he who is called Christ); when he comes, he will show us all things.' [26] Jesus said to her, 'I who speak to you am he.'

Haacker marshals an impressive case in favour of the thesis that the phrase under discussion harks back to a debate between Jews and Samaritans, probably centred upon Gen. 49: 8-12, Jacob's blessing on Judah (which understandably posed problems for Samaritan interpreters):[32]

This hypothesis becomes a certainty when we reflect that the saying concerning Judah in Genesis 49 occurs within the framework of Jacob's Blessing. In her conversation with Jesus the Samaritan woman had already spoken of 'our father Jacob', whose name is associated with the

gospel, particularly in material likely to be owed either directly to the redactor or to tradition which he has extensively developed' ('Attitudes to Judaism', 351-2).

[30] Bultmann, 175.

[31] 'Gottesdienst'. This is easily the most penetrating of the spate of articles that have appeared on this subject in recent years. See also I. de la Potterie, ('"Nous adorons"'), who, however, has no time for source criticism, which, he says, poses more problems than it resolves (pp. 85-6).

[32] 'Book 2 of the Samaritan Chronicle, like the Jewish Chronicler, takes the passage to refer to David and Solomon, and thereby precludes, no doubt intentionally, any eschatological (messianic) interpretation' ('Gottesdienst', 121).

place of the encounter, and subsequently invoked 'our fathers'. Once its
key-phrase is seen to be drawn from, of all places, Genesis 49, Jesus' reply
hits the bull's eye.[13]

Even if certainty seems too strong a claim for Haacker's thesis,
and the details of his reconstruction must in the nature of things
remain in doubt, his explanation of the present state of the text
(*überlieferungskritisch*, as he points out, rather than *literarkritisch*) is
powerful and convincing. The missionary thrust into Samaria
reflected in this story will obviously have preceded (by how long it
is impossible to say) the angry encounters between the Johannine
group and the Jewish authorities illustrated in the Gospel from ch.
5 onwards.[14] It is worth bearing in mind that as we know from
Josephus, although the Samaritans were in certain circumstances
prepared to identify themselves as Ἰουδαῖοι, they would desist from
doing so as soon as the *religious* differences had been brought out
into the open.[15] And that the contrast between Samaritans and
Jews at this point is predominantly religious can hardly be contested. None the less the passage does cohere more easily than
Lowe himself has spotted with his general view that Ἰουδαῖοι is to
be translated 'Judaeans'. After all, the immediate context is the
opposition between two sacred mountains, Gerizim and Sion, and
when Jerusalem is explicitly mentioned it is natural to take the
Ἰουδαῖοι that follows as referring in the first place to the people of
that region—the Judaeans. If it be objected that such a rendering
cannot but distort the sense of the passage as a whole, then one
must reiterate that this is not a problem for the interpreter but for
the translator, handicapped as he is by the conceptual distinction
between Jews and Judaeans which the Greek word alone neither
contains nor imposes. (The same can be said of the other passage
that causes Lowe problems: 'I have always taught . . . in the
temple, where all Ἰουδαῖοι come together' (John 18: 20): although
the primary reference here must be a broad one to Jews from all
parts of the world coming to worship in Jerusalem, it would be
patently absurd to leave the Judaeans out!)

How then is the assertion that 'salvation is from the Judaeans/

[13] 'Gottesdienst', 122f.
[14] This is not to endorse Raymond Brown's view that the wave of theological
speculation reflected in ch. 5 was actually precipitated by the admission of
Samaritan converts into the Johannine group (*Community*, 36–40).
[15] *AJ* 11. 340–4; cf. Lowe, 'Who were the Ἰουδαῖοι?', 125 n. 75.

Jews' to be interpreted in the light of the Gospel as we know it, and how would such an integral reading differ from that implied in the original context? If, as I have suggested, the passage recalls a missionary thrust from south to north in the early days of the Johannine community, then one might suppose that this mission did in fact originate in Judaea. (Ch. 1 similarly reflects an even earlier mission further north, designed to persuade the people of Galilee that Jesus was the Messiah.) Whatever additional meanings the term Ἰουδαῖοι acquired from its usage in the Fourth Gospel there is then no need to reject an original association with Judaea in the dictum 'salvation is from the Ἰουδαῖοι'. Quite simply, Judaea is conceived as the country of origin of Jesus the Messiah (John 1: 41; 4: 25) and *as such* the source of salvation.

Lowe asserts (it is another occasion of difficulty for him) that 'Jesus' supposedly Judean origin . . . is hardly in evidence anywhere in John's Gospel (except conceivably at John 4: 44)'.[36] This is not so, since the Prologue too, as Wayne Meeks has shown, evinces the same basic conviction that Judaea is Jesus' ἴδια πατρίς, the place where he truly belongs but can no longer find a home.[37] Meeks points out that the verb μένειν, so much part of the evangelist's developed theology, is used of Jesus' sojourns in Galilee (1: 39f.; 2: 12; 7: 9), Samaria (4: 40), Transjordan (10: 40), and Ephraim, when 'he no longer went about openly among the Judaeans' (11: 54), but never of his visits to Judaea and Jerusalem.[38] There is thus evidence, strongly supported in ch. 4 itself, of a movement from Judaea to Galilee and (less significantly for the Gospel as a whole) Samaria. Such a movement is more than just a historical echo of Jesus' various journeys: it indicates a passage, a transplantation even, of a message (a gospel in the original sense) from the place where it first sprang up to a more welcoming soil.

This is not the place to argue in detail how the antipathy between north and south is reflected elsewhere in the Gospel. (The evidence is well laid out by Meeks.) But there is no reason to suppose that it was motivated from the outset by especially deep theological concerns. Indeed the passage which best illustrates it, John 7: 40-52 (from which the term Ἰουδαῖοι is significantly

---

[36] 'Who were the Ἰουδαῖοι?', 125 n. 77.
[37] 'Galilee'. Thyen gives further support for this view: 'Heil', 171 n. 38.
[38] 'Galilee', 167.

absent), is a fairly simple, synoptic-type controversy story, centred straightforwardly upon the messianic claims characteristic of the foundation charter of the community (if that is not too pretentious a title for the signs source), the twin titles of 'prophet' and 'Messiah'.

By the time the Gospel was completed, the word Ἰουδαῖοι had acquired, all too evidently, much more sinister connotations. But the evangelist never repudiated the basic tradition that the original home (πατρίς, ἴδια) of the Messiah/Saviour was Judaea. This is shown by his readiness both to preface his work with a hymn testifying to this truth and to build some of his most profound theological reflections into a simple account of an early mission in Samaria.

(d) Judaeans in Galilee?

The only other texts that present difficulties for Lowe's argument occur close together towards the end of ch. 6 (verses 41 and 52).[39] Lowe affirms that in the following chapter, where the Gospel speaks of Jesus' fear of the Judaeans, the opening words, 'after this', refer to a confrontation between Jesus and Ἰουδαῖοι in the synagogue at Capernaum (John 6: 59). 'Thus the text as it stands forces us to understand these to have been Judaeans too *in some sense*.'[40] This is perhaps acceptable at the level of integral interpretation (though one is entitled to ask, Judaeans in what sense?), but almost ever since the advent of critical exegesis dangerous cracks have been detected in the bridge between chs. 6 and 7,[41] and few scholars would be happy with an argument resting on this ramshackle structure alone. (In any case if there were Judaeans in Galilee in any numbers, Jesus would scarcely have been able to

[39] Most observers of the Johannine Jews have some difficulty in squeezing these two instances into their general theories; for the Ἰουδαῖοι in ch. 6 are neither Judaeans in any obvious sense, nor religious authorities, nor even uniformly hostile, since they bicker among themselves (γογγύζειν, 6: 33; μάχεσθαι, 6: 52) about how to take the words of Jesus. See the comparative table drawn up by U. C. von Wahlde on pp. 49f. of an article yet to be considered: 'Johannine "Jews"'. An exception is J. W. Bowker, who makes these texts the corner-stone of his theory that the one section of Judaism 'which almost always appears as taking up a position of unquestioning and invariable opposition to Jesus . . . is not the Jews, it is the Pharisees': 'Origin and Purpose', 400. Why I disagree with this view will emerge later.

[40] 'Who were the Ἰουδαῖοι?', 120 (my italics).

[41] e.g. Wellhausen, *Evangelium*, 28, 34.

evade them by staying there!) Of course there is no reason why Jews should not have been in Galilee; indeed, in the broad sense the Galileans had just as good a title to the name Ἰουδαῖοι as their fellow-Jews further afield in the diaspora.[42] All the same, if Lowe is right in his contention that elsewhere in the Gospel Ἰουδαῖοι refers to Judaeans, some explanation must be sought for the shift of reference in this single passage.

One possible explanation is that ch. 6, or at least this section of it, was composed at a time when the regional connotations of Ἰουδαῖοι had become faded or blurred—sufficiently at any rate to allow the evangelist to employ the term in a setting in which, as soon as one's attention is drawn to the geographical oddities, it can be seen to be about as much in place as a hornet in a bee-hive.[43] And if the incongruity slips past most readers unobserved, this might be because the evangelist has succeeded in foisting upon the Judaeans those qualities of blindness and obduracy which make them the obvious candidates at any point in the story where interlocutors with just such characteristics are required—even though their internal dissensions here jar somewhat with the stereotype. Here we can refine slightly upon Lowe's assertion that even the Ἰουδαῖοι operating in Galilee were 'in some sense' Judaeans. Within the Gospel as a whole their role of uncomprehending questioners is roughly that which is associated with the Judaeans elsewhere, most pertinently in the preceding chapter.

In view of the other unusual features of the passage in which they occur we may prefer to leave these two instances in ch. 6 out of account. If we opt for this course then we can see that wherever Ἰουδαῖοι is used of actual human beings with a role to play in the narrative, these are natives or inhabitants of Judaea. But to say this is to say very little: the nature and significance of the role they play is left undefined, and the reasons for assigning it to them unexplored. Nor, I suspect, would Lowe himself be satisfied with such a conclusion. For he is anxious to, as it were, contain the infection, to argue that without further specification Ἰουδαῖοι not only can but must refer to Judaeans; and at the close of his article

---

[42] See e.g. Josephus, *BJ* 2. 232 (a particularly clear instance): πόλλων ἀναβαινόντων Ἰουδαίων ἐπὶ τὴν ἑορτὴν ἀναιρεῖταί τις Γαλιλαῖος. More generally see *BJ* 2. 195 ff.

[43] Such a suggestion would fit in well with Barnabas Lindars's thesis, argued on totally other grounds, that ch. 6 did not belong to the first edition of the Gospel but to the second: *Behind the Fourth Gospel*, 47–50.

he speaks of 'the Palestinian use of Ἰουδαῖος to distinguish Judaeans from Galileans etc.'[44] as the one that is characteristic of the gospels in general. Such a usage, if established, would indeed be singular: it would be like using the word 'Poles' to *distinguish* the inhabitants of Poland from Poles living abroad. Here it is not enough to show that the term is constantly employed to refer to natives of the country concerned—which in any case is a fact too obvious to require proof, possibly even a tautology. One would need, surely, *separate words* (poles apart) for natives and expatriates, which is what we do not have.[45] In the whole of his long article I have detected only one isolated instance (which Lowe labels 'instructive') of such a use, and that is Jos. *AJ* 17. 254ff., in which, as he says, 'Josephus states first that many Galileans, Idumeans and people from Jericho and Perea had come to Jerusalem to celebrate Pentecost, where they were joined by αὐτοὶ Ἰουδαῖοι. Since all had come to a Jewish festival, and the Jewish areas of Palestine were precisely Galilee, Perea, Judaea and Idumea, αὐτοὶ Ἰουδαῖοι here indisputably signifies *the Judeans in the strict sense.*' But as Lowe admits, 'later in the same passage he relates how the Romans attacked the Ἰουδαῖοι, now meaning *the whole crowd*',[46] which makes it clear that the word itself does not carry the required specification.[47] Much more typical of Josephus' usage is his distinction between οἱ ἐν τῇ Ἰουδαίᾳ κατοικοῦντες and αἱ τρεῖς τοπαρχίαι προσκείμεναι (*AJ* 13. 50) or between two groups of Ἰουδαῖοι, the first οἱ ἐν τῇ Ἰουδαίᾳ and the second οἱ ἐν Ἀλεξανδρίᾳ κατοικοῦντες (*AJ* 14. 113).

But if Ἰουδαῖοι has a broader extension than either 'Jews' or 'Judaeans' we should even so be grateful to Lowe for alerting us to the dangerously misleading inaccuracy of what he calls 'the current mistranslations'.

[44] 'Who were the Ἰουδαῖοι?', 130

[45] Unsurprising in itself, the ambivalence of the Greek word reflects an identical ambivalence in the Aramaic word יהוד—one that had existed at least since the 5th century. Thus in transcribing the phrase חרי יהודא—'freemen of the Jews'/'Jewish freemen' (Cowley, 30: 19), a copyist made a significant slip, writing instead חרי יהוד—'freemen of Judaea'/'Judaean freemen' (Cowley, 31: 18), obviously without noticing the difference. This establishes the local reference. But later in the same letter the writer (Yedoniah) speaks on behalf of יהודיא כל בעלי יב—'Jews, citizens of Elephantine' (30: 22/31: 22; cf. line 26 of both documents). Similarly (to take but one further example) one can contrast יהודין זי יב (20: 2) with יהודיא די ביהוד (Ezra 5: 1).

[46] 'Who were the Ἰουδαῖοι?', 105 n. 14.

[47] Here it is given by the little word αὐτοί!

(e) Authorities

Before addressing the second big question, that of role or function, we may strive for a little more precision in the first. If Jesus' adversaries are Judaeans, what kind of Judaeans are they? Lowe does not bother with this extra refinement; and when others wonder out loud whether it is perhaps the authorities rather than the general populace who are held in the evangelist's sights, it is of Jewish rather than of Judaean authorities that they do the wondering. In fact this neat distinction between the Jewish people (with whom on the whole the evangelist had no quarrel) and their official representatives (the real target of his resentment) is for many not a complementary but an alternative way of clearing the Fourth Gospel from the ugly suspicion of anti-Semitism. Thus Urban C. von Wahlde, who has industriously collated the views of a large number of earlier commentators, concludes: 'although a current trend in scholarship is to see the Johannine Jews as comprising both the common people and the authorities, upon close examination we found that there is little or no reason for seeing the Johannine Jews as common people except for the case of 6: 41, 52'.[48] (A further hint of certain peculiarities in the use of the term in this chapter.)

There is no need to contest von Wahlde's findings that with this couple of exceptions every instance of what he calls the characteristic Johannine usage involves a reference to Jewish (or Judaean) authorities. Unfortunately, however, this result is not itself of any great moment. For what John writes, usually at any rate, is not οἱ ἄρχοντες or some equivalent expression like οἱ ἐν τέλει, but simply οἱ Ἰουδαῖοι, and this in spite of the fact that such terms as ἄρχοντες, ἀρχιερεῖς, and even Φαρισαῖοι are known and available to him. Like many others, including Lowe, von Wahlde fails to distinguish between sense and reference. Long ago Bultmann had pointed out that in the Fourth Gospel 'the different types of rich and poor, tax-gatherers and prostitutes, the sick seeking to be healed and the questioners eager for knowledge, have disappeared. Only when the material used by the evangelist demands it, do we meet individual people.'[49]

He drew the correct conclusion that the Jews in the Fourth

---

[48] 'Johannine "Jews"', 54.   [49] *Gospel*, 86 n. 5.

Gospel have a symbolic role and that this is one of the features that set it apart from the other three. To insist, with however painstaking a precision, on the *reference* of the term is still to fall short of the *sense*.

This distinction, which is important for my argument at this point, is not quite the same as the well-known Fregean distinction,[50] though it can be explained by starting from Frege's most famous example, that of the morning star and the evening star, which both have the same reference (the planet Venus) but, obviously, different senses. One can answer the question, 'What is the morning star?' satisfactorily by saying, 'It is actually a planet', and the further question, 'Which planet?' by 'The planet Venus'. And the same two answers would serve equally well to identify the evening star. But what (though he does not say so) is presumably the source of Frege's example, a couplet attributed to Plato in the *Greek Anthology*,[51] shows that the simple business of identification may be a long way from giving a full understanding of the *meaning* of the two terms. In fact in some contexts one could give a perfectly proper answer to the question, 'What does "morning star" mean?' without mentioning the planet Venus at all. Such a precise identification is certainly irrelevant to an understanding of the Greek couplet.

Similarly the question asked by both Lowe and von Wahlde falls outside the realm of exegesis and in any case is incapable of eliciting the *kind* of answer exegesis requires. For the Fourth Gospel is not an unpretentious and impartial record of events concerning certain individuals and groups: it is a work of literature, and since this is so what really counts towards understanding the various characters is a knowledge of their role or function within the whole.[52]

In works of pure literature, like the majority of plays and

[50] G. Frege, 'Über Sinn und Bedeutung'. The word *Bedeutung* means 'meaning', which makes it a very clumsy tool for the use to which Frege puts it: 'reference' is vastly more apt. Frege applied the term to sentences as well as to proper names, and reached the conclusion that all sentences with the same truth-value (*Wahrheitswerth*), i.e. true or false, have the same *Bedeutung*.

[51] Ἀστὴρ πρὶν μὲν ἔλαμπες ἐνὶ ζωοῖσιν Ἑῷος· | νῦν δὲ θανὼν λάμπεις Ἕσπερος ἐν φθιμένοις (*Anth. Graec.* 7. 670).

[52] There is no reason why what is obviously true of individual characters (Judas the traitor, Thomas the doubter) should not also apply to groups and gatherings. The specific role and function of several specific characters in John has been studied by Eva Kraft, 'Personen'.

novels, one can *identify* the characters simply by consulting a list
of the dramatis personae. Who is Oswald? Steward to Goneril. In
the case of the gospels, which resemble 'historical' plays or novels
in this respect, the matter is more complex. They derive much of
their material, and most of their characters, from outside their
own world of discourse (an obvious possible exception is the
beloved disciple in John).[53] So it is certainly legitimate to attempt to
answer the question, 'Who were the Ἰουδαῖοι?' as Lowe does, by
appealing to external as well as to internal evidence. But we can
no more understand the gospels by answering this and similar
questions of *reference* than we can understand a play of
Shakespeare by scanning the list of dramatis personae. Exegesis
demands a total reading: the *sense* we attach to the characters
(Hamlet's indecisiveness, Macbeth's ambition, Othello's jealousy)
proceeds from and is justified by a reading of the work in
question.[54]

Here, however, the interests of the exegete by no means
coincide with those of the historian.[55] Of course the gospels furnish
evidence—of a kind—for a historian asking general questions
about the reference of various terms (Scribes, Pharisees, chief
priests, Ἰουδαῖοι) at the time of their composition. But here history
and interpretation must be allowed to go their separate ways. The
wilful obduracy of the Ἰουδαῖοι of the Fourth Gospel does not prove
that this is how the real Ἰουδαῖοι actually behaved, any more than
the portrayal of Richard III in Shakespeare's play of that name is
reliable evidence for the character of the historical Richard.
Certainly the historian has a right to stake a claim in this territory
and his claim must be respected; but with this proviso the exegete
too must be permitted to work his own lode. In a work of literature, especially one with as urgent a rhetoric as that of the Fourth
Gospel, the important question concerns the role or function of the
various characters: this is what I have called *sense*.

---

[53] One may also wonder whether characters such as Nathanael, Nicodemus, and
Lazarus have been invented *ad hoc* by the evangelist.

[54] Not that one can sum up any of these characters in a word. Even personages
of a size to spark off bright new adjectives (Pickwick, Quixote, Tartuffe) always
elude the grasp of the wordmakers.

[55] The relationship between exegesis and history exhibits a kind of master/slave
dialectic which brooks no merging of roles.

2. FUNCTION

Bultmann writes of the symbolic function of the Jews in one of those gleaming little cameos of compressed insight that stud the pages of his commentary.[56] Given that he soars high above the *story* level which is as far as any question concerning identity or reference can reach,[57] what he has to say can scarcely, as far as it goes, be faulted; nor, in my view can it be put more succinctly. Accordingly, I quote it here for the sake of completeness:

The term οἱ Ἰουδαῖοι, characteristic of the Evangelist, gives an overall portrayal of the Jews, viewed from the standpoint of Christian faith, as the representatives of unbelief (and thereby, as will appear, of the unbelieving 'world' in general). The Jews are spoken of as an alien people, not merely from the point of view of the Greek readers, but also, and indeed only properly, from the standpoint of faith; for Jesus himself speaks to them as a stranger and correspondingly, those in whom the stirrings of faith or of the search for Jesus are to be found are distinguished from the 'Jews', even if they are themselves Jews. In this connection therefore even the Baptist does not appear to belong to the 'Jews'. This usage leads to the recession or to the complete disappearance of the distinctions made in the Synoptics between different elements in the Jewish people; Jesus stands over against the Jews. Only the distinction between the mass of the people and its spokesmen occasionally proves to be necessary for the Evangelist's presentation of his theme; but this, characteristically, is often drawn in such a way that the Ἰουδαῖοι, who are distinguished from the ὄχλος, appear as an authoritative body set over the Jewish people. Οἱ Ἰουδαῖοι does not relate to the empirical state of the Jewish people but to its very nature (*Wesen*).[58]

What then can be added? About the role of the Jews as such, nothing at all. But since we are now concerned with sense

[56] Bultmann's masterly treatment of the central question still leaves room on the periphery for two other problems: (*a*) the *untypical* usages (discussed in the first part of this article); (*b*) the employment of different terms (discussed in what follows).

[57] Theoretically one could ask about the sense (function) of the Ἰουδαῖοι without budging from the *story* level, because the distinction between sense and reference does not overlap with that between the *story* level and what is variously thought of as the allegorical, symbolic, or theological meaning of the Gospel. On the lower level the function of the Ἰουδαῖοι is to display the surprising unreceptiveness to Jesus' message of his own people in his own lifetime. On the higher level (which, following the basic insight of Clement of Alexandria, I prefer to think of as the spiritual meaning of the Gospel), it is hard to see any point at all in questions restricted to reference.

[58] *Gospel*, 86–7.

or meaning, and since meaning, as de Saussure taught the structuralists, is conveyed by contrasts or oppositions (not always binary), one can still put questions about those other actors (aside from the ὄχλος and the ἄρχοντες to whom Bultmann alludes) who appear now and then alongside the Jews, either supporting them or blending with them or even elbowing them aside. I am thinking of such terms as Φαρισαῖοι, ἀρχιερεῖς, and, most mysterious of all, κόσμος.

Important though their role is, the Jews are not ubiquitous in the Fourth Gospel, and it is worth asking why. Why in particular, when they play such an important part in the passion narrative, does Jesus not name them at all in his urgent warnings to his disciples the previous evening?

(a) Pharisees

It is widely held nowadays that 'Pharisees' in this Gospel (and most pertinently in chs. 7 and 9) is virtually a synonym for 'Jews' and belongs to the same level of redaction.[59] (Even Bultmann thinks this about ch. 9.) Thus Martyn mentions but does not examine the opinion of Wellhausen and Spitta that 9: 18–23 were added by the evangelist to his source.[60] But like Ernst Bammel, I believe that 'the Pharisees-passages reflect controversies between the Christian community and shades of opinion within the Jewish world. They represent old valuable tradition.'[61] What we have in 9: 18 is not just a shift in nomenclature but a radical hardening of attitudes. In fact the blind man himself, whose cure foreshadows and symbolizes his conversion, is not present at the interrogation of his parents that leads to the sentence of excommunication. One senses at this point that the decision has already been taken, the rift is inevitable. Not so in the earlier conversation between the Pharisees and the blind man: the Pharisees debate among themselves on familiar subjects along familiar lines. What the blind man eventually says of Jesus, ὅτι προφήτης ἐστίν, v. 17, constitutes a

---

[59] e.g. Wengst: 'the two concepts appear together and are mutually explanatory'. An inspection of all the relevant texts shows that 'Judaism emerges as a one-dimensional phenomenon, pharisaical in kind' (*Bedrängte Gemeinde*, 42). Notwithstanding my reservations, I find Wengst's discussion careful and thorough.

[60] *History*, 13 n. 31.

[61] 'John did no miracle' 197. This fine article deserves more widespread recognition.

relatively modest claim, one that had been made for Jesus from a very early stage. The same is true, of course, of 'Messiah', but by now this had evidently gathered a lot more weight. The Pharisees make a brief reappearance at the end of the chapter, in a conclusion (9: 40-1) which as it stands is a brilliant example of Johannine irony. Originally, however, the question they put to him (*Μὴ καὶ ἡμεῖς τυφλοί ἐσμεν;*) could have been a genuine plea for enlightenment.

I have already mentioned the little controversy story at the end of ch. 7. Its true beginning is in 7: 32, where the chief priests and Pharisees (an alliance yet to be elucidated) send out officers (*ὑπηρέται*) to arrest Jesus. This discussion too is conducted on a relatively low level, arising out of claims already made for Jesus in the signs source. At the opening of the following chapter (8: 12-20) the Pharisees are still present. Here the subject-matter is richer, since Jesus brings up the topic of his Father (neither term nor topic occurs in ch. 7); but whatever interpretation one puts on this passage, there is a natural break at 8: 20. The Jews of 8: 22 *can* be identified with the Pharisees of 8: 13, but such an identification, on the level of integral interpretation, is no reason for refusing to recognize separate strata at this point. Besides, the debate here (on the conditions of legally admissible testimony) is an ordinary rabbinical-style argument, very unlike the refutation by riddle, typically Johannine, that follows.

The one passage that might be thought perhaps to tell against the distinction I have been advocating between Jews and Pharisees occurs in ch. 12: *ὅμως μέντοι καὶ ἐκ τῶν ἀρχόντων πολλοὶ ἐπίστευσαν εἰς αὐτόν, ἀλλὰ διὰ τοὺς Φαρισαίους οὐχ ὡμολόγουν ἵνα μὴ ἀποσυνάγωγοι γένωνται* (12: 42). This verse is odd in more ways than one. In general, chs. 11 and 12 present a rather different view of the *Ἰουδαῖοι* from the rest of the Gospel. Apart from 11: 8, 54, two of the three passages where the *Ἰουδαῖοι* can only be Judaeans, they are presented in a sympathetic light: 11: 19, 31, 36, 45; 12: 9, 11. So there is already some doubt about the level of redaction of these chapters. At 12: 42 the Pharisees, in distinction from the authorities, are credited with the power of dismissal from the synagogue, whereas earlier (11: 46; 12: 19) they are tacitly assumed to be identical with those same authorities. Bammel says of the mention of the Pharisees here and at 3: 1 'this is redaction level' without further explanation.[62] Presumably the passage was written after the composition of ch. 9 (to which it unambiguously alludes) had been completed; but it is puzzling (and possibly a weak point in my argument) that the evangelist has not written διὰ τοὺς Ἰουδαίους at this point or, as elsewhere, διὰ τὸν φόβον τῶν Ἰουδαίων (cf. 7: 13; 9: 22; 20: 19). One possible explanation, though not one that can figure as part of the exegesis, is that the writer was thinking directly of the Pharisees at Yavneh.

However these passages are finally interpreted, we must distinguish here between two separate theses. First, there is the general thesis that in the great majority of instances commonly accepted as 'typical' the term Ἰουδαῖοι occurs in passages which suggest that the rift between Christians and Jews is either imminent or has already taken place. Secondly, there is the thesis that the Pharisee passages, or at any rate the most important of them, reflect an earlier stage in the history of the Johannine community, when real debate with the leaders of the parent community was still possible and still in fact going on. The latter thesis nicely coheres with the former but is not required to establish it.

(b) Passion narrative

In considering the role of the Ἰουδαῖοι in the passion narrative we may best begin with the story of the arrest, which is as close as the Fourth Gospel ever gets to the synoptic tradition. The first verse for examination, 18: 3, contains no explicit mention of the Ἰουδαῖοι. (They are waiting in the wings.) It is convenient to set out John and the corresponding passage in Mark in parallel columns. (It is to be noted that in Mark and Matthew the arrest follows immediately upon the account of the prayer in the Garden, which John of course omits.)

Mark 14: 43 (= Matt. 26: 47)	John 18: 3
καὶ εὐθὺς . . . παραγίνεται ὁ Ἰούδας εἷς τῶν δώδεκα, καὶ μετ' αὐτοῦ ὄχλος μετὰ μαχαιρῶν καὶ ξύλων παρὰ τῶν ἀρχιερέων καὶ τῶν γραμματέων καὶ τῶν πρεσβυτέρων.	ὁ οὖν Ἰούδας λαβὼν τὴν σπεῖραν καὶ ἐκ τῶν ἀρχιερέων καὶ ἐκ τῶν Φαρισαίων ὑπηρέτας ἔρχεται ἐκεῖ μετὰ φανῶν καὶ λαμπάδων καὶ ὅπλων.

[62] I think Bammel is right, and that it belongs to the level of redaction at which, as we shall see in the next section, the Pharisees are assigned a role in the planning and preliminaries of Jesus' arrest.

These texts are different enough to make any theory of direct dependence unlikely, but close enough to point back to a common tradition. Since apart from two exceptions stemming from the Matthean redaction (Matt. 21: 45; 27: 62) the curious conjunction of ἀρχιερεῖς and Φαρισαῖοι is confined to John, we may suppose that it is the evangelist or one of his school who has substituted Φαρισαῖοι for the γραμματεῖς and/or πρεσβύτεροι he presumably inherited. Leaving aside the σπεῖρα (what was a Roman cohort doing here?), we may notice the presence of the ὑπηρέται, who figure in an earlier story of an (attempted) arrest, a story in which, as here, they were sent by οἱ ἀρχιερεῖς καὶ οἱ Φαρισαῖοι (7: 32; cf. 7: 45). What is more, it was these same 'chief priests and Pharisees' who according to John engineered Jesus' arrest and execution in the first place. Here too there is a fairly close parallel, this time in Matthew:

Matt. 26: 3	John 11: 47–53
(cf. Mark 14: 1; Luke 22: 2)	Συνήγαγον οὖν οἱ ἀρχιερεῖς καὶ οἱ
Τότε συνήχθησαν οἱ ἀρχιερεῖς καὶ	Φαρισαῖοι συνέδριον . . . εἷς δέ τις
οἱ πρεσβύτεροι τοῦ λαοῦ εἰς τὴν	ἐξ αὐτῶν Καϊάφας, ἀρχιερεὺς ὢν
αὐλὴν τοῦ ἀρχιερέως τοῦ λεγο-	τοῦ ἐνιαυτοῦ ἐκείνου, εἶπεν αὐτοῖς
μένου Καϊάφα, καὶ συνεβουλεύ-	. . . ἀπ᾽ ἐκείνης οὖν τῆς ἡμέρας
σαντο ἵνα τὸν Ἰησοῦν δόλῳ	ἐβουλεύσαντο ἵνα ἀποκτείνωσιν
κρατήσωσιν καὶ ἀποκτείνωσιν.	αὐτόν.

John has expanded an inherited tradition to include Caiaphas' famous prophecy. And once again he has replaced πρεσβύτεροι (or whatever) by Φαρισαῖοι. In this case, obviously, there is no room for the ὑπηρέται who for John are the natural agents of the Sanhedrin (named only here in this Gospel). This is also true of 11: 57.

At the arrest of course, the chief priests and Pharisees are not physically present. The chief priests will play an important part in the subsequent drama; not so the Pharisees, who now drop out of the story altogether. They have made positively their last appearance, and so they bow out, leaving the stage to the Ἰουδαῖοι who, along with the ἀρχιερεῖς who represent them (19: 21), are the true villains of the passion story.

In 18: 12 the narrative takes a new turn: the talking over, the arrest is effected: ἡ οὖν σπεῖρα καὶ ὁ χιλίαρχος καὶ οἱ ὑπηρέται τῶν Ἰουδαίων συνέλαβον τὸν Ἰησοῦν καὶ ἔδησαν αὐτόν (there is no synoptic parallel to this verse).

Are we to conclude from the evidence so far presented that John makes no distinction between the chief priests and Pharisees on the one hand and the Ἰουδαῖοι on the other, that he uses the two terms equivalently and indifferently? That would be an over-simplification. Clearly *in this case* the Ἰουδαῖοι and ἀρχιερεῖς have the same reference, and the identification is a fateful one. For the remainder of the passion narrative they can no longer be properly distinguished: the chief priests having been formally convicted of plotting Jesus' death, now the Jewish people are seen to be demanding it from the only authority with the power either to pass the sentence or to carry it out. In none of the other gospel accounts does the term Ἰουδαῖοι occur except in the expression βασιλεὺς τῶν Ἰουδαίων—a nugget of tradition[63] exploited by John with his habitual irony, nowhere more tellingly employed than here. But by replacing the synoptic ὄχλος with the more specific term οἱ Ἰουδαῖοι, far from exonerating the general populace from complicity in Jesus' death, John is inculpating them all the more.

But where does this leave the Pharisees? To begin with one must distinguish the passages discussed in the last section (where the Pharisees, as we saw, have survived in older stories reworked by the evangelist) from the deliberate conjunction of chief priests and Pharisees, which never occurs without some connection, direct or indirect, with the passion. The evangelist may, it is true, have inherited a tradition of the Pharisees' bitter hatred of Jesus (according to Mark they begin plotting his death very early indeed: Mark 3: 6); but it does seem that in these texts he has introduced them, so to speak, on his own recognizance. (And no doubt it is on the same level of redaction that the puzzling 12: 42 took its present shape.)[64] Martyn argues persuasively for the view that the chief priests, as actual contemporaries of the earthly Jesus, represent the *einmalig* level of the drama (i.e. the level at which the narrative refers to the events and people of Jesus' own day); the Pharisees, on the other hand, represent what he calls 'the Gerousia of John's own city', since after the fall of Jerusalem they are the ones

---

[63] This is in fact the only point in the whole Gospel where John's use of Ἰουδαῖοι converges with that of the Synoptists.

[64] See above, n. 62.

who picked up the reins of power in Jewish communities every-where.[65]

Attractive as Martyn's theory is, it relates to the Pharisees, not to the Jews. If the evangelist sees the Pharisees, along with the chief priests, as engineering Jesus' downfall in the first place, we must not forget that they vanish from the scene altogether before the actual arrest and leave it to the Jews, along with the chief priests, to press for Jesus' execution. So it is not just the Pharisees that attract his ire and resentment: it is the Jewish people as a whole who are made the symbol of the human shadow.

(c) The world

Any comprehensive reading of the role of the Ἰουδαῖοι in the Fourth Gospel must reckon not only with their frequent appearances but also with their disappearance—from the close of the Book of Signs until the beginning of the passion narrative. The evangelist himself draws attention to this by the device of making Jesus refer back to an earlier statement that the Jews had found particularly enigmatic: 'as I said to the Jews so now I say to you, "Where I am going you cannot come"' (13: 33; cf. 7: 36; 8: 22). The significance of this remark changes slightly in the new context because the perplexity of Jesus' new audience, though just as great as that of the Jews, is of a different order.

Given the setting of the farewell discourse, there is obviously no room for any direct confrontation with the Jews. Their physical absence at this point is not only unsurprising but necessary. The problem lies elsewhere, in the fact that when Jesus tells his disciples of the persecutions they will soon have to endure he warns them not against the Jews but against 'the world'. At one juncture he mentions the synagogue ban: ἀποσυναγωγοὺς ποιήσουσιν ὑμᾶς (16: 2). The shift from the singular to the plural is made earlier in the passage, at 15: 20; so the plural cannot be said to be unexpected. 'They' of course are the Jews, but their role has already been usurped by ὁ κόσμος—the world; and though they are not far away (who else had the power to expel people from the synagogue?), they are not named.

In the Prologue, a general observation about the world's un-receptivity to the light (1: 10) had been narrowed down to focus

[65] *History*, 72–3.

on a single state (τὰ ἴδια) and a single nation (οἱ ἴδιοι) soon to be specified as οἱ Ἰουδαῖοι. In the body of the Gospel, where the sullen hostility of these same Ἰουδαῖοι is a major theme, the movement of the Prologue is reversed, and after Jesus' retirement from the public scene the narrator's record of the unreceptivity of the Jews is followed by Jesus' own prophetic warning of the active hostility of the world. In the farewell discourse, where the word κόσμος occurs no fewer than 20 times (not counting ch. 17), there are no instances of the positive usage found elsewhere in the Gospel.[66]

Although neither in the Prologue nor in the Gospel proper is there any formal identification of Ἰουδαῖοι and κόσμος,[67] in both cases the reader is invited by the context to make the identification for himself. Here once again we must be careful to distinguish between sense and reference. One might argue that the world envisaged in the farewell discourse, like that of the Prologue, is really a very tiny one, a single nation; nevertheless it is experienced by the evangelist and his community as a *world*. The bleak metaphysical statement of the Prologue, ὁ κόσμος αὐτὸν οὐκ ἔγνω (1: 10) is echoed in a warning to the disciples: εἰ ὁ κόσμος ὑμᾶς μισεῖ, γινώσκετε ὅτι ἐμὲ πρῶτον ὑμῶν μεμίσηκεν (15: 18). But these do not emerge out of the cosmic gloom of Gnosticism; rather they are the consequence of the intersection of tradition and experience. The sad failure of divine revelation (Wisdom/Logos) to enlighten the world in which it shone culminated in the rejection, by his own people, of that revelation incarnated in Jesus. The Christian community, hurt and bewildered by its own experience of rejection, could only make sense of it by interpreting it as a re-enactment of the career of its founder.[68] Yet Jesus does *not* say: 'if *the Jews* hate you, remember that they hated me first'. Why not?

On what we have called the *story* level this question poses no problems. We can simply say that the situations are different: the behaviour of Jesus, living as he did at a time when the inhabitants of Judaea moved in constant fear of Roman reprisals and repression, naturally alarmed the religious authorities: 'It is good

---

[66] Especially 3: 16–19 and in the expression τὸ φῶς τοῦ κόσμου (8: 12; 9: 5; cf. 1: 9; 12: 46).

[67] Unless one counts 8: 23, where the Jews (ὑμεῖς) are said, unlike Jesus, to be ἐκ τούτου τοῦ κόσμου. The additional οὗτος, which certainly affects the sense, is only found once in chs. 14–17 (16: 11), but is frequent elsewhere: 8: 23; 9: 39; 11: 9; 12: 25, 21; 13: 1; 18: 36.

[68] See Wayne Meeks's deservedly famous article, 'Man from Heaven'.

that one man should die for the people.' The dangers faced by his followers are no longer localized in this way—their profession of faith in Jesus (15: 21—$\delta\iota\grave{\alpha}$ $\tau\grave{o}$ $\check{o}\nu o\mu\acute{\alpha}$ $\mu o\nu$) will incur the enmity of the world at large. Of course such an answer is unsatisfactory: both Caiaphas' prophecy and Jesus' warning are intended to resound far beyond the confines of the rooms in which they were uttered. But if after scrutinizing the role of the Jews in the Gospel you conclude that the evangelist intends to portray them not just as the adversaries of Jesus but as a continuing threat to the well-being of the community, then you are left with the task of explaining why all direct reference to the Jews is dropped as soon as the situation of the community becomes the specific focus of interest. That writers on the role of the Jews in the Gospel mostly ignore this problem is I suppose to be explained by the fact that if the locus of one's inquiry is a word or an expression, one tends to leave out of consideration passages where the word or expression in question is not employed. Which, at least in this instance, is surely a matter of regret.

If in asking what in the world the world is doing here the questioner wants an answer on the level of *explanation*, the genesis of the ideas that dominate the Gospel, then the answer might be expressed in terms of the Gnostic myth of the endemic enmity of the world and its unnamed ruler. But on the level of *understanding*, that is of the meaning of the Gospel, any answer must include the distancing effect of a word ('world') which takes the author beyond the realm of immediate experience, a true dissociation of sensibility.

3. CONCLUSIONS

Compelled to choose between Lowe, anxious to prove that John's Ἰουδαῖοι are properly confined to an area on the edge of the Mediterranean smaller than Wales, or von Wahlde, removing from the evangelist's purview all but a handful of highly placed officials, and the vast, visionary exegesis of Bultmann, dissatisfied with anything less than an archetypal symbol of the sinfulness of mankind, one would, I think, have to opt for Bultmann, if only because he shows an incomparably greater understanding of the *meaning* of the Gospel. But is such a choice inescapable? Niels Dahl, one of the most penetrating and astute of recent writers on the Gospel, does not think so. Commenting on Bultmann's general thesis (which he accepts) that the Jews are the representatives of the world in its hostility to God, he adds: 'it is, however, equally important that the *Jews* are those who represent the world'.[69] Bultmann, for whom even the humanity of Jesus was no more than a contingent vehicle of divine revelation, would undoubtedly disagree with this proviso, which he would regard as a glorification of the happenstance, an illegitimate and dangerously mistaken exaltation of the importance of historical fact. We must acknowledge, I think, that we have to do here with interpretative options which proceed as much from the personal metaphysic of the individual exegete as from the book they are interpreting: the choice is between the historical, the theological, and the historico-theological.

The issue is further complicated by the exciting suggestions of J. Louis Martyn, who adds an extra dimension to the historical approach with his theory of a two-level drama, a two-tier universe and the consequent need of stereoptic vision. In an essay of as restricted a scope as this it would be foolish to do more than note the range of interpretative possibilities. It can be stated with some assurance though that to offer an interpretation of John or any aspect of his Gospel—from Jews to judgement, from Pharisees to fig-trees—without getting beyond the sheerly historical or referential is tantamount to hooding the eagle or seeling his eyes.

Before concluding it may be worth offering some final observations on the two distinctions which have guided the discussion.

(a) Sense and reference

Perhaps no question in New Testament studies, certainly none of such importance, has been worse affected by the confusion between sense and reference than the one we have been considering. But however carefully it is drawn there must remain some area of possible disagreement. If the Fourth Gospel were a work of pure literature the sense of οἱ Ἰουδαῖοι, as I have argued, would be entirely determinable from within the work itself. Since this is not so, what we have seen to be the fundamental ambivalence of the word continues to present problems that cannot be properly elucidated without inquiring into the genesis of the Gospel. Bereft, apart

---

[69] 'Johannine Church'.

from a few scattered instances, of the kind of contextual clues
which make it so easy to establish the reference throughout the
much more voluminous writings of Josephus, we require more
historical evidence before we can be sure whether Lowe is correct
in his conclusion that it was Judaeans, not Jews in general, that
the evangelist had in mind. And here the reference could affect the
sense because of the delicate matter of what Frege calls 'die
verknüpfte Vorstellung'. Galileans, Jews themselves, will have
thought very differently about Judaeans. (And would it *mean* the
same thing to say, 'the people of Samaria have no truck with the
people of Judaea' as to say, 'Samaritans have no truck with Jews'?)

(b) The two levels of understanding

Up to now I have distinguished between the *story* (avoiding the
question-begging term 'history') and the meaning of the Gospel.
This distinction is of course a modern version of the old distinction
between letter and spirit, or the literal and the allegorical. In the
topic we have been considering Bultmann's interpretation is surely
the right one, but such confidence would in many cases be
misplaced, partly because of the many unanswered questions
regarding the genesis and growth of the text, partly because of the
exceptional subtlety of the author and the delicacy of what one
might call his interpenetrative technique.

(c) The question why

Out of the answers to the first two questions (who were the
Ἰουδαῖοι and what function do they fill?) there emerges a third
question (why?) which probes into the link between the who and
the what: why does the writer assign *this* role to *these* people?
This, unlike the other two, is a historical question. Why are the
Ἰουδαῖοι (Jews or Judaeans as the case may be) selected along with
the κόσμος to serve as the central symbol of negativity in a Gospel
which, unlike the other three, is strongly marked by an ethical
or soteriological if not a cosmological dualism? He could have
chosen οἱ ἄρχοντες, with the possibility of a conceptual link with ὁ
ἄρχων τοῦ κόσμου: this would have retained the reference argued
for by von Wahlde and provided a satisfactory sense as well.
Alternatively, if he wanted to invite the kind of stereoptic reading

Martyn attributes to him, he could have made more use than he does of the phrase ἀρχιερεῖς καὶ Φαρισαῖοι (which seems rather to reflect a different level of redaction). Or he could have further extended his use of ὄχλος (of which there are already 20 instances in the Gospel)—a general and unspecific term which would not have drawn undue attention to the Jewishness of Jesus' adversaries.

This difficulty, although for the most part passing unobserved,[70] is a real one: one reason why Lowe's thesis is so unsatisfactory as it stands is that it fails to explain *why* the evangelist should have evinced such hostility to the inhabitants of the tiny province of Judaea. Indeed Lowe does not even raise the question or feel its force. Here I can only sketch in a provisional answer in successive stages.

1. One might start by asking if there is anything in the tradition that might have furnished some platform, however narrow, for the edifice which came to be built. Indeed there was: the belief shared by all the evangelists that Jesus' message was rejected by his own people and the seed of his word sown on poor and unreceptive soil. The inscription on the cross, which Pilate says is not to be erased, itself affords eloquent testimony to this rejection: 'King of the Ἰουδαῖοι', king of those whose faith and confidence he failed to elicit. It would be hard to overvalue the significance of this one small fact: it is of the kind that resonates in the memory and generates myth. But if its presence in the tradition explains where the fourth evangelist derived the motif it does nothing to account for the use he made of it.

2. In the second place it might seem as if the opposition between Galilee and Judaea so persuasively argued by Meeks might give Lowe's thesis the stiffening it needs. For if an important episode in the history of the Johannine community had been somehow linked with the fortunes of a group of Galilean (and later, maybe, Samaritan) converts, then we might be able to give a plausible explanation of the deliberate blackening of the name of the Judaean nation throughout the Gospel. Of course we should still be left with the task of explaining the allegorical significance sub-

---

[70] Among those who *have* felt the need for an answer is Carl von Weizsäcker, who, writing in 1864, attributed the bitterness of the Gospel to a sustained resentment on the part of the evangelist arising out of some soul-searing experience he had undergone at the hands of the Jews. *Untersuchung*, 187.

sequently invested in these same Judaeans; but at least we could see why, given such an history, the Judaeans would naturally have been picked for the role of Jesus' adversaries.

Unfortunately such an explanation overlooks the very restricted space occupied by the theme of Galilean acceptance versus Judaean rejection. Only in two places (4: 43 ff. and 7: 47–52) is it at all prominent and in neither is the required thesis easy to sustain. In the first, in ch. 4, the passage from Judaea to Galilee is, it is true, given unmistakable emphasis: it serves to bracket both the story of the woman at the well (4: 3, 43, 45) and that of the nobleman's son (4: 46, 54). But as it happens the key word Ἰουδαῖοι is missing. Its nearest occurrence is in the phrase 'Salvation is from the Ἰουδαῖοι' (4: 22; cf. 4: 10). So the weight of contrast between those who rejected Jesus and those who welcomed him is borne by *Judaea* and *Galilee* (and Galileans, who are said, oddly, to have 'seen' what Jesus did in Jerusalem: 4: 45).

This might be dismissed as of no significance were it not for the fact that no Ἰουδαῖοι, at least by that name, figure in the second episode either. In this Jesus is championed unexpectedly by Nicodemus, who pops up out of nowhere to answer a mindless objection voiced not by the Judaeans but by the *Pharisees*: Μή τις ἐκ τῶν ἀρχόντων ἐπίστευσεν εἰς αὐτὸν ἢ ἐκ τῶν Φαρισαίων; (7: 48). The reader who recalls that Nicodemus was both ἐκ τῶν Φαρισαίων and an ἄρχων τῶν Ἰουδαίων (3: 1) can appreciate the ironic humour of his riposte, as he sides with the crowd of those 'ignorant of the law' (7: 49) and actually quotes the law in reply. This allusion to Nicodemus' authoritative position among the Ἰουδαῖοι is at best flickering and indirect: not enough to offset the fact that it is not they but the Pharisees who occupy the centre of the stage.

This is not to deny the significance of the Galilean connection in this passage: both Nicodemus (explicitly) and the crowd (implicitly) are closely associated with this northern province from which neither Christ nor prophet could be expected, so that the story sardonically suggests the discomfiture of the sophisticated south by the unlettered north. But the Ἰουδαῖοι as such—active enough earlier in the chapter—play no part whatever in this little episode.

So while the north/south opposition may well have fed into the community's traditions and given an extra impetus to the polarizing tendencies that permeate the Gospel as we have it, it is not a sufficiently strong theme to account for the role the Ἰουδαῖοι are eventually asked to assume.

3. One of the minor puzzles can be cleared up relatively simply. This is the evangelist's readiness to speak of Jesus (a Judaean) and his disciples (Jews) as if they were of a different race and nation from the Ἰουδαῖοι. Josephus uses a similar device when he records how a certain Justus urged the citizens of Tiberias 'to take up arms and form an alliance with the Galileans, whose hatred of Sepphoris will make them willing recruits' (*Vita* 39; cf. 325). For Sepphoris, although one of the three largest towns of Galilee (*Vita* 123) and named by the Romans as its capital (*Vita* 38), had abandoned the Galilean cause (*BJ* 3. 61: ἀποστῆναι Γαλιλαίων). Josephus, whose usage, like John's, is possibly affected by his personal interests here, might seem to imply that the people of Sepphoris are not really Galileans; but of course that cannot be his intention. Again like John, he expects his readers to supply the necessary qualifications for themselves.[71]

4. This parallel from Josephus, though mildly illuminating, sheds no light at all on the real difficulty, which is that the fourth evangelist's antagonism towards the Ἰουδαῖοι, grounded though it may have been upon local rivalries, was predominantly religious and ideological. This is particularly true of the tense and acrimonious debates, especially in chs. 5, 8, and 10, that give the Gospel much of its distinctive character. Jesus goes so far as to call his adversaries children of the devil (8: 44) and they, time and again, sought to kill him for his blasphemies. What still needs to be explained then is the extraordinary polemical thrust of the Gospel—noticed long ago by Bretschneider, who pointed out how closely it resembles in this respect the work of the second-century apologist Justin.[72]

5. Once again it is Josephus, a contemporary of the evangelist, who offers some glimmer of light in this rather dark and impenetrable tunnel. Just occasionally in his substantial corpus are found glimpses of a usage of Ἰουδαῖοι different from its habitual reference to those of Jewish race, whether in Judaea or elsewhere. In one of his rare animadversions on the name itself, he tells us that it is

---

[71] Sean Freyne believes that by Josephus' day 'attitudes had hardened to the point that this very specialized use of the term "Galileans" was justified without taking account of its purely geographical associations': *Galilee*, 125.

[72] Carolus Theophilus (Karl Gottlieb) Bretschneider, *Probabilia*, 118-19.

derived from the tribe of Judah and dates ἐξ ἧς ἡμέρας ἀνέβησαν ἐκ Βαβυλῶνος (*AJ* 11. 173), suggesting that it properly belongs to the returning exiles (Jeremiah's basket of good figs) rather than to those who were left behind—a comment that supplements the earlier snippet of information that it was the same people (the returned exiles) who were responsible for the reconstruction of the Temple (11. 84). Book 11 concludes with the strange story of Alexander and the Samaritans, plus a postscript to the effect that Shechem provided a refuge for people accused of violating the dietary laws or the Sabbath regulations 'or any other such sin' (11. 346), who fled from Jerusalem protesting their innocence.

Counterbalancing this picture of Shechem as a centre of religious dissidents inhabited, Josephus tells us, ὑπὸ τῶν ἀποστατῶν τοῦ Ἰουδαίων ἔθνους (11. 340), is another picture, opposed and facing, of a Jerusalem reserved for the good and the pure. We are informed that soon after the re-dedication of the Temple, the priests and the Levites 'killed the passover lamb for all the returned exiles, for their fellow priests, and for themselves; it was eaten by the people of Israel who had returned from exile, and also by every one who had joined them and separated himself from the pollutions of the peoples of the land to worship the Lord, the God of Israel' (Ezra 6: 20-1).

Earlier, speaking of those who endeavoured to frustrate the efforts of the returned exiles to rebuild the Temple as the עַם הָאָרֶץ (4: 4), the Chronicler had made no distinction between these and 'the adversaries of Judah and Benjamin' (4: 2); and Josephus, who has Ezra as a source at this point, bluntly identifies the same group as the Samaritans (*AJ* 11. 19-30, 84-8).[73]

Whatever the precise relationship between the עַם הָאָרֶץ and the Samaritans, there seems to have been a real connection between the people of the north and those southerners who remained behind at the exile and subsequently earned the disapproval of the powerful group (*the Ἰουδαῖοι?*) of which Ezra, the *bête noire* of the

---

[73] R. J. Coggins, commenting on Ezra 4: 4, declares that 'there is no reason to link them [sc. the people of the land] with the Samaritans', *Samaritans*, 66-7; and there are certainly difficulties (notably the use of the term in Hagg. 2: 4 and Zech. 7: 5) in the way of this. But Josephus, a contemporary of the fourth evangelist, does appear to do so; and Coggins himself, speaking of Second Isaiah, had already concluded of 'the northerners and . . . those who had remained in Judah during the exile' that 'these two groups came to be identified with one another, and both would be dismissed as no part of the true people of God' (op. cit. 37).

Samaritans, came to be a leading representative. And so it may be no coincidence that Jesus, besides being associated with the עַם הָאָרֶץ (John 7: 49), treated the Ἰουδαῖοι as aliens and failed to rebut the charge that he himself was really a Samaritan (8: 48).

6. It is widely held nowadays that relations between the synagogue and the Johannine Christians were finally severed as a direct result of the activities of the Pharisees at Yavneh under the leadership of Gamaliel II.[74] But however attractive and plausible, this hypothesis does not explain all the features of the evangelist's use of οἱ Ἰουδαῖοι. It seems that at the most important stage of its development the Johannine community must be located among the sects and parties of the Second Temple whose very existence the canonical documents of the period do so much to conceal. The Samaritans may not have been the only people of Jewish race reluctant to call themselves Ἰουδαῖοι when religious affiliations were in question.

Finally, it is perhaps worth adding that while the *meaning* of the term Ἰουδαῖοι in the Gospel, its allegorical and symbolic function, is unaffected by such findings, they do raise the possibility that none of the previously suggested *identifications* has quite succeeded in hitting the mark.

[74] The scholar most widely associated with this view is J. L. Martyn, who offers a particularly subtle and interesting version of it. But the theory of a nexus between the proceedings at Yavneh and the Fourth Gospel dates back at least as far as 1861, when M. von Aberle called the Gospel 'der Absagebrief gegen das restaurirte Judenthum' ('Über den Zweck', 94).

3

Bridging Ambiguities

How does newness come into the world? How is it born?
Of what fusions, translations, joinings is it made?

(Salman Rushdie, *The Satanic Verses*)

The newness I am concerned with here is the claim of a human
being to be equal to God—for such was the charge brought against
the Jesus of the Fourth Gospel by those it calls 'the Jews'. My
theme, then, expressed in the deplorable exegetical jargon that is
hard altogether to avoid, is Johannine christology: specifically the
challenge to Jewish monotheism as this finds expression in the
pages of the Gospel. How could such a challenge, from within the
Jewish tradition, be mounted by or on behalf of someone known to
be a human being, 'whose father and mother are known'? Perhaps
we should start by discounting the possibility that it was actually
made by the real, historical Jesus of Nazareth; but if we do this we
are left with the task of explaining how John the Evangelist came
to depict him as a divine or semi-divine being, claiming equality
with God. If in sober fact he never made such a claim, then the
real historical Jews are unlikely to have maintained that he did;
and in that case the confrontations we find in the pages of the
Fourth Gospel, though ostensibly concerned with the career of
Jesus, must reflect a very different struggle: one between the
Christ-party and the Jewish establishment much later in the first
century. The scholar who first argued this hypothesis in any detail
was J. Louis Martyn.[1] His allegorical reading of the Gospel is still,
in my opinion, by far the best hypothesis available of the meaning
of the Gospel, and in what follows I shall simply assume it to be
broadly correct.

The same assumption is made by Wayne Meeks, in a recent
article.[2] He starts with a summary of John 5: 18, which 'says that
the plot to have Jesus killed began because Jesus was "making

[1] *History and Theology.*   [2] 'Equal to God.'

himself equal to God"'. This assertion, he continues, 'can hardly be historical, so we must seek an explanation for it in the history of the Johannine circle'. But first he offers a brief analysis of Jesus' response to the charge, stressing its ambiguity:

On the one hand, Jesus claims to do nothing 'of himself' (vv. 19, 30). He is merely like a child who imitates 'whatever he sees his father doing' (v. 19). He is the perfect agent, who does not seek what he wants, but only 'the will of the one who sent me' (v. 30). He does not 'come in his own name' nor seek human 'glory' but comes in the name of the Father and receives glory from the one God (vv. 41–44). On the other hand, he does what God does: raises the dead, conducts judgement, and has 'life in himself' (vv. 21–22, 25–29). And the Father has granted him the authority to do these things precisely 'that all may honor the Son as they honor the Father' (v. 23).[3]

Nothing in this response, it is worth remarking, is calculated to dissipate the Jews' understandable *malaise* (and indeed their only mistake was to assert that Jesus was '*making himself* equal with God').[4] The evangelist does not pretend that they would have been satisfied with Jesus' answer or have gone quietly home to supper with all their misgivings allayed. On the contrary, the next time the accusation is levelled against Jesus it follows an assertion on his part that 'the Father and I are one' (10: 30). On the third occasion it is the reason offered to Pilate for demanding Jesus' execution (19: 7).

An impartial observer dropping in during one of the exchanges between Jesus and 'the Jews', or witnessing the outbreak of murderous hostility recorded at the end of ch. 8, might well be reminded of those fierce family rows whose surprising virulence is intelligible only if they are heard against the background of a long history of mutual incomprehension and mistrust. And in fact this debate marks the end of a long vendetta. The issue is a religious one, exacerbated by the conviction on each side that the other is distorting or defacing the legacy of the past. Hence the need to find something in their shared tradition to account both for the accusation of ditheism and for the ambiguity of the response.[5] 'As know-

---

[3] 'Equal to God', 311.

[4] As has been observed by C. K. Barrett, *Essays*, 24.

[5] On this see my *Understanding*, 137–51. David Aune has pointed out to me that having heard only one side of this quarrel, we are in no position to make any reliable reconstruction of the original debate. No doubt 'the Jews' would regard John's account as biased and distorted, and their own version of the events leading

ledgeable Jews themselves,' Meeks asks, 'how could the shapers of the Johannine tradition have come to speak of Jesus in a way that the Jews took to be self-evidently blasphemous?'[6]

In answering this question Meeks makes a number of standard observations before going on to remark that 'the key clue to our mystery' may lie in Nils Dahl's suggestion[7] that the divine δόξα of Jesus seen by Isaiah (John 12: 41) and his 'day' seen by Abraham (8: 56) point to a Christian appropriation—and christological interpretation—of the visions (interpreted as theophanies) of certain patriarchs and prophets. Along with the other traditions alluded to by Meeks, these surely helped the Johannine group to fill in the picture of Jesus' unique relationship with God. But there is still a piece of the puzzle missing.[8]

It may be helpful here to remind ourselves of the solution proposed by Rudolf Bultmann, the well-known hypothesis of a lost Gnostic document upon which the evangelist drew freely. The question is, though, if you abandon this hypothetical source, what are you going to put in its place? And if you believe, as I do, that the roots of the Gospel are Jewish, how are you going to account for these bold new ideas? 'How does newness come into the world? How is it born? Of what fusions, translations, joinings is it made?' If we cannot find a source what are we to look for instead: a tradition, an influence, a background, a catalyst, a miraculous divine intervention, or simply the ineluctable processes of history?

Many important features of John's christology are rooted fairly

---

to the breakup would be completely different. Yet *something* must have happened to precipitate the row, and with due caution we should be able to hazard a reasonable guess concerning the points of divergence between the two parties. On the subject of one-sided narratives see Norman R. Peterson, *Rediscovering Paul*, esp. pp. 10-14, under the heading, 'History as Story'. In the case of John the matter is further complicated by the twofold perspective of the Gospel, for the evangelist is often more interested in his own present than in the surface story. The real closure of the former is to be sought not in Jesus' execution (which is where the surface story directs the reader's attention) but in the community's expulsion from the synagogue. It is a fair guess that 'the Jews' would have alluded to this in terms more suggestive of apostasy than of excommunication.

[6] 'Equal to God', 310.
[7] 'Johannine Church', 128-9.
[8] The same problem is addressed, from the opposite end, so to speak, in a thoughtful piece by Lars Hartman, 'Johannine Jesus-Belief', which starts by assuming the monotheism of the author of the Gospel and his readers, and concludes by half-admitting that this assumption is too frail to withstand the probing to which he subjects it: 'we have put more questions to the evangelist than the text he left behind gives any answers to' (p. 99).

obviously in specific Jewish traditions. That the Prologue is indebted to speculations about the role of wisdom in God's plan for the world was pointed out long ago by Rendel Harris[9] and is now widely admitted. The figure 'like a man' of Daniel 7 is equally clearly the not-so-remote ancestor of the Johannine Son of Man. That the important mission motif has to be explained against the background of Jewish ideas of prophecy and agency is well established.[10] All the various titles bestowed on Jesus in John 1, including the enigmatic 'Lamb of God', are recognizably and for the most part indisputably Jewish. The *merkabah* tradition alluded to by Dahl[11] also assists our understanding.

Yet none of these religious allusions and debts, remarkable as many of them are, appears to have provoked in 'the Jews' the same kind of blazing anger as what they saw to be a direct claim to equality with God—which, as Meeks recognizes, is virtually a charge of ditheism. In particular, neither the term Logos nor the title Son of Man finds any place, either then or later, in credal confessions. Nowhere do we come across the affirmation, 'Jesus is the Logos' or 'Jesus is the Son of Man'.

In searching for what lies behind the fierce debates of the Fourth Gospel, we should be on the look-out for some analogue, on the other side of the Jewish–Christian divide, of the claims that aroused the ire of Jesus' antagonists, for otherwise we shall not even begin to comprehend how this seemingly impassable chasm came to be bridged. Hitherto scholarship has failed to come up with a satisfactory explanation of the strangely elusive claim, hovering between ditheism on the one side and subordinationism on the other, that characterized Johannine christology at the point at which it offended the deepest religious sensibilities of 'the Jews' and aroused them to a response that was, quite literally, murderous.

Crucial to my argument is the observation that neither the term Logos nor the title Son of Man can provide what we are looking for, since neither, if we follow the Gospel account, was the object of Jewish ire and indignation. The Logos is not found outside the Prologue; and although the title Son of Man is important to John, and can be seen hovering on the edge of the debate in ch. 8, it is

---

[9] 'Origin.'
[10] See especially Peder Borgen, 'God's Agent'.
[11] 'Johannine Church', 129.

some way from the heart of the controversy: and this, the true focus of this blazing row, is what we are after.

At this point I must acknowledge a debt to what is, in my opinion, one of the best but at the same time least regarded studies of John's Gospel to have appeared in the last twenty years: Jan-Adolf Bühner's thesis, *Der Gesandte und sein Weg* (1977). Bühner's central interest is in tracing the link between the angel-motif and the prophet-motif in the tradition; and he goes so far as to say that 'the fusion or blending (*Verbindung*) of prophet and angel will prove to be the real key to answering the history-of-religions question concerning Johannine christology'.[12] What I wish to propose instead is that the key to any understanding of what lies behind the claim or charge of ditheism in the Gospel is what amounts to an angel christology *tout court*. This proposal, though related and indebted to the observations of other scholars,[13] has never, to my knowledge, been put forward so directly. Shying away, for some four decades, from the rather extreme views of Martin Werner,[14] Christian scholars have only recently begun once again to admit the importance of the 'Christ as angel' motif in the post-apostolic period, from the Shepherd of Hermas to Cyprian, from Justin to Origen. No one, apparently, has thought that it might shed light on the fierce christological debates in the Fourth Gospel.

To establish this case we must first of all undertake a rapid survey of some OT texts in which angels play a significant role.[15]

---

[12] *Gesandte*, 271. Cf. p. 427. There is clearly much to be said for Bühner's suggestion. Like angels, prophets were regarded as speaking with the voice of God (e.g. Deut. 18: 18-20; Jer. 1: 9): no wonder that the later Jewish tradition, as Bühner has shown (pp. 341-73), insisted on the identity of the prophet and the angel/messenger. Having commented elsewhere upon the relevance of the prophet and agent/emissary motifs to the Fourth Gospel (*Understanding*, 308-17), I do not wish to elaborate upon it again, for my argument here moves in a somewhat different direction.

[13] Notably, besides Bühner, Adolphine Bakker, 'Christ an Angel?'; Christopher Rowland, *Open Heaven*, 94-113; Larry W. Hurtado, *One God*.

[14] *Entstehung*.

[15] For an excellent survey of the relevant material see Peter Schäfer, *Rivalität*, 1-40. The most recent survey is that of Michael Mach, *Entwicklungsstadien*. Mach stresses that for a full coverage of the biblical evidence one must also deal with the heavenly-host passages, but my concern here is with God's special angel or envoy.

I. THE ANGEL OF THE LORD

We must begin by putting a question mark over the word 'the'. The grammatical peculiarity that makes it impossible for Hebrew to distinguish between the determinate and the indeterminate form of יהוה מלאך is seldom noticed. Nor does much help come from the rarer form מלאכי, which can in principle refer either to one of the speaker's messengers or to his one and only messenger. The Elohist version of the Hagar story in Gen. 21: 17 uses the indeterminate מלאך אלהים (*contra* RSV), and this is also how the LXX generally introduces the angel/messenger when he appears for the first time in any particular episode: Gen. 16: 7; 21: 17; 22: 11; Exod. 3: 2; 4: 24 (not in MT); Judg. 2: 1; 6: 11; 13: 3; 2 Kingdoms 14: 7; 4 Kingdoms 1: 3. Important exceptions include Gen. 24: 7; 31: 11; Exod. 14: 19; 23: 20; 32: 34 (ὁ ἄγγελός μου); Num. 22: 22 (ὁ ἄγγελος τοῦ θεοῦ, where MT has מלאך יהוה). It is doubtful, however, if such data as these permit any wide-ranging inferences concerning the intentions of the original authors, since both the Elohist and, more obviously, the LXX writers, are offering *interpretations* of an earlier tradition. Had the earliest writers felt the need to distinguish between *the* angel and *an* angel they would doubtless have found some way of doing so.

A further difficulty, underlined by Walter Baumgartner, is the variety of roles assigned to the מלאך יהוה.[16] (I use the definite article here simply to conform to English usage.) We cannot be sure, for instance, that the consolatory angel/messenger of the Hagar stories, the liberating angel of the Exodus narrative, the exterminating angel of 1 Chron. 21: 12, and the guardian angel of the pious (Pss. 34: 8; 35: 6) are the same—or different!

For the purposes of my argument, however, it is sufficient to notice the impossibility, in several of the narratives in which the מלאך יהוה plays a prominent part, of properly distinguishing between God and his messenger. In the stories of Hagar (Genesis 16 and 21), Jacob (Gen. 31: 11-13), Gideon (Judges 6), and the parents of Samson (Judges 13), the oscillation is rapid and the effect disconcerting, even disturbing. Throughout Genesis 18 there is a similarly subtle and rapid shift between the Lord introduced by the narrator in Gen. 18: 1 and the 'three men' whom Abraham

[16] 'Zum Problem.'

(unaware of what the reader has already been told) sees by the oaks of Mamre (Gen. 18: 2), and also between the Lord and the two men in ch. 19, sometimes reflecting the narrative and reader axis, at other times the perspective of the characters in the story. We know that when he wishes God can intervene directly in human affairs, but he does not always choose to do so, and when, instead, he selects a messenger to act on his behalf, the reader is afflicted by the same perplexity as the human protagonist. Even in the delightful story of Balaam's ass, where the angel figure occupies the centre stage throughout, Balaam understandably reads the word that the angel bids him speak (Num. 22: 35) as the word put into his mouth by God (22: 38).

The divine messenger (מלאך אלהים, indefinite) who appears to Hagar in Genesis 21 tells her in one verse (17) that 'God has heard the voice of the boy where he is', and in the next, speaking *as* God, 'I will make a great nation of him.' Jacob, ten chapters further on, has precisely the same experience (31: 11-13). In Exodus 3, though it is the מלאך יהוה who appears to Moses (v. 2), it is God (v. 4) or Yahweh (v. 7) who speaks, and the ensuing discussion is with God (ch. 3) or Yahweh (ch. 4). In Judges 6 the angel of the Lord who appears to Gideon begins: 'The Lord is with you' (v. 12), but when Gideon speaks the Lord himself answers him, and is then addressed directly in his turn. In Judges 13, the angel of Yahweh who appears to the wife of Manoah is described by her to her husband as a 'man of God' (איש אלהים, divine man?), whose 'appearance was like that of an angel/messenger of God, most awe-inspiring'. When Manoah eventually asks his name, he receives the reply, 'Why do you ask my name, it is too wonderful' (13: 2-21), and the angel figure promptly ascends to heaven in the flame of the altar of sacrifice. When it is all over, Manoah exclaims in alarm, 'We shall surely die, for we have seen God' (Judg. 13: 22).[17]

That no firm distinction can or should be drawn between God and his angel/messenger is graphically demonstrated by the use Hosea makes of the story of Jacob's wrestling match in Genesis 32. In the original account Jacob's antagonist is referred to simply as 'a man' (v. 24), but Jacob himself has no doubt that he has 'seen

---

[17] Cf. Gen. 16: 13; 32: 30. Could there possibly be a hidden allusion to this tradition in Jesus' words to Philip: 'Anyone who has seen me has seen the Father' (John 14: 9)?

God face to face' (v. 30); so it is not surprising that Hosea, recalling this episode, places God and the angel/messenger in synonymous parallelism (12: 4-5; ET 12: 3-4).

All interpretation runs the risk of misunderstanding, but in these passages the risk is particularly acute, since it is evident that they are all crucially and deliberately inexplicit. Did Hagar, Jacob, and Manoah actually see God, as they claim to have done? The answer to this question is withheld: to say either yes or no would be to miss the whole point. Is the eponymous hero of Brecht's *Der gute Mensch von Sezuan* a man or a woman? The answer implied in one English version, *The good woman of Sezuan*, betrays both Brecht's secret and the translator's inadequate grasp of it. Is the Jungian *persona* (the closest analogy I can find) to be identified with the self? Yes and no. In both these instances we have to do with a relationship so close that from one angle it can only be construed as identity. One might also think of Wittgenstein's duck-rabbit, or rather hare (*Hase*) that can be seen as the head of a duck or of a rabbit but never as both. Here, though, there could be no question of ever identifying the two heads, so the analogy is imperfect.

2. THE LIBERATING ANGEL

The chief angel/messenger figure is the one who guided Israel out of Egypt. The key passage, picked up in Num. 20: 16 and Judg 2: 1, is this:

Behold I send an angel/messenger before you, to guard you on the way and to bring you to the place which I have prepared. Give heed to him, and hearken to his voice, do not rebel against him, for he will not pardon your transgression; for my name is in him. (Exod. 23: 20)

What looks like an early reaction to the whole idea of a liberating angel and an attempt to belittle his role is found in a verse from Third Isaiah. The text of Isa. 63: 9 (לֹא צָר וּמַלְאָךְ פָּנָיו הוֹשִׁיעָם) is generally emended in modern editions to conform to the LXX: οὐ πρέσβυς οὐδὲ ὁ ἄγγελος ἀλλ' αὐτὸς κύριος ἔσωσεν αὐτούς. Thus צָר becomes צִיר and וּמַלְאָךְ פָּנָיו becomes וּמַלְאָךְ פָּנָיו, breaking the construct link. The liberating angel vanishes and redemption is attributed to God himself, or rather to his face or presence.

The threat posed by Exod. 23: 20 is deftly disposed of by the

LXX translator. Throughout, as J. W. Wevers has observed, this writer 'avoids any interpretation that might identify the angel with Yahweh, his name is not within him; he is not himself the Lord—his name is rather upon him—nor can he forgive sins; rather he can and must carry out God's orders as his messenger.'[18] In the following verse, MT virtually identifies Yahweh with his messenger: 'But if you hearken attentively to *his* voice and do all that *I* say, then I will be an enemy to your enemies and an adversary to your adversaries.' For קֹלוֹ LXX reads τῆς φωνῆς μου: the voice is now the voice of Yahweh, and the fruitful ambiguity yields to an edifying exhortation that could cause no offence to the most pious of pious ears.

The *Mekilta of R. Ishmael* handles the problematic text with some subtlety. It concludes the Tractate Kaspa with a discussion of Exod. 23: 19 ('You shall not boil a kid in its mother's milk'). The next Tractate, Shabbata, which is also the last, takes up the midrash at Exod. 31: 12 ('And the Lord spoke to Moses'): 'Directly and not through an angel (מלאך) nor through the emissary (השליח).' Thus the midrash breaks off just before the offending verse that describes the liberating role of the מלאך יהוה, and when the commentary is resumed, some eight chapters further on, it indirectly repudiates this role with a remark ostensibly addressed to the nature of God's communication with Moses. Since there is nothing in 31: 12 to make one suspect the presence of an intermediary (and why would God need one when addressing Moses?), we can only suppose that it is the threateningly intractable Exod. 23: 20 that has provoked the vehement denial with which the new tractate, Shabbata, commences.

What the *Mekilta* hints at is tackled head on by the Passover Haggadah, which first illustrates Deut. 26: 8 by quoting Exod. 12: 12 and then expatiates upon each clause in succession:

'For I will go through the land of Egypt in that night': I, and not an angel. 'I will smite the first-born in the land of Egypt': I and not a seraph. 'And against all the gods of Egypt I will execute judgements': I, and not the emissary (השליח).

[18] *Notes*, 369-71.

As in the *Mekilta*, the angel (מלאך) can scarcely be other than the
liberating angel of Exod. 23: 20. The two texts are clearly related.[19]

Like the *Mekilta*, *Leviticus Rabbah* takes God's address to Moses as
a starting-point for an attempt to do away with the role of the
liberating angel. But there is a significant difference. Whilst the
more recent midrash acknowledges that the problem text is picked
up both in Num. 20: 16 and in Judg. 2: 1, it preserves God's
transcendence by identifying the angel in the former with Moses
and that in the latter with Phinehas. Thus earthly מלאכים are
firmly identified as prophets. There are heavenly מלאכים too, but
there is apparently no danger of their usurping God's authority.

We may conclude then that the ambiguity and oscillation between
Yahweh and his angel that is found elsewhere in Exodus, as in
Genesis, Numbers, and Judges, appears in Exod. 23: 20 in an
especially direct and dangerous form. When adapting or commenting upon this passage, however, later Jewish authors, starting with
LXX, do their best to conceal the indiscretion, not wishing to leave
room for an angel figure who, credited with an independent
existence, might be thought to be related to Yahweh not as an ally
or amanuensis but as a rival.

These misgivings may be thought to be justified by the use to
which the Exodus tradition was put elsewhere, first in the
Apocalypse of Abraham and secondly in the Gospel of John.[20]

The angel Yaoel, who plays such an important part in the
pseudepigraphon, and whose name is clearly a conflation of
Yahweh and El, alludes to Exod. 23: 20 in his address to
Abraham: 'For your sake I have indicated the way of the land'

---

[19] As is recognized by Judah Goldin, 'Not by Means of an Angel'. Goldin also
refers to the *Mekilta* on Exod. 12: 12, which cites Exod. 12: 29 ('Now it was the
Lord who smote the first-born') and makes the same addition: 'not by means of an
angel and not by means of an emissary'. Apart from the last instance the determi-
native form השליח is used. Goldin fails to notice this fact, but as Bühner has observed
(*Gesandte*, 327), it must have some significance. Bühner thinks that Israel's
guardian angel is probably the intended reference. For more texts and further
comment see Schäfer, *Rivalität*, 48–50.
[20] See too *Understanding*, 142–4. The angel of the *Apocalypse of Abraham* closely
resembles the Metatron of the late (5th or 6th century AD) *3 Enoch*, also called 'the
lesser Yahweh' (12: 5), and is relevant to the history of the rabbinical controversies
told by Alan F. Segal in his *Two Powers*. John Day has drawn my attention to a
bowl inscription, again some centuries after the New Testament, which invokes an
angel called Yehoel. See J. Naveh and S. Shaked, *Amulets*, 163.

(10: 14). Literally fulfilling the divine promise, 'my name is in him' (Exod. 23: 21), and assuming the role of the liberating angel, he resembles the Jesus of the Fourth Gospel in professing to be the emissary of God ('I am sent to you' (10: 6, 13)) and claiming the authority of his name (10: 8). Subsequently (17: 3) the same name, Yaoel, is given to God. Jesus too declares that he has been sent by God and shares in the authority of his name (John 5: 43; 10: 25). God has made him a gift of his name (17: 11) and he has manifested it (17: 1) and made it known to his disciples (17: 26).

3. THE *ANGELUS INTERPRES*

We can scarcely blame the biblical writers for failing to provide us with all the material we would need for a comprehensive *Überlieferungsgeschichte* of the traditions that interest us. By the time Daniel was composed, in the second century, the heavenly realm was peopled by a throng of angelic beings, some of whom had particular names and carried out particular functions. As Christopher Rowland has argued, an early stage of what must have been a gradual transformation is reflected in Ezekiel.[21] The awesome Yahweh figure of chapter 1 reappears in chapter 8, once again 'in the appearance of a man' (8: 2, following LXX in reading אִישׁ (ἀνδρός) for MT's אֵשׁ). By now he has stepped down from his throne and exhibits the form, as Rowland says, of 'an agent of the divine purpose'. Like the מלאך יהוה of many earlier stories, he addresses the human seer with the authoritative voice of God, and is the first of what would prove to be a whole series of angelic figures who, like him, would have a human shape but be readily recognizable as heavenly messengers with the task of communicating divine mysteries to the few chosen souls privileged to receive these and to pass them on to the wise. Ezekiel's description of the man-like figure is drawn upon in the final part of Daniel (ch. 10) for his own portrayal of an angel whom it is hard not to see as a later avatar of 'the angel of the Lord'.

Meanwhile a number of angels (and other night riders) had appeared in the first major section of Zechariah, including 'the angel of the Lord' and the prophet's *angelus interpres*. At first the angel of the Lord plays an intercessory role (1: 12), but sub-

---

[21] *Open Heaven*, 95–8.

sequently the reader may scent a whiff of the old equivocation, when the words addressed to Satan, 'the Lord rebuke you' (3: 2), are attributed not, as we should expect, to the angel of the Lord mentioned in the previous verse, but to Yahweh himself.

Elsewhere, in another development that anticipates a regular rabbinical ploy, any possible ambiguity (perceived as dangerous or undesirable?) is blocked out, and English translations are compelled to shift from 'angel' to 'messenger': 'Then Haggai, the messenger of the Lord (מלאך יהוה), spoke to the people with the Lord's message (במלאכות יהוה), saying, "I am with you, says the Lord"' (Hag. 1: 13). The name of Malachi, the last of the canonical prophets, is left untranslated, and eventually the figure of the Lord's messenger (מלאכי, 3: 1) appears to be identified with Elijah (3: 23; ET 4: 5). (This is certainly how Matthew reads him (Matt. 11: 10, 14).)

In many pseudepigraphical writings such as *The Testaments of the Twelve Patriarchs*, one gets no sense of any possible confusion between the Lord and his angel, who plays a largely intercessory role (*T. Levi* 5: 6; *T. Dan* 6: 5; *T. Ash.* 6: 40; *T. Ben.* 6: 1). In the *Letter of Jeremiah*, engrossed as it is with the condemnation of idolatry, we read: 'Say in your heart, "It is thou, Lord, whom we must worship". For my angel is with you and is watching your lives' (vv. 5–6). The angel of the Lord, purged of all his eloquent opacity, is now no more than a benign fairy godmother, posing not the slightest threat to monotheistic orthodoxy.

Such a variety of response and interpretation makes it impossible to generalize about the Jewish understanding of angels in the Second Temple period. My impression is that all the writers quoted are coming to terms, one way or another, with a tradition perceived by some as valuable, and therefore to be absorbed and adapted, by others as dangerous, and therefore to be suppressed. Aware, however, of the danger of reading one's own interests into texts which cannot be supposed to share the curiosity and concern of subsequent scholarship, I must leave this as a conjecture.

Despite this hesitation, I believe that a reasonable case has already been made for the view that the מלאך יהוה tradition provides the most plausible and obvious explanation of John's presentation of Jesus as the emissary of God. The pages of the Bible are crowded with a host of intermediary figures—word, spirit, name, priests, and prophets, not to mention dreams and visions—that represent God in his dealings with humanity; but nowhere else is there such an obvious analogue to the tantalizing equivocation that makes it impossible, when assessing the christology of the Fourth Gospel, to settle definitively either for ditheism or for subordinationism. Searching in the Jewish tradition for remnants of a possible bridge that could lead across to John's provocatively ambiguous portrayal of Jesus' relationship with the God who sent him (the Father–Son relationship is another story) where else should we look?

In the next section of this chapter the case will be strengthened by the consideration of three further pieces of evidence.

4. THREE DIVERGING PATHS

To do justice to the colourful diversity of the Jewish heavens at the turn of the era, teeming as they are with angelic life, a painter would have to operate with the bravura of a Bosch. The resulting picture would not be without internal contradictions, so perhaps it is better to think of a tapestry woven over a long period by several hands. Despite some disagreement in form and content, one persistent motif, reaching back to the original מלאך יהוה tradition, may be traced throughout. Three versions of this are particularly relevant to this study.

(a) 4 Ezra

Centuries earlier than *4 Ezra* the strength of the מלאך יהוה tradition may be seen from the role played by 'the angel of the presence' in *Jubilees*. From chapter 2 onwards it is he who fulfils the task of dictating to Moses the history of creation and much else besides; so the voice of the angel is equivalent to the voice of God. When recounting the story of Hagar, this 'angel of the presence' attributes the angel's role to another, 'one of the holy ones' (17: 11), whereas when he comes to the story of the sacrifice of Isaac he himself assumes the responsibility of preventing Abraham from sacrificing Isaac: 'And I called out to him from heaven and said to him, "Abraham, Abraham"' (18: 10). He evidently feels more directly involved in the fate of Isaac than in that of Ishmael. A little further on '*the Lord* called Abraham by his name *again* from heaven' (18: 14), and the reader sees very clearly that the old equivocation has lost none of its power to mystify and bemuse.

In *4 Ezra* the *angelus interpres* has a name, Uriel. In other respects the difficulty of distinguishing him from the God who sent him is exactly the same as before. Although the author is a contemporary of the fourth evangelist, it is unlikely that they were acquainted with one another, and the marked resemblance in their handling of the angel/emissary theme must be put down to the striking persistence, within the Jewish religious community, of this particular tradition.

In 5: 31 the angel appears for the second time. As his conversation with the seer proceeds, there is a point at which we suddenly become aware that it is no longer, apparently, the angel who is speaking, but God: 'you cannot discover my judgement or the goal of the love that I have promised my people' (5: 40). This is only one of numerous passages in which the angel is either addressed by a title that seems more appropriate to the deity (so 4: 38; 5: 41; 7: 45, 58, 75) or talks as if God is speaking through his mouth (5: 40, 42; 6: 6; 8: 47; 9: 18–22). In chapter 7 there is another abrupt and unannounced change of subject: the angel opens the dialogue, but Ezra again addresses his reply to God (7: 17).

Elsewhere (12: 7–9) Ezra turns to God to pray for enlightenment and it is the angel who replies. In chapter 13 our first impression, after another prayer addressed to 'the Most High', is that God himself is responding; but we then realize that 'the Most High' is being spoken of in the third person, and this continues until the end of the chapter—except for one reference to 'my son' (or, more probably 'my servant') (13: 37). All this leaves us thoroughly confused—not for the first time. At the close of chapter 13 the angel promises Ezra further revelations and the explanation of wondrous matters (13: 56), but then promptly vanishes: in the concluding chapter God deals with the seer directly.

How the first readers of the book responded to these bewilderingly rapid and frequent transitions we can only guess. We should bear in mind, however, that they must have been used to precisely the same comings and goings, toings and froings, in the Bible itself. Certainly a deconstructionalist critic would have a field-day with all these texts, though a sense of sportsmanship might make him refrain from taking pot-shots at all those sitting ducks and immobile rabbits. A less hostile reader might well simply assume that Uriel, the angel of Ezra's visions, had taken the place of the biblical מלאך יהוה.

(b) The Magharians

Whether or not the tenth-century Qaraite writer, Ya'qūb al Qirqisānī, to whom we owe our knowledge of the Magharians (cave-dwellers?), was right to place them before Jesus and Christianity, what is recorded about the convictions of this sect forms an interesting comparison with our other examples. With some of its members reported as regarding laughter as unlawful, it can scarcely have been the most attractive of religious groups. What is significant about the Magharians is their literal interpretation of the 'angel of the Lord' passages in the Bible, 'for they assert that these are descriptions of an angel, who created the world'.[22] A similar view, Qirqisānī tells us, was held by Benjamin al-Nahāwandī, another Qaraite writer, who lived in the preceding century: 'He maintained that the great Creator created one angel and it was this angel who created [the] whole world, and who sent the prophets and despatched [sic] the messengers, and performed the miracles and made commandments and prohibitions and it is he who brings about whatever comes to pass in the world, and not the prime Creator.'[23] It seems, then, that the Magharians, believing the angel of the Lord to be a real being, created by God,[24] concluded that he acted as a kind of demiurge. Jewish monotheism is evidently much more severely threatened by such a doctrine than by any of the other texts that we have considered so far. Indeed, with only the slightest of deviations we would be dealing with an embryonic Gnosticism, with the angel of the Lord transformed into an evil, oppositional God instead of what the Magharians appear to have thought him to be, a compliant master-of-works.

After outlining Qirqisānī's views, H. A. Wolfson goes on to suggest that they should be conflated with reports of the eleventh-century Muḥammad al-Sharastānī concerning a sect that appears in his work, probably by a scribal error, under the name of

---

[22] B. Chiesa and W. Lockwood (eds.), *Ya'qūb al-Qirqisānī*, 134–5.

[23] Ibid. 147–8.

[24] Cf. Epiphanius on the Ebionites: οὐ φάσκουσι δὲ ἐκ Θεοῦ πατρὸς αὐτὸν [i.e. Christ] γεγεννῆσθαι, ἀλλὰ ἐκτίσθαι, ὡς ἕνα τῶν ἀρχαγγέλων, μείζονα δὲ αὐτῶν ὄντα (*Adv. Haer.* 30: 16, PG 41: 433C).

Maqāriba.[25] Here the created angel, like that of Qirqisānī's Magharians, is used as an explanation of anthropomorphism, and like that of his Nahāwandī, is said to have mediated the revelation of the Law. It contains, however, Wolfson points out, three additional elements: '(1) that the angel through whom the Law was revealed and to whom all the anthropological narratives of the Hebrew Bible refer, could be sent down by God among men to act as His representative; (2) that the angel was actually sent down by God to act as His representative among men; (3) that it is this belief of theirs that was later followed by Arius.'[26] Apart from the association with Arius, evidently a conclusion of Sharastānī himself, it is hard to see how much closer we could get to one of the fundamental tenets of the fourth evangelist. Even if, which seems unlikely, we should be thinking of two sects rather than one, the work of these two medieval authors, drawing on evidence that is now lost to us, shows more clearly than anything else outside the New Testament how easy it was, once the first fatal step of hypostasization had been taken, to pass from a characteristically Jewish belief to one which is actually much closer to Christianity. It is perhaps not surprising that no record of the existence of this sect has come down to us through official rabbinical channels.

(c) *Justin Martyr*

My final example, looked at in the light of the preceding argument, is so remarkable as to appear shocking. Here at last, despite Justin's disclaimers, is an honest-to-God ditheism, for the angel/messenger of God, no longer to be confused with 'the Father and Creator of the universe', is nevertheless pronouncing himself to be divine. Basing himself on the statement in Exod. 3: 2 that 'the angel of the Lord appeared to Moses', and conveniently forgetting that it is God (MT אלהים, LXX κύριος) who is said to have called to him out of the bush (3: 4), he does not hesitate to misquote the crucial text when condemning the Jews for their perversity:

So much is written for the sake of proving that Jesus the Christ is the Son of God and his Apostle, being of old the Word, and appearing sometimes

---

[25] H. A. Wolfson, 'The Pre-Existent Angel'. Norman Golb disagrees: 'It is evident that the only source which can be relied upon with confidence for the description of the Maġārīya is Qirqisānī' ('Who were the Maġārīya?', 350). But see now the very full discussion of Jarl Fossum, 'Magharians'.

[26] 'The Pre-Existent Angel', 92.

in the form of fire, and sometimes in the likeness of angels; but now, by the will of God, having become man for the human race, He endured all the sufferings which the devils instigated the senseless Jews to inflict upon Him; who, though they have it expressly affirmed in the writings of Moses, 'And the angel of God spake to Moses in a flame of fire in a bush, and said, I am that I am, the God of Abraham, and the God of Isaac, and the God of Jacob,' yet maintain that He who said this was the Father and Creator of the universe . . . The Jews, accordingly, being throughout of the opinion that it was the Father of the universe who spake to Moses, though He who spake to him was indeed the Son of God, who is called both Angel and Apostle, are justly charged, both by the Spirit of prophecy and by Christ Himself, with knowing neither the Father nor the Son. . . . And that which was said out of the bush to Moses, 'I am that I am, the God of Abraham, and the God of Isaac, and the God of Jacob, and the God of your fathers,' this signified that they, even though dead, are yet in existence, and are men belonging to Christ Himself.[27]

Justin's exegesis, though apparently based on a simple blunder, actually marks the natural end of a trajectory that had started many centuries earlier. If we place the Fourth Gospel where it belongs, at a slightly less advanced point on the same curve, Justin's argument loses some of its power to shock. However crude and uncompromising, it is not unrepresentative of what Christians had come to believe. But what of the Jews, and in particular what of the adversaries of Jesus who are given that name in the Fourth Gospel? Did they see Justin's argument coming? Had they already confronted it? Is John's angel christology simply a more delicate and sophisticated variety of Justin's heavy-footed apologia?

5. CONCLUSION

In response to the question how the hypothesis advanced in this chapter differs from or improves upon earlier suggestions, my answer is that the perplexingly rapid shift of perspective demanded

---

[27] *1 Apol.* 63. Oskar Skarsaune, *The Proof from Prophecy*, holds that Justin made use of a testimony source here, arguing from the fact that his three quotations from Exodus 3 'show remarkable accordance with each other against the LXX' (p. 47). But one would scarcely expect them to diverge! Subsequently, in *Dial.* 59–60, Justin takes a different tack, allowing Trypho to observe: 'He who was seen in a flame of fire was an angel, and he who conversed with Moses was God, so that both an angel and God, two together, were in that vision' (*Dial.* 60. 1; cf. Philo, *De Vit. Mos.* 1. 71).

by the biblical and pseudepigraphical texts is matched very clearly, *at precisely the point where the theory requires it*, by a similar oscillation between the claims attributed to Jesus in the Fourth Gospel, where we experience the same difficulty in saying whether Jesus is claiming divinity with the Father or acknowledging his complete dependence. The pendulum swings back and forth between the two poles in such a way that we cannot arrest it at either pole, or indeed at any point in between, without radically misrepresenting the evidence. One vital element in the theory has long been recognized: the Jewish law of agency that posits a theoretical identity between sender and sent alongside a suspended awareness of the difference between the two. The other element, just as vital, is required to explain the particularity of the mission of Jesus, where God is the sender and Jesus his angel emissary. Clement of Alexandria was to say later of Christ that he has been called 'the face' (τὸ πρόσωπον) of the Father (*Stromata* 5. 6. 34, 1)—the word that is regularly used in the LXX to translate the Hebrew פָּנִים. Put into Latin this would be *persona*, and the Jungian term conveys with some precision the essential relationship between God and the face he presents to the world, first through an unnamed angel/messenger and then definitively, as Christians believe, through Christ.

Why has this explanation, so close to the assumptions of many of the leading Church Fathers, never been advanced by critical scholarship? The most likely reason is that the Jesus of the Fourth Gospel, human and divine, does not *look* like an angel. But he does behave like one, and in many places assumes the role, not just of a prophet (for the prophets were never confused with the God in whose name they spoke) but of the clearly 'angelic' Son of Man. What is notable about the so-called Son of Man in Daniel is that, unlike most of the other individual angels in the book, he has no name,[28] simply an appearance and a role. Like other angelic figures,[29] in Daniel and elsewhere, he *resembles* a (son of) man; consequently, resemblance being a reciprocal relationship, when the Johannine Jesus takes over the role of the Son of Man, he has

---

[28] John Day has argued 'that the overall redactor of the book of Daniel wished to equate the one like a son of man with the angel Michael', *God's Conflict*, 165. But the author of Daniel 7 presumably had no such intention, nor is it the impression received by the reader.

[29] e.g. Gen. 18: 2; 19: 10; 32: 24; Judg. 13: 11; Ezek. 9: 2; Dan. 8: 15; 9: 21; 10: 16, 18; 12: 6–7; *1 Enoch* 87: 2; 90: 14.

no need to alter his own appearance: he looks like an angel after all.

What, though, has been explained in this chapter? *Ab esse ad posse valet illatio.* Since Johannine Christianity emerged from Judaism, it must have been possible for it to do so, in the form, moreover, in which the Gospel shows it to have existed. There must have been a bridge (particularly important but having left few obvious traces) probably connected with the more prominent bridge that leads back to the Danielic Son of Man. Yet the discovery of a bridge does not amount to an explanation of how it came to be crossed; nor does it entail the conclusion that the passage was somehow an inexorable necessity. Just because a new religion did *de facto* come into existence does not mean that it had to do so. With no space to include any reflections on the Father–Son relationship which is the other facet of Johannine christological thinking, my purpose has been to inquire into certain conditions of the possibility of the new religion, not to offer a causal explanation of its actual genesis.

4

The Signs Source

Taken together, the two books of Robert Tomson Fortna, the first published in 1970 and the second eighteen years later,[1] represent the most thorough and sustained attempt ever made to reconstruct the alleged narrative source underlying John's Gospel, and to assess the theological purpose of the source and of its redactor. Yet despite the claims of certain scholars,[2] there is as yet no consensus concerning the extent or nature of the postulated source, and some continue to question its very existence. Indeed it would be more accurate to speak of a *dialogue des sourds* in which the opposing camps confront one another across an apparently unbridgeable divide and make little or no attempt to respond to one another's arguments.[3] This situation is surely not to be tolerated in the world of academia, where, at least in principle, scholars are supposed to move together towards a common understanding of the truth through reasoned argument and debate. The persisting disagreement is the more surprising when one reflects that 'partitionist' theories have been around for the best part of two centuries,[4] and signs-source theories for one and a half.[5] No doubt the majority of such theories lie buried in decent obscurity: one might think that

[1] *The Gospel of Signs* (1970); *The Fourth Gospel and its Predecessor* (1988).

[2] e.g. Robert Kysar, 'Source Analysis'. In a concluding note, Kysar recognizes 'the existence of a sizable body of scholars who continue to maintain that source analyses of the fourth gospel of any kind are fruitless and impossible speculation' (152 n. 1). The consensus of which he speaks is really a conspiracy of the like-minded, its weakness exposed by the publication, a decade or so later, of H.-P. Heekerens's *Zeichen-Quelle*.

[3] For instance, Fortna totally ignores Heekerens's detailed objections to certain of his arguments (*Zeichen-Quelle*, 23–4, 34–9), and all but ignores Donald A. Carson's sustained attack in 'Current Source Criticism'. Carson, in his turn, fails to get to grips with some of Fortna's strongest arguments. Charles Kingsley Barrett's predominantly negative review of Fortna's *Gospel of Signs* in *JTS* 22 (1971), 571–4 is largely taken up with a criticism of Fortna's reconstruction of the first sign story and allows his central arguments to pass without comment.

[4] The earliest I know is that of J. Chr. R. Eckermann, *Über die eigentlich sicheren Gründe* (1796). Cf. Siegfried Schulz, *Untersuchungen*, 48 n. 3.

[5] The first being Alexander Schweizer, *Evangelium Johannis* (1841). Cf. Gilbert van Belle, *Semeia-Bron*, 11–13.

had Fortna's theory been as frail as these it too would have been effectively throttled by its critics, with the result that he would have been in no position to publish a 'sequel' many years later. Yet this is scarcely an argument. How then are we to account for the fact that the most long-lived of all Johannine source theories, the signs source, has neither gained the scholarly consensus that its advocates, deaf to all protests, appear to take for granted, nor yet been consigned to inglorious oblivion?

One reason is the contrast between the instinctive distaste of conservative scholars for anything that smacks of literary reconstruction and the irrepressible urge of the more adventurous to keep on mounting expeditions in search of sources. But this difference falls outside the sphere of rational discussion. For our purposes a more important reason is that the proponents of the theory claim too much for it, while its opponents concede too little. By expanding possibilities into probabilities and then treating these as if they were certainties the advocates of what is still, after all, only a hypothesis present a relatively easy target for the heavy guns of their adversaries. These, in consequence, are dispensed from the necessity of doing battle on a less favourable terrain. To facilitate the following discussion the subject may be divided into four interlinked but distinguishable topics: the existence of the source; its extent; its reconstruction; its purpose. There is, however, a fifth topic, closely associated with the question of the *extent* of the source and to be treated alongside it. This is the theory of the signs *gospel*, propounded and defended, in slightly differing forms, in Fortna's two books. The essay that follows, then, comprises five main sections, plus a postscript.

I. EXISTENCE

Because of the interrelatedness and interdependence of most biblical scholarship it can be salutary, from time to time, to pay heed to a solitary voice which, *cantans extra chorum*, sticks determinedly to its own line. Such a voice is that of the Oxford scholar James Matthew Thompson, who, in a series of articles written for the *Expositor* between 1915 and 1917,[6] anticipated by some years

---

[6] See bibliography for a list of these articles. In my own book, *Understanding*, 33 n. 78, I failed to give due credit to Thompson's pioneering studies.

the better-known work of Alexander Faure.[7] At the time Thompson
wrote Johannine source criticism was still a German bailiwick;[8]
although he shows some awareness of the early work of Spitta, he
evidently did not know it at first hand,[9] and his own writing is
fresh and individual. In his third article he observes that

> there runs through the narrative portions of the first twelve chapters of
> the Gospel a single and definite point of view with regard to Jesus' σημεῖα;
> they are uniformly emphasized both as a proof of His divine mission and
> as a proper ground of religious faith. The significance of this point of view
> is enhanced by the fact that it does not extend to the second part of the
> Gospel, and is either ignored or adversely criticised in the discourses of the
> first part. The conclusion (xx. 30–31), then, so far as its mention of σημεῖα
> is concerned, is shown to correspond to certain definite portions of the
> Gospel, which have an individuality of their own. It does not summarise
> the whole gospel or represent the point of view of the other parts.[10]

Elsewhere Thompson says of the concluding verses of chapter 20
that they are 'ludicrously inadequate as a summary of the most
characteristic doctrine of the Gospel';[11] but had the evangelist
been as convinced as Thompson was of the inappropriateness of
this conclusion, he would surely have composed an alternative
ending of his own. It *can* be read so as to include the resurrection
appearances as signs. Fortna suggests that for the redactor of the
signs gospel the resurrection was itself the ultimate sign, and, even
more intriguingly, that for the evangelist this place was occupied
by Jesus' death.[12] But these can only be guesses: how can we be

---

[7] 'Quellenscheidungshypothese.'

[8] William Sanday, in a book dedicated to 'my American friends', ranks Benjamin
Wisner Bacon among the partitionists, commenting, in his lofty way, that he 'has
been to Germany and learnt his lesson too well' (*Criticism*, 24). But Bacon, though
prepared to be counted, along with Wellhausen, as a 'revisionist', rejects the appellation 'partitionist': cf. *Fourth Gospel*, 480–1.

[9] In the first of his articles ('Disarrangement', 422 n. 1) he alludes to Spitta's
Geschichte (1893); but he makes no mention of Spitta's later, equally important
work, *Johannes-Evangelium* (1910), nor, for that matter, of Hans Hinrich Wendt,
Schichten (1911). So Thompson scarcely deserves Ronald Knox's jibe, in *Absolute
and Abitoflhell*, 3, that in 'setting out the Gospel Truths t'explain', he 'Thought all
that was not German not germane.'

[10] 'Structure', 525–6.

[11] 'Appendix', 145. Not surprisingly, Thompson does not get everything right.
But even his errors are illuminating, for instance his assertion that the second
half of the Gospel promotes a different and higher view of Christ than is found in
the first. He is right about the difference, wrong to assert that it is confined to the
second half of the Gospel.

[12] Most clearly in *Predecessor*, 250; see also pp. 204, 212, 214, etc.

sure of what a redactor had in mind in taking over a conclusion
for his work which, *ex hypothesi*, he did not compose himself? Here
if anywhere it is legitimate to invoke the spectre of the intentional
fallacy. No doubt the *meaning* of the word σημεῖον (a sign, emblem,
or token pointing to some reality beyond itself) is sufficiently
general to allow a thinker as subtle as John to apply it, indirectly,
to events such as Jesus' crucifixion (already compared, in 3: 14, to
the bronze serpent set up or elevated by Moses in the desert) or his
resurrection (as an outward sign of the inward glory perceptible,
to the true believer, in all Jesus' actions). Nevertheless, in all
the occurrences of the term that can reasonably be ascribed to
the signs source, the *reference* of σημεῖον is consistently that of a
miraculous act performed in the sight of the disciples in order
to promote faith in Jesus. On any reading of the evidence this
reference is extended, in 20: 30, either to Jesus' death, or to his
resurrection, or to both; and this extension involves such a grind-
ing wrench that we must surely recognize it, along with
Thompson, Faure, and innumerable other scholars, as one of the
Gospel's salient aporias. Here, I think, Charles Kingsley Barrett[13]
and Barnabas Lindars[14] are simply wrong.

Thompson goes on to argue, as Faure was to do, that 20: 30–1
fits best towards the end of chapter 12, where the first part of the
Gospel is brought to a solemn close and the evangelist sums up its
results (12: 37–43). Of this (preliminary) conclusion he says that it

was obviously written from the point of view of one who thought that
Jesus' object was to evoke faith by working miracles, and who wished
to account for the comparative failure of this attempt. It contains no
suggestion of deeper faith or wider issues. It is a fitting conclusion for those
incidents and passages which we have just enumerated [i.e. the miracle
stories], but a most inappropriate one for some other parts of the chapters
which precede it. It shows, moreover, no consciousness of the second part
of the Gospel (chap. xiii.–xxi.), in which (except for xx. 30) the word
σημεῖον does not occur at all. It is therefore strong evidence for the
independent existence of a narrative-Gospel, one of whose characteristics
was a belief in the apologetic aim and value of Jesus' miracles.[15]

---

[13] 'There is no reason why he [the evangelist] should not be making his own
comment on a wider range of material' (*Gospel*, 575).

[14] 'This verse can be quite reasonably understood as it stands, in spite of the lack
of connection with the passion and resurrection accounts. . . . Why should it not be
John's own conclusion to the Gospel?' (*Behind the Fourth Gospel*, 31).

[15] 'Structure', 523.

In his first book, Fortna, who knows Thompson's work and is usually alert to the presence of aporias, fails to observe how awkward the end of chapter 20 appears in its present context; he remarks, puzzlingly, that if the passion source was part of the longer signs source, the mention of signs in 20: 30 'is not so surprising'.[16] In fact, by extending the source to include the passion narrative, 'he cuts the ground away', as Lindars observes, 'from one of the original arguments for the hypothesis of the Signs Source itself'.[17]

The other strong indication of the existence of a signs source is to be found in 4: 54. Here is how Faure stated the case:

We can rediscover the traces of just such a miracle book (a βιβλίον σημείων Ιησοῦ or whatever it was called—there may have been more than one collection) in the miracle stories of the Gospel itself: we have simply to glance over the stories peculiar to the Gospel, the two Galilean miracles in chapters 2 (the marriage-feast of Cana) and 4 (the Johannine equivalent of the centurion from Capernaum), the two Jerusalem healing-miracles (the cripple in chapter 5 and the blind man in chapter 9), and the raising from the dead in chapter 11.[18] Even if these have been torn apart and gradually expanded (this is also true of the miracles in chapters 4 and 5) the stories betray even so their earlier interconnectedness and their original character. Yet despite all the insertions the opening words of the first two miracles have been preserved: ἐποίησεν ἀρχὴν τῶν σημείων ὁ Ἰησοῦς ἐν Κανᾶ τῆς Γαλιλαίας (2: 11); τοῦτο πάλιν δεύτερον σημεῖον ἐποίησεν ὁ Ἰησοῦς (4: 54). Moreover the journeys and other events that intervene between these two stories do not disguise the fact that their situation is the same. And having undergone fewer expansions than the others, they show that it was originally a matter of short, factual stories, simply told.[19]

---

[16] *Gospel*, 198. Equally puzzling is the observation of Lamar Cope that 'the conclusion in 20: 30-31, which is so fitting for a Signs Gospel and so inappropriate for the present Gospel, is very difficult to explain if the Signs Gospel did not contain the death/resurrection story' ('Earliest Gospel', 18). The death/resurrection story, taken in conjunction with the preceding discourse and prayer, is precisely what makes the present ending so problematic. Fortna now thinks that the signs source and the passion source were 'almost certainly' once separate, 'as their contrasting genres indicate: a collection of miracle tales on the one hand and a continuous narrative of Jesus' death on the other' (*Predecessor*, 118), an opinion scarcely consistent with the view argued later that the signs source 'was already a *gospel*—a primitive and bare one, by later standards, but a gospel nevertheless' (ibid. 205). Is there an aporia here?

[17] *Behind the Fourth Gospel*, 30.

[18] Faure thinks that the story of the feeding of the five thousand, along with what he calls the 'sea miracle', was borrowed from the Synoptics and added later.

[19] 'Quellenscheidungshypothese', 109-10.

Faure goes on, as Thompson had done before him, to link this 'miracle account' with 12: 37 (τοσαῦτα σημεῖα) and 20: 30 (πολλὰ ἄλλα σημεῖα).

It seems to have been left to Bultmann to make the final, clinching observation that the enumeration which concludes the second miracle must be taken from the source, 'since it ignores 2. 23'.[20] How could the evangelist have referred to the curing of the official's son as 'the second sign' when he had already asserted that 'many people, seeing the signs which he was performing, believed in him' (2: 23; cf. 3: 2)? Here is an obvious contradiction. It certainly looks on the face of it that two independent narratives have been stitched together at this point; and most of the recent proponents of the source theory adopt this solution, arguing that when inserting the second sign recorded in his source the evangelist did not attempt to harmonize the story by removing the word 'second'.[21] This does not, of course, mean that all the questions are solved. Why, for instance, having followed his source in enumerating the first two signs, did the evangelist fail to

---

[20] *Gospel*, 209 n. 2. Eduard Schwartz had already spotted the discrepancy but he noted simply that the Galilean miracles (1: 11; 4: 54) are narrated as if the 'many signs' which Jesus had performed earlier (*gleich am Anfang*) in Jerusalem counted for nothing ('Aporien', 116). The numbering, he says, is not idle or frivolous (*müssige Spielerei*), but 'a deliberate attack on Luke or on the *Vorlage* of Matthew and Luke' (p. 510). In 4: 45 we are told about the welcome accorded to Jesus by the Galileans who, having gone to Jerusalem for the feast, had seen 'all that he had done' there on that occasion. The word σημεῖα is not used here, but the problem generated by this passage, immediately preceding as it does the 'second' miracle-story, is of the same order.

[21] Urban C. von Wahlde, the only modern scholar to have offered an analysis of John's narrative source that can be said to rival that of Fortna, has an alternative solution. Maintaining that *all* uses of the word σημεῖα in the sense of miracles come from the source, he suggests that this was the second sign performed by Jesus *during his trip from Judaea to Galilee* (the other being his uncanny display of knowledge about the Samaritan woman's marital status earlier in ch. 4) (*Earliest Version*, 94). But there are two objections against this theory: (*a*) If, as is probable, ἐλθὼν ἐκ τῆς Ἰουδαίας εἰς τὴν Γαλιλαίαν means 'having returned from Judaea to Galilee' it cannot include a reference to an event that took place in Samaria; (*b*) in any case, a feature common to all Jesus' miracles is that they were performed 'in the sight of the disciples' (20: 30), which cannot be said of Jesus' conversation with the Samaritan woman. Yet another solution is offered by Heekerens, who quotes (twice—*Zeichen-Quelle*, 24, 123) Matthias Rissi: 'It is the place that matters, not the number. Cana comes to be a sign of faith, while Jerusalem remains obstinate' ('Hochzeit', 84). But the absence of the name 'Cana' (supposedly a key-word) ruins this suggestion too. (Fortna (*Predecessor*, 299 and n. 140) holds that the emphasis on Galilee in both 2: 11 and 4: 54 comes from the evangelist.)

enumerate the rest?[22] (Fortna has his own solution to this problem, which we shall come to in the next section.) There are a number of possible answers,[23] but perhaps the simplest is that after this point the evangelist, for whatever reason, began to change the *order* of his source; and in fact many commentators had already suspected that chapters 5 and 6 have been transposed. (Archbishop Bernard, who himself switches the two chapters round, tells us that this suggestion had been made as early as the fourteenth century by Ludolph of Saxony.)[24]

The arguments for the *existence* of a Johannine signs source are surely overwhelming. Furthermore, like most good theories, the theory propounded by Thompson and, independently, Faure, is clear, elegant, and bold. With sufficient ingenuity, one can think of more complex explanations which, because of the nature of historical inquiry, can never be ruled out in principle. H.-P. Heekerens, for instance, has proposed that the three Galilean miracles (in chapters 2, 4, and 21) were added to the Gospel by a later redactor who, eager to underline the theological opposition between Galilee and Jerusalem, chopped up his mini-source into three pieces, inserted the first two of these in different places of the narrative, and used the third to introduce a quite separate appendix,[25] deliberately depriving it, in so doing, of its signs status. Heekerens does not speculate about the kind of situation in late first-century Palestine that might have prompted this move; and to prefer his theory to the much simpler thesis argued by Thompson and Faure is rather like returning to the Ptolemaic theory of planetary orbits after knowing Copernicus.

Nevertheless it is possible to admit that John had a signs source and to maintain at the same time that it is virtually irrecoverable and therefore of no practical use in exegesis. If we can agree that the source existed the next question is what it comprised.

---

[22] Jürgen Becker thinks that the source itself may have stopped counting because, as he points out, all its readers could count up to seven (*Evangelium*, 114). But on the same reasoning they could also count up to two!

[23] Carson appears to think ('Source Criticism', 421) that the multiplicity of possible answers invalidates them all—as if the exegete, confronted with such an *embarras de choix*, cannot but be left as nonplussed as Buridan's ass.

[24] *St John*, vol. i, p. xvii, n. 1.

[25] *Zeichen-Quelle*, 121–2.

2. EXTENT

The author of the source tells us that he made a selection from a larger stock of σημεῖα at his disposal (20: 30). We cannot be sure just how many stories he picked out. Fortna suggests ten or, more probably, seven as a likely number;[26] but if he is also correct in his view that the miraculous catch of fishes recorded in chapter 21 belonged to the source then this must mean that the evangelist himself did not feel obliged to include everything he found. In default of evidence to the contrary it seems reasonable to assume that all the miracle stories in the first half of the Gospel were taken from the source; but there is some doubt about at least two of these. Faure, as we have seen, thought that the evangelist drew upon the Synoptics for his account of the feeding of the five thousand, and the way that the story of the raising of Lazarus is constructed, interweaving narrative and revelatory dialogue, makes it hard to be sure that it was extracted from the same parcel as the rest. What is more, although these are all miracle stories and most of them are referred to directly or indirectly as σημεῖα (the healing of the cripple in chapter 5 is an exception)[27] there are many *kinds* of miracle involved, and we would be unwise to assume that they can be classified as belonging to a single genre.[28]

Heekerens challenges the widespread assumption that the remaining, non-Galilean miracle stories were drawn from the source.[29] In my view this challenge, which largely depends upon an improbable interpretation of the πάλιν δεύτερον of 4: 54, is unconvincing; though perhaps it leaves just the shadow of a doubt. But the story that presents the most serious problems is one that Heekerens himself accepts.

This is the miraculous catch of fishes, relegated to the appendix of the Gospel, but providing a clue to its provenance in the concluding verse: τοῦτο ἤδη τρίτον ἐφανερώθη Ἰησοῦς τοῖς μαθηταῖς

---

[26] *Gospel*, 101.

[27] Although this miracle is nowhere called a sign in the present Gospel, it is clearly the 'one work' referred to by Jesus in 7: 21. For the most part the terms σημεῖα and ἔργα have the same extension in the Gospel.

[28] C. H. Dodd distinguishes at least three types in his careful and instructive discussion of these stories in *Historical Tradition*, 174–232.

[29] 'There is nothing to be said for R. Bultmann's hypothesis that the original numeration of the first two miracles is to be extended to *all* the miracles of the Gospel' (*Zeichen-Quelle*, 26).

ἐγερθεὶς ἐκ νεκρῶν (21: 14), reconstructed by Fortna as τοῦτο (ἤδη) τρίτον ἐποίησεν σημεῖον Ἰησοῦς. Here, he suggests, the redactor (whom in his first book he takes to be the evangelist, in his second 'the author of the appendix') 'has retained the original τοῦτο ἤδη τρίτον, appropriate in the source as adjectival, making it here a clumsy adverbial phrase'.[10] This, it must be said, is an attractive interpretation, which has the advantage of placing the miracle as the third of a series of Galilean stories in the postulated source. Fortna himself, however, acknowledges that 'the assignment of this story to the source is much more hypothetical than for the other miracles,'[11] and concludes by speaking of it as 'only a more or less intelligent guess'.[12] Yet even if we leave aside the signs in chapters 6, 11, and 21 as only doubtfully belonging to the source there is still enough to authorize the fundamental distinction between source and redaction that the theory demands.

Here, though, is where the real difficulties begin. Few of the advocates of the theory have been content to restrict it to the miracle stories. Even William Nicol, who confines himself to what he calls the 'sēmeia source', believes that 'it would probably have contained more, even of the other narrative material in John'.[13] Fortna himself makes it clear in his first book that contextual (by which he chiefly means the presence of aporias) must take methodological precedence over ideological criteria (*Tendenzen*). Yet there is a series of remarks in the introduction to his second book that betray his affinity to the school of German rationalism in which 'partitionist' theories took their rise. He speaks of the strange juxtaposition of 'earthly signs alongside otherworldly teaching against them, the heavenly revealer of pure Christian theology doing deeds that are frankly temporal and even coarse';[14] and although much of what he says clearly does not apply to the other stories (and certainly not to the passion narrative), he

---

[10] *Gospel*, 96.

[11] *Predecessor*, 66.

[12] Ibid. 67. The 'third' of the received text fits its present context perfectly well, since of the three appearances recorded in ch. 20 the first, to Mary Magdalene, was not 'to the disciples'. Fortna (*Predecessor*, 66) says that it is anomalous, because the previous two appearances are not numbered. But if, as he now thinks, the evangelist was not the author of the appendix then one can understand why a later redactor might wish to impress upon his readers that the new episode is the natural sequel of what went before.

[13] *Sēmeia*, 6.

[14] *Predecessor*, 3.

appears to have slipped from a signs-source theory to a narrative-source theory without, as far as one can tell, any strong reason apart from his own powerful conviction of 'the all-but-intolerable tension between *narrative* and *discourse*'.[35]

As far as *The Fourth Gospel and its Predecessor* is concerned this matters little, since with one exception all the material from the first half of the Gospel that Fortna assigns to the source (the temple episode, the priests' plot, the anointing, and the triumphal entry) is now assigned to the passion sequence. The exception is the introduction to the source: what follows the Prologue in chapter 1. This passage differs from the body of the Gospel in a variety of ways, especially in its virtually exclusive concentration upon messiahship (in a number of guises) and in the curiously passive role assigned to Jesus throughout. The reasons for assigning it to the signs source are very strong, although the reconstruction, especially of the first section, is quite tricky. My own view, put very succinctly, is that there are no good grounds for denying that this is where the signs source began,[36] that elements of it are to be found in the miracle stories of the first half of the Gospel, and that it concluded with 20: 30–31a.[37]

One other passage remains to be considered: 7: 1–9. There is a genuine aporia here because in urging Jesus to go up to Jerusalem so that his disciples there may see his works, his brothers imply that he has not yet performed any signs there (in spite of the story in chapter 5). Fortna observes that 'as a matter of fact, the saying of the brothers implies that Jesus *has* "worked" in Judea, since it is taken for granted that he has disciples there';[38] but Jesus had disciples in Galilee before he had begun to perform any signs (they were invited to the wedding at Cana), and just as we are told that he made converts in Samaria through the testimony of one woman

---

[35] *Predecessor*, 1. If the evangelist himself had been disturbed by the contrast between narrative and discourse, he would not have bothered to combine them. The truth is that he *needs* discourse: without it he would not have a Gospel.

[36] Having defended this view in my book (*Understanding*, 280–90), I will not argue it afresh here.

[37] Whether the rather grim conclusion, 12: 37–40, belonged to the source is hard to determine. Fortna now thinks (*Predecessor*, 137) that it was composed when the signs source was fused with the passion narrative to make a single Signs Gospel. Taken in conjunction with the temple episode and the priests' plot, it was, he argues, intended to answer the question how the messianic worker of signs could have been executed by official decision. But it is not inconceivable that the outcome of the signs source was more pessimistic than Fortna believes likely.

[38] *Gospel*, 196.

(4: 39) his fame may have preceded him to Jerusalem too. Jesus' initial reluctance to go up to Jerusalem exactly matches, as Bultmann notes,[19] the protest he makes to his mother at Cana (which, as will be argued below, was part of the source), and establishes a neat pattern of a double series of signs, first in Galilee, then in Jerusalem—a theory that Fortna himself argues for on other grounds. Here then is another likely candidate for inclusion in the source.[40]

The conclusion must be that arguments of varying degrees of persuasiveness can be put forward for including particular passages in the source, but that no agreement about its extent is likely to be forthcoming. Yet the difficulty of determining how exactly the signs source was composed should not prevent us from acknowledging the strength of the evidence for its existence.

3. A SIGNS GOSPEL?

The pages Fortna devotes to arguing his new thesis are very compressed. He sets out to prove that the signs source (SQ) and the passion source (PQ) were combined, before the evangelist took them over, into a signs *gospel*, and concludes with an appeal to the reader: 'Have we not, then, found good reason to speak of a unified pre-Johannine source, a Gospel of Signs?'[41]

This reader, for one, is unconvinced: not one of Fortna's four arguments stands up to critical examination.

1. Fortna opens his case with a discussion of what he admits to be only a 'handful of instances of *stylistic overlap* between PQ and SQ'. Now there is something very odd about this argument. All of the six 'elements of style that can be regarded as characteristic of the pre-Johannine material' have already figured in a list of stylistic features used, in Fortna's earlier book, to support the (on

---

[19] Gospel, 289 n. 1.

[40] Not that this passage is free from difficulties (see Ashton, *Understanding*, 330-2). 7: 5, for instance, tells us that even Jesus' brothers (who were urging him to go up to Jerusalem to perform wonders) did not believe in him. This can only be an uncomprehending gloss. Schwartz ('Aporien' (1908), 117) remarks upon the perplexity it caused John Chrysostom: καὶ ποία, φησίν, ἀπιστία ἐνταῦθα; παρακαλοῦσι γὰρ αὐτὸν θαυματουργῆσαι . . . καὶ δοκεῖ μὲν ἡ ἀξίωσις δῆθεν φίλων εἶναι (*In Joannem Hom.* 48, PG 8, col. 270).

[41] *Predecessor*, 214.

the face of it) very different thesis that signs and passion were composed *by the same author* to make up a 'Gospel of Signs'. In so far as the stylistic evidence can be given any weight this indeed is the direction in which they point. Yet in *Predecessor* they are taken as 'evidence that *the same editorial hand* appears to have reworked, and to that degree stylistically integrated, the two once-separate sources or bodies of tradition—and to have done so prior to the work of 4E'.[42] To establish this case Fortna would have to show that the verses or parts of verses in which these stylistic features occur in his source(s) are to be attributed, not to the original author(s) but to the pre-Johannine redactor. Since he makes no attempt to do this we are justified in passing on to the second of his arguments.

2. Finding no aporias to justify his assumption of a seam in 12: 37–40, Fortna asserts that 'if on the level of style the source's author [redactor?] has retouched the preexisting narrative and on the level of structure has joined . them together smoothly, the *Johannine composition* does not show this kind of smoothing. Thus, the pre-Johannine join of the two kinds of material [i.e. the SQ and the PQ] is to be found in the present Gospel not at a point of Johannine transition but still in the same pre-Johannine passage.'[43] This argument is very compressed and exceedingly difficult to follow. It begins by tacitly admitting the absence of any textual evidence that the SQ and the PQ ever existed independently. The hard evidence (aporias) is confined to the break between (*a*) the two sources in combination and (*b*) the new material Fortna ascribes to the evangelist. Yet in what follows the existence of a pre-Johannine join is simply assumed, and Fortna appears to regard it as significant that this join is to be found (!) in a pre-Johannine passage. But where else would one expect to find it? The whole argument is very puzzling.

3. The third argument is also a little hard to grasp: 'Underlying the Johannine unity is an earlier tension, which is not evidence against the earlier combining of signs and passion but on the contrary the circumstance that required it: the discontinuity of signs and passion due only to the separate origin of SQ and passion tradition.'[44] One can concede this tension (it plays an important part in the argument of Ernst Käsemann that the passion is a mere

[42] *Predecessor*, 208.   [43] Ibid. 210.   [44] Ibid. 211.

postscript to the Gospel);[45] but though it may not count as
evidence *against* Fortna's thesis, how is it evidence *for* it? Why
should the joining operation not have been performed by the
evangelist himself?

4. The final piece of evidence, which Fortna regards as the
strongest, is 'the fundamental *theological unity* in the two halves
and its sharp difference from the theology of the finished Gospel'.[46]
Fortna argues that PQ and SQ share a common christology,
mainly characterized by the absence of the themes of 'salvation
(soteriology)' and 'revelation (epistemology)' so central to the concerns of the evangelist. No doubt he is right about the interest they
share in the messiahship of Jesus, but this is equally true of many
other early Christian sources. More important, apparently, is their
lack of interest in the evangelist's central concerns; but this can
scarcely be regarded as a strong unifying factor either.

These criticisms do not, of course, mean that Fortna is wrong in
his supposition that the narrative source was unified before the
evangelist adopted it as the basis of his own work. Indeed, some of
the stylistic (or, I would suggest, grammatical)[47] resemblances
between the signs and the passion narrative indicate that the
two authors shared a common linguistic background (dialect?).
Perhaps the author of the passion narrative took over and adapted
the work of his older colleague. Nor does the fact that Fortna has
not produced enough evidence to substantiate his thesis invalidate
all his subsequent comments on the redactional work of the evangelist. But his new thesis is beset by many of the weaknesses that
prompted him to discard his original signs-gospel theory.
Consequently, although we cannot discount the *possibility* of a pre-

---

[45] *Testament*, 7.

[46] *Predecessor*, 213.

[47] Notably the last on Fortna's list of six, the use of a singular verb with a double
subject (*Predecessor*, 209; cf. *Gospel*, 216). Such a usage is much more indicative of
a shared dialect than a common author. But in this instance the breakdown does
not permit us to make any wide-ranging inferences, with 4 occurrences in Fortna's
SG (1: 35, 45; 2: 2; 4: 53), 3 in PQ (2: 12 (?); 18: 1b, 15), and 2 in 4E (3: 22; 4:
12). When listing the stylistic references Fortna does not distinguish between the
passion source in the proper sense and the passages in the first half of the Gospel
that he believes to have introduced it. It is worth noting, however, that out of some
66 examples of 'pre-Johannine' stylistic characteristics, only 4 belong to the latter
category, one of them being the especially dubious 2: 12. (The others are instances
of what Fortna regards as characteristic pre-Johannine uses of ἐκ: 12: 2, 4; 13: 21;
cf. *Predecessor*, 209 n. 498.)

Johannine join, it remains preferable, methodologically speaking, to treat the two sources separately, as is done by the majority of authors who adopt a redaction-critical approach. In the rest of this chapter I shall confine my comments to the signs source as such.

4. RECONSTRUCTION

If we grant that the arguments in favour of the *existence* of a signs source are overwhelming, and are prepared, provisionally at any rate, to suppress our doubts about its *extent*, then we are still not entitled to conclude that it can be *reconstructed* with equal certainty in the form in which the author left it. Fortna insists that it is recoverable, and that the indications of the evangelist's interfering hand are clear enough to enable us to proceed with some confidence. Is he right? A thorough reassessment would have to be almost as long as his defence of his own proposals.[48] What follows is simply a series of illustrative probes, almost inevitably weighted on the side of disagreement. To be fair, it should be added that his own estimate of the accuracy of his reconstruction is no higher than about seven on a scale of one to ten.[49]

(a) 1: 19–34

Fortna himself admits that his analysis of this passage 'is unusually intricate and contains a number of uncertainties'.[50] The problem here is that two versions of the same episode (the testimony of John) have been rather clumsily stitched together, and there is even some doubt about whether the main responsibility for this is to be laid at the door of the evangelist. Be that as it may, disagreements concerning the reconstruction of the passage as a whole, especially the first half, do not entail any serious dispute over meaning. The suggestion that the source originally opened with the words introducing John in 1: 6–7 is of course speculative, but these two verses cannot have belonged to the *Vorlage* of the Prologue, and they furnish an excellent introduction to the postulated source.

---

[48] As an example of a full-scale review (of an equally complex but rather different set of proposals), cf. Frans Neirynck *et al.*, *Jean et les Synoptiques*.
[49] *Predecessor*, p. xii.
[50] Ibid. 34.

(b) 2: 1-11

The little dialogue between Jesus and his mother is what for most readers gives this story its special piquancy. Fortna regards the contradiction between what Jesus says and what he does as one of the Gospel's aporias, and he attributes the initial exchange to the evangelist: 'Its meaning is that the request for a miracle, even from Jesus' own mother, is inappropriate when compared to his greater purpose, the enactment of his "hour". . . . What matters above all is Jesus' death, for that is what his *hour* refers to. . . . His mother's request, though it will be met, is premature.'[51] But 'hour', in the story, does *not* refer to Jesus' death, for once he has begun to confront his approaching passion then the time for working miracles has not just arrived but is already past! In John 2: 4 'my hour', exceptionally, refers to the start of Jesus' splendid public career. When the evangelist takes over the term on his own account he uses it in a different way to refer to the hour of glorification.[52] In the source, Jesus' reluctance is overcome by his mother, just as in 7: 1-9 his hesitations over whether to ascend to Jerusalem to perform miracles for the benefit of the disciples are overcome by his brothers.

(c) 4: 46-54

One would not expect Fortna's reconstruction of this key passage to diverge sharply from that of earlier scholars. This, as we have seen, is one of the texts singled out by both Thompson and Faure when they argued the case for a separate source. Even a conservative scholar like C. H. Dodd feels obliged to offer an explanation of 4: 48, so much at variance with the generally positive attitude to Jesus' miracles found elsewhere in the Gospel: 'Unless you see signs and wonders you will not believe.' Disdaining, as usual, to throw his hat into the ring and to tangle with other scholarly interpretations, Dodd first points out the unusual features of the verse and then comments: 'All this suggests that there is originally

---

[51] *Predecessor*, 55-6.

[52] 'Witness', 'believe', 'hour', 'sign', 'works', 'son of God', 'sent' are all terms whose reference or meaning shifts once they have been incorporated into the work of the evangelist. Fortna recognizes that this is a common ploy, and often signals his awareness of it by giving an alternative rendering when he comes to the analysis of the evangelist's redaction.

a non-Johannine element in the dialogue.'[53] The weakness of this observation is apparent, because Dodd makes no attempt to explain why the evangelist should wish to insert such a saying into his narrative. At this point the strength of the signs-source hypothesis should be manifest.[54]

(d) 11: 1-45

The very extent of the material that needs to be surveyed in order to cover this particular story suggests that it is different in kind as well as in extent from the others. Rudolf Schnackenburg comments upon the different conclusions reached in earlier attempts to reconstruct the source: Wellhausen, Spitta, Wendt, Hirsch,[55] and of course Bultmann. He himself offers a new version. Fortna, in his first book, attempts a totally different reconstruction, with the story of the Samaritan woman inserted between 11: 15 and 17. He retracts this suggestion in his second book, and makes other minor modifications as well, at the same time admitting that 'separation of source and redaction in chapter 11 is more difficult than in any of the other miracle stories'.[56] Von Wahlde offers a version that accords with his other theses.

This story presents us, unquestionably, with some difficult puzzles, starting with the very first verse, where we are told that Lazarus came from the same village as Mary and her sister, Martha, but are given no hint that he was actually their brother. But in a story in which, as C. H. Dodd remarks, 'word and action form an indivisible whole, to a degree unique in the Book of Signs',[57] the work of reconstruction is especially hazardous. Not that all the attempts are wrong, but only one can be right, and the

---

[53] *Historical Tradition*, 192.

[54] Especially as it is expounded by Rudolf Schnackenburg, in an exceptionally brilliant defence of the theory: 'Zur Traditionsgeschichte'. Von Wahlde, in his discussion of 4: 48, agrees that it 'has been added on to the original signs material' (*Earliest Version*, 93), but then criticizes Fortna for assigning it to the Johannine redactor, observing that 'there is little literary evidence for this' (p. 94 n. 64). Thus he evades the difficulty that the verse creates for his view that *all* the occurrences of σημεῖα to mean miracles belong to the source. Contrast this with Fortna's statement (*Predecessor*, 237) that the term is used twelve times by the evangelist (2: 23; 3: 2; 4: 48; 6: 2, 26, 30; 7: 31; 9: 16; 10: 41; 11: 47; 12: 18, 37) as against five surviving pre-Johannine instances (2: 11, 18; 4: 54; 6: 14; 20: 30).

[55] *Gospel*, ii. 513 n. 3.

[56] *Predecessor*, 104.

[57] *Interpretation*, 363.

complexity of the material should warn us not to be too confident about the reliability of our own opinions.

These examples are perhaps enough to show that it is possible to take issue with Fortna at almost every point of his reconstruction. His confidence in the 'recoverability' of the source is surely misplaced. This does not mean that the attempt is not worth making, for the work of reconstruction throws up a large number of incidental observations that cannot but enhance our understanding and appreciation of the Gospel as a whole. The most important question, however, is left unanswered: can we be sufficiently confident of the general nature of source and redaction to make reliable inferences about the theological purposes of both? This is what Fortna claims to do—but it is here that he may appear most vulnerable to the arguments of his critics that his project is too ambitious to be realized in a way that can carry conviction.

5. PURPOSE

Because of the manifold uncertainties in any attempted reconstruction of the source we might be tempted to conclude that there is little point in attempting to determine its character and purpose; the pretence that it is possible to distinguish these from those of the redaction ascribed to the evangelist may appear equally futile. We have seen that Fortna himself does not claim more than a 70 per cent probability for the accuracy of his reconstruction, yet the large measure of uncertainty does not seem to worry him. Should it? He is not in the position of a builder, responsible, before starting his work, for checking and replacing timbers whose soundness he has reason to doubt. Fortna's house of theory is fully constructed, furnished, and inhabited; yet insecure and draughty as it is, he moves through it with ease and assurance.[58] We have already remarked upon the gap between scholars who accept the general viability of the signs-source hypothesis and those who either dismiss it out of hand or regard it as virtually useless for the purposes

---

[58] He seems to have modified his views since 1974, when, having remarked in his review of *Sēmeia* (*JBL* 93 (1974), 119) that Nicol neglected to provide an exhaustive reconstruction, he observed that without this no precise redaction-critical investigation is possible.

of exegesis. This is where the gap yawns most widely. Who is right?

The first point to stress is the a priori unlikelihood that an author will take over and adapt a document with which he whole-heartedly disagrees. Here the balance of probability lies heavily in favour of expansions and modifications rather than of any radical recasting. On this score Fortna cannot be faulted. Recognizing that the primary purpose of the source is to insist upon Jesus' messianic status, he does not make the mistake of saying that the evangelist has no interest in this. As an argument *ad hominem* one may point out that Marinus de Jonge, one of the most determined critics of all source theories, stresses that John is dissatisfied with any *merely* messianic view of Jesus, but constantly seeks to deepen and extend this in a variety of ways.[59] On this point the two scholars are agreed. It is not that John no longer subscribes to the traditional belief that 'Jesus is Messiah'; but by the time the Gospel has been composed the twin titles of 'Messiah' and 'Son of God' have gathered all the additional significance attached by John to the special relationship between Jesus and the Father.

Where the difference between source and redaction is marked by a genuine aporia, as in 4: 48, the critic can operate with some confidence. In many cases, however, where the seam is less obvious, it is necessary to employ some other criterion; and here the risk of circularity is palpable. A good example is the notion of Jesus' self-manifestation found in the conclusion of the Cana story in chapter 2 and in the commencement and conclusion of the miraculous catch of fishes in chapter 21, and marked in all three cases by the use of the verb φανεροῦν. Other critics, for example Boismard, have used this similarity as an additional argument for assigning the latter episode to the source; but for Fortna the idea of self-manifestation belongs to the theology of John, and so in both passages he eliminates φανεροῦν from his reconstruction,[60] which reads, in the first passage: [τοῦτο πρῶτον ἐποίησεν σημεῖον] ὁ Ἰησοῦς,

---

[59] 'Jesus' kingship and his prophetic mission are both redefined in terms of the unique relationship between Son and Father' (*Stranger from Heaven*, 52).

[60] 1: 31, where there is another occurrence of the term, is also eliminated from the source; it is found too in 7: 4 (part of a passage with strong claims to be includ-ed in the signs source), and in 9: 3, introducing the miracle of the man born blind. This little problem is far from resolved. Marie-Émile Boismard concludes that 'le verbe "manifester" est un terme quasi technique, dans la littérature juive et dans le quatrième évangile, pour parler de la "manifestation" du Messie, en tant que Messie, au moment où il va commencer son ministère' (*Moïse ou Jésus*, 51-2).

and in the conclusion of the second: τοῦτο (ἤδη) τρίτον [ἐποίησεν σημεῖον] Ἰησοῦς.[61]

One of the greatest weaknesses of Fortna's work is his failure to investigate the all-important notion of Messiah in any depth or to place the source in context in the prehistory of the Johannine community. Without any social or historical back-up, source criticism (and redaction criticism, for that matter), proves a brittle and inadequate investigative tool. In the signs source, he says, 'a number of titles—Christ, Elijah, the Prophet, Son of God, Lamb of God, King of Israel—cluster together to convey an essentially single theological affirmation: that Jesus is the Messiah of Jewish expectation'.[62] But the composite Messiah pictured by Fortna would have been unrecognizable to any Jewish sect of the period. Furthermore, one can scarcely imagine how this curious construct, a kind of bionic man, would have been expected to behave. The serious questions raised by recent scholarship concerning the meaning of the term 'Messiah'[63] and the challenge to widespread assumptions concerning the extent of messianic hopes at the turn of the era[64] are surely relevant to Fortna's work; but he pays them no heed. Nor does he attempt to answer J. Louis Martyn's objection that miracles played little part in the traditional Jewish expectation of the Messiah.[65] Finally, he does not explain why a document primarily concerned to affirm Jesus' messianic status should make so little reference to this after the introduction. The net result is a strangely abstract piece of literary detective-work.

According to Fortna the dominant factor in the evolution from the messianic faith of the source to the developed christology of the Gospel was 'the powerful creativity of one mind—the Evangelist's—making dramatic use of an older work'.[66] But he refrains from speculating on what might have prompted the burst of theological creativity that has to be assumed. Thus he overlooks, or at any rate stands back from, the angry and anguished conflicts

[61] In *Predecessor* Fortna appears to allow that some element of self-manifestation (though not of glory) may be attributed to the source. See pp. 50, 53, 58.

[62] *Predecessor*, 228–9.

[63] Especially in a series of brilliant articles by Marinus de Jonge, starting with 'The Use of the Word "Anointed" in the Time of Jesus', NT 8 (1966), 132–48.

[64] Above all in J. Neusner *et al.* (eds.), *Judaisms and Their Messiahs*.

[65] *History and Theology*, 84–7.

[66] *Predecessor*, 224.

that must have preceded the rupture between the Johannine group and the parent synagogue. In doing so he deprives himself, it seems to me, of a potentially powerful tool for explaining the literary and theological trajectory that he pursues with such persistence.

Fortna might not unreasonably retort in response to these remarks that it is unfair to criticize him for not doing what he never set out to do in the first place. He can scarcely be blamed for not having written the book that certain of his readers might have wished to see. His work, moreover, like that of Bultmann, which it resembles in its single-minded consistency, is arguably greater than the sum of its parts. If the *overall* account that he offers in his exegesis of the narrative sections of the Gospel and in his analysis of their redaction proves a more effective aid to understanding than any alternative explanation, then we should not allow any residual reservations concerning particular details to prevent us from accepting its general validity. Fortna himself makes the point admirably: 'what is presented here is a hypothesis whose vindication is not finally based on arguments about criteria but on its usefulness in coming to terms with this elusive and insistent Gospel'.[67]

This, then, is the crucial question—the acid test. In the attempt to understand the development of the Gospel can the signs-source theory be replaced without loss? Or will, say, Lindars's much more flexible theory, which postulates the absorption and adaptation of a whole series of independent traditions, serve equally well?[68] After all, this theory too works in conjunction with the (surely necessary) hypothesis of a Christian thinker with a powerfully creative mind, working upon a whole series of traditional stories or sayings and transforming them into vehicles of his own theological vision. Does the suggestion that he received all or most of these in a single document with a consistent theological thrust actually help us to penetrate more deeply into the intentions of the redactor?

A proper answer to this question would entail a detailed criticism of the whole of Part 2 of *Predecessor*, where, in a series of brilliant vignettes, Fortna examines a number of theological motifs

[67] *Predecessor*, p. xii.
[68] The fruitfulness of Lindars's approach is evident from a whole series of articles, beginning with 'John and the Synoptic Gospels: A Test Case'.

(Messiah, Signs and Faith, Salvation, etc.) and endeavours to demonstrate how the evangelist, without repudiating the single-minded insistence of the source upon Jesus' messiahship, enfolds the old material in his new faith. Within the limits of this essay, however, a more general answer must suffice.

1. For the most part Fortna's insights concerning *the theology of John* neither depend upon nor derive from the details of his source theory. His most important insights concern the messianic thrust *of the source itself*. Such a source, viewed as a missionary document directed to traditionally minded Jews within the synagogue, enables us to understand how the message concerning Jesus established itself within a community some of whose members were later utterly to repudiate it.

2. Underlying Fortna's two books is the assumption that the evangelist had in front of him as he wrote—on his desk, so to speak—the work of his 'predecessor', and that he built his own book on or around this in a sustained burst of creative energy. True, he admits that 'one cannot know in advance *how many* . . . stages in the gospel's literary history it will be necessary to postulate in order to account for the aporias'.[69] But conscious of the danger 'of unnecessarily complicating the critical task', he starts with the provisional assumption that there were only two principal stages in the formation of the Gospel: 'basic document' and 'redaction'. Fully acquainted as he is with the hypothesis of multiple stages, one may wonder if Fortna has given it sufficiently serious consideration.

The cure of the cripple in chapter 5 furnishes us with a good example of a passage for which Fortna's initial assumption cannot stand. According to him the conclusion of the actual miracle story ($\mathring{\eta}\nu$ $\delta\grave{\epsilon}$ $\sigma\acute{\alpha}\beta\beta\alpha\tau\text{o}\nu$ $\grave{\epsilon}\nu$ $\grave{\epsilon}\kappa\epsilon\acute{\iota}\nu\eta$ $\tau\mathring{\eta}$ $\mathring{\eta}\mu\acute{\epsilon}\rho\alpha$, v. 9) was added by the evangelist,[70] but this is too simple: the controversy dialogue, linked, as Harold W. Attridge has argued,[71] with 7: 18–26, must have been appended at a period when the community was still engaged in halakhic debate with the Pharisees.

Forced, then, to query one of the basic methodological assumptions underlying Fortna's work,[72] we may prefer to adopt a more

---

[69] *Gospel*, 3.
[70] *Gospel* 52; *Predecessor*, 117.
[71] 'Thematic Development'; see too Herold Weiss, 'Sabbath'.
[72] It is true that in outlining the principle of the source/redaction model (*Gospel*,

flexible approach. Even where there is no obvious seam to indicate the interference of a second hand, we must at least acknowledge that the changing situation of the community is likely to leave its mark upon a work which, however indirectly, reflects the relationship of the community with 'the Jews'.

3. No analysis restricting itself to the narrative sections of the Gospel can do full justice to its conceptual richness, since it must omit at least a third, and probably more, of the Gospel as we have it. And if we confine ourselves to the signs source itself, including every passage that may be reasonably supposed to have belonged to it, we will have scarcely more than a tenth of the Gospel to work with. So it is not surprising that while we can derive from this material valuable insights into the nature and purpose of this supposedly pre-Johannine document, it does not give us much help in determining the theological preoccupations of the evangelist. Any recognizably Johannine addition or insertion (such as the manifestation of glory at the end of the Cana episode) is seen to be such because the motif it exhibits belongs clearly and unmistakably to the evangelist's concerns as these emerge elsewhere in the Gospel. A good half of the evangelist's work is to be found in the controversy stories and discourses, and the kind of redaction criticism commended and practised by Fortna can make no headway without constantly appealing to these for inspiration and confirmation. To see how John treated his sources we must understand him already; and the results of any internal redaction criticism cannot, in the nature of things, bring any new revelation.

4. These comments may appear dismissive, but they are not intended as such. In the two decades following the appearance of J. Louis Martyn's *History and Theology* in 1968, there have been few better books on the Fourth Gospel than Fortna's *Predecessor*. But the value of his masterly summary of Johannine theology lies not in his source theory as such but in his theological analyses of individual passages.

8), Fortna qualifies his presupposition by the words 'so long as it is feasible', but in his extended application of the method in the second half of *Predecessor*, he betrays no awareness of its fragility. Thus he fails to draw the proper inferences from the concession he makes to Attridge at the end of his discussion, allowing that parts of the Johannine material beginning at 5: 9b with parts of ch. 7 'belong to the same Johannine stage of these two obviously complex chapters' (*Predecessor*, 117 n. 259).

6. POSTSCRIPT

All modern Johannine scholars, except those opposed in principle
to any diachronic study of the Gospel's growth and development,
have broadly accepted the thesis that it was published in a number
of editions, and that informed guesses may be made concerning
the scope and purpose of each of these. In my book *Understanding* I
took over this thesis unreflectingly and unquestioningly—from
Brown, Lindars, Schnackenburg, and others. This idea now seems
to me, if not entirely inappropriate, at least somewhat misleading.
The notion of successive editions fits readily enough in a culture
accustomed to printed books, but has only a limited application
before the fourteenth century. Criticizing the obsessive desire of
modern literary historians to give a precise date to the works of
medieval authors, John Benton argues that these

could keep their personal copies of a manuscript for many years, allowing
other copies to be made at different stages of development but maintaining
their capability to shape the work, to correct it, and allow it to develop.
Copies of such texts made at different dates are like sketches of a growing
child, each an authentic representation of a given stage, no one more
representative than another.[73]

Similarly, of the 'takes' or states of a particular etching by, say,
Rembrandt all may be authoritative but none definitive.[74]

No doubt it was possible in any age for an author to turn back
to a work that he or she had regarded as finished and to tinker
with it, even to add to or subtract from it. What is more, authors
and composers with a creative life of more than a decade or so
may rework material that has been lying unused for many years.
'I made this, I have forgotten—And remember', writes T. S. Eliot
in his poem *Marina*, and a little later introduces virtually
unchanged a line which, following the advice of Ezra Pound, he
had omitted years earlier from *The Waste Land*: 'The garboard
strake leaks, the seams need caulking'. Similarly, a recent bio-
grapher of Goethe writes of his 'ability to transform the nature and
quality of a literary work simply by adding to it—an ability

[73] '778: Entering the Date', 5.
[74] e.g. the etching entitled *Ecce Homo*, extant in eight states and radically
reworked in the sixth, in which the foreground crowd has been burnished out and
replaced by two dark cellar arches.

nowhere more apparent than in the sixty years long development of his *Faust*'.[75] But the point about the *Urfaust* is that it remained unpublished in Goethe's lifetime: to think or speak of it as if it were an early edition of the work is simply wrong. Nor is the facsimile of the uncut version of *The Waste Land* an *edition* in any ordinary sense of the word.

Here, then, is yet another reason why we should be wary of treating Fortna's postulated pre-Johannine synthesis of signs and passion as a *Gospel*. If it did exist it will have been at best a rough draft of what was to come later. Only when we can point to complete reworkings, prompted by drastic alterations in the life of the Johannine community, should we begin to think of a second edition.[76] That there were two distinct editions of the Gospel in the strong sense remains a real possibility, one I myself favour. But it is not the only possibility; and we should remain open to a more flexible approach.

[75] Nicholas Boyle, *Goethe: The Poet and the Age*, i. *The Poetry of Desire* (*1749–1790*) (Oxford, 1991), 86.

[76] If, along with many others, we think that the presence of John 15–16 alongside John 14 entitles us to speak of separate editions, perhaps we should remember Act IV, Scene iii of Shakespeare's *Love's Labour's Lost*, where two versions of part of one of Berowne's speeches lie side by side.

5

The Shepherd

I. INTRODUCTION: SOME METHODOLOGICAL OBSERVATIONS

Unlike commentaries, in which questions on a huge variety of topics (historical, literary, theological, etc.) are frequently heaped hugger-mugger on top of one another, essays on particular sections or chapters of the Gospel are for the most part quite carefully focused. Whole books have been written on the passage, scarcely more than twenty verses, that is the topic of this chapter, some making only cursory allusions to the remainder of the Gospel. One of the most recent of these proclaims by its title its intention to deal with the shepherd discourse *in its context*,[1] but with one exception the contributors to this volume understand 'context' to refer to what immediately precedes and follows, not to the Gospel as an integrated whole. The oddity of this procedure should not be allowed to pass unnoticed. Newcomers to the arcane science of biblical exegesis may be surprised, even astonished, by the determined restraint of those whom the Germans call *Neutestamentler*, their ability to confine their attention to a chapter, a section, a phrase, sometimes a single word.[2] 'What literary critic', Mary Ann Tolbert challengingly enquires, 'would characteristically write essays on only one or two pages of a short story, much less one or two paragraphs?'[3] Not a few essays on the Synoptic Gospels put a ring round one brief paragraph and proceed to focus on this to the exclusion of everything else: the word 'pericope' (which always reminds me of the little rings that my mother used to cut from a slab of pastry when preparing jam or treacle tarts) seems to have been coined in order to confer upon this procedure the weighty authority of academe. This authority, it might be argued, is adequately assured by the acknowledged

---

[1] *The Shepherd Discourse*, ed. J. Beutler and R. T. Fortna, p. 3.
[2] In his massive study of the term ἀλήθεια in the Johannine writings, *La Vérité* (2 vol., 1128 pages), Ignace de la Potterie does not even bother to include in his purview the terms ἀληθής and ἀληθινός.
[3] *Semeia*, 53 (1991), 206.

achievements of form criticism. Maybe so, but the methods of form criticism are not always appropriate to the study of the Fourth Gospel, and the mere utterance of the word 'pericope' is not enough to justify our singling out particular sections and treating them in isolation from the rest.

In fact the passage that concerns us here (10: 1–21) *cannot* be properly discussed in isolation. It is tied to the remainder of chapter 10 by three verses (26–8) which briefly recapitulate the shepherd theme; and many scholars, as we shall see, argue for a closer connection with the preceding chapter also. In this respect the shepherd discourse differs from the allegory of the vine (15: 1–17), a passage which it otherwise resembles both in tonality and genre. This has borrowed from the surrounding discourse something of the brooding awareness of Jesus' imminent departure that pervades these chapters. Yet as a literary unit it is more coherent, more tightly knit, and more easily treated apart. Besides, it follows a firmly stated conclusion ('Let us be off'). Chapter 9 finishes much less abruptly.

If, for the moment, we leave aside the problem of the link between chapters 9 and 10, and—provisionally—consider the shepherd discourse as a unit, then it is worth pausing to reflect upon what other questions may be addressed to the text.

In *Understanding the Fourth Gospel* I suggested that questions concerning any literary work may be grouped under four headings: (1) content; (2) author or origins; (3) readership or situation; (4) the work itself. *Mutatis mutandis* the same groupings may be applied to individual passages.

1. The question of content, the nature of the material, is easy to overlook because we tend to assume that we *know* what we are dealing with here.[1] Most modern exegetes, confident of understanding the central picture of Jesus as the good shepherd, remain unworried by the impossibility of identifying the subsidiary figures with any certainty.

2. Certain commentators, notably Rudolf Bultmann and Jürgen Becker, have attributed the shepherd discourse to the ecclesiastical redactor; but this view is no longer widely held and in what follows I shall simply assume that the author is John, the fourth evangelist. In so far as one is justified in speaking of a source here,

---

[1] I return to this point in Section 5 of this chapter.

there is no reason to look beyond the Old Testament, though perhaps 'influence' is a better word.[5]

3. The question of readership and situation raises more problems, and we shall see that the answers to this illuminate the *meaning* of the text.[6]

4. In any consideration of the work itself the meaning should be paramount, but present-day exegetes are often more concerned with details of structure and organization.[7] More important, surely, is the question of genre: what *kind* of text is this? Should we be thinking in terms of allegory, parable, or riddle?[8] (All are possible renderings of the Greek word παροιμία.)

One of the most recent books concerning this passage is a collection of studies delivered as papers to the SNTS Johannine Writings Seminar in two successive meetings in 1985 and 1986.[9] How comprehensively does it cover the four areas I have just targeted? The only paper to address most of the issues (though without always clearly distinguishing between them) is John Painter's 'Tradition, History and Interpretation in John 10'; but Painter's failure to consider the question of genre (he leaves the word παροιμία untranslated throughout) is a serious weakness. The best of the other papers are two that deal with the background of the passage, the first (by Johannes Beutler) focusing on the Old Testament, the second (by John D. Turner) concentrating on the Graeco-Roman conceptual sphere and inquiring into possible relationships with Gnosticism. Of the four remaining papers, those by Ulrich Busse and Hartwig Thyen are concerned with context, the former with the relationship of the passage with what immediately precedes and follows, the latter attempting to tie it in

---

[5] Or even 'background', the term used in two of the articles (by Beutler and Turner) in the collection cited in n. 1, and regularly employed in studies that search for connections with earlier writings, biblical or otherwise. One thinks of Eric Auerbach's word *hintergründlich*, quaintly translated as 'fraught with background'.

[6] A very different approach, yet clearly belonging to the same area of discourse, may be found in an essay by Robert Kysar: 'Johannine Metaphor'. This is an example of reader-response criticism.

[7] A typical example of this approach is to be found in the article by Jan A. Du Rand in the collection cited in n. 1: 'A Syntactical and Narratological Reading'. Du Rand disembowels the text and carefully exposes its entrails to public inspection. He may be right to insist that 'the text itself should be allowed to speak for itself to communicate effectively to the reader' (p. 97); but why does it have to be drawn and quartered first?

[8] Robert Kysar, 'Johannine Metaphor', has a fourth suggestion—metaphor.

[9] See n. 1.

with the whole Gospel. Both of these, then, are looking at 'the work itself'; so too, from a different perspective, is Jan A. Du Rand: 'A Syntactical and Narratological Reading of John 10 in Coherence with Chapter 9'. Finally, M. Sabbe, in an essay which, like those of Beutler and Turner, can be placed within the second circle (author and origin) studies 'the relationship of John 10 with the Synoptic Gospels'.

Of all these papers Painter's, as its title suggests, is the only one to treat the subject diachronically, and consequently the only one to take the same line as an essay by Rudolf Schnackenburg published the year before the seminar group had begun to turn its attention to the shepherd discourse. Schnackenburg remarks, apropos of the shepherd discourse, that the real puzzle in this passage ('was rätselhaft oder doch umstritten bleibt') is 'the genesis, formation, composition, and insertion of the shepherd discourse into the broad context of the whole Gospel (*in den Zusammenhang des Evangeliens*)';[10] and he goes on to observe that the difficulties and perplexities of current Johannine scholarship can be illustrated from this characteristic example. But within a year this diachronic emphasis had clearly gone out of fashion. With a single exception (Painter) the members of the SNTS Johannine Writings Seminar either assume or argue that the passage is to be taken as it stands and belongs integrally to its context, 'as a continuation of Jesus' argument with the Pharisees and "the Jews" of chapter 9'.[11] Nevertheless, flying in the face of this

---

[10] 'Hirtenrede', 142.

[11] *Shepherd Discourse*, 3. Hartwig Thyen in particular declares roundly that 'as a literary *work*, John's Gospel is not the end-result of some anonymous "process of growth" that can be described along lines determined by the history of traditions or religions (as if texts, like trees, lay down "year-rings"), but rather the outcome of a production-process (ποίησις) in the course of which it has gained its autonomy in the face of the original intentions of its author and equally of the ostensible (*ostensiv*) relations to the world of its first addressees' (p. 118). Johannes Beutler, one of the editors, supports the view that the shepherd discourse belongs where it is and cannot otherwise be interpreted meaningfully. This opinion, he says, 'is holding its own and even gaining ground' (p. 19). Ulrich Busse too argues for a 'close inter-lacing of all parts of the text of chapter 10 with the wider context' and asserts that this 'renders any version of rearrangement unlikely' (p. 9). It is to be noted, however, that in arguing for the integrity of chapters 9 and 10, Beutler and Busse depend upon two different readings of v. 7. The latter argues that the most widely attested and commonly accepted reading, ἡ θύρα, 'destroys the coherence of the text' (p. 10), and opts for ὁ ποιμήν instead. The former disagrees, and conducts his analysis of the structure of the passage on the assumption that ἡ θύρα is right (p. 20). (This is reminiscent of an identical quarrel between Wellhausen (ποιμήν)

broad agreement, the editors conclude by raising, as 'possibly the most interesting issue', the question how the various approaches represented in the collection relate to each other: 'Especially, the more and more urgent problem of the reciprocal relation between diachronic and synchronic readings of the text comes to the fore.'[12] This is the challenge to which I now wish to respond.

Four preliminary remarks may be helpful. In the first place there is nothing in the Beutler–Fortna volume to suggest how the various contributors might take up the editors' challenge without radically altering their own approaches and in three cases (Busse, Beutler, Thyen) their attitudes. For how could we expect someone who contests the very legitimacy of a diachronic reconstruction, as Thyen certainly does and as the other two appear to do, to avail himself of its findings?

The second point is this. The enterprise is crammed with difficulties. It is at least theoretically possible that the text we are attempting to dissect may transform itself before our eyes, even as we are wielding the scalpel. The situation for which the author is writing may have altered, and with it the focus and significance of his material. Indeed, there is no a priori guarantee that the author is the same in both cases. *Ex hypothesi* we have to take it for granted that we are dealing with a different, expanded text; but we also have to reckon with the possibility that the genre of the piece has been altered as well.

In the third place an exercise of this kind is obviously pointless unless it sheds some additional light upon the text. Although we must begin from where we stand (there is no other starting-point available), we must be able to infer from the present state of the text something of its earlier history, and possibly too of the situation of the community during the same period. Conversely, we are entitled to expect that the prehistory of the text may help us to understand its present state. The inquiry, then, is dialectical, with the past illuminating the present, and vice versa.

Finally, it should be stressed that whilst exegesis never deals in certainties, speculative exegesis is especially hazardous: the bolder the speculation the greater the uncertainty. Yet facts, in so far as they are ascertainable, may sometimes be less helpful in the quest

and Schwartz (θύρα) in the first decade of the century.) Anyone determined to establish the coherence of the passage will have no trouble in coping with either reading.

[12] *Shepherd Discourse*, 4.

for understanding than informed guesswork. No doubt the student is right to be wary of unreliable guides and even perhaps to spurn their offer of assistance. On the other hand, when the commentaries place before our bewildered gaze what in some cases may be dozens of pieces of information, why should we be expected to put the jigsaw together for ourselves without, so to speak, any visual aid? This box arrives, unfortunately, with no helpful picture on the lid, nothing to which one might point as evidence of the correctness of one's reconstruction. Indeed, in this case we are obliged to manufacture our own jigsaw, to cut and shape its pieces before we can begin to assemble them: in order to construct we have to begin by deconstructing. (The work of commentators is often deconstructive in a similar way.) But deconstruction is never an end in itself; and it is surely preferable to try and put the pieces together than to leave them scattered on the table.

Accordingly, I propose to do three things: first, to chart a possible scenario of the prehistory of this passage, starting from the hypothetical first edition; secondly, to reconstruct as best I can the history of the period between the two editions by considering how the elements of which it is composed may reflect the increasingly fraught relationships between the newly established Johannine community and the 'synagogue' from which it is now excluded; thirdly, to offer an interpretation, in the light of this study, of the passage as it now stands. Finally, by way of an appendix, I will offer some reflections on an aspect of the text rather taken for granted in what precedes: its world of discourse.

2. THE FIRST EDITION

There are three main difficulties standing in the way of a synchronic reading:

1. After the opening paragraph, which looks like a parable, or possibly an allegory, the evangelist interrupts his explanation by giving it a name. He calls it a παροιμία, a word which in many contexts could equally well be translated 'parable' or 'allegory' (the RSV has 'figure'), but in the present context, in view of the evangelist's own explanation, may well mean 'riddle':[13] 'This

---

[13] Cf. Prov. 25: 1, where παροιμίαι are called ἀδιάκριτοι (hard to make out); Sir. 39: 3 and 49: 17 (ἀπόκρυφα). The *Suda* glosses the word παροιμία as λόγος ἀπόκρυφος.

παροιμία Jesus addressed to them, and they did not understand (οὐκ ἔγνωσαν) what he was saying to them' (10: 6). (The word δέ, which I have translated 'and', is a much weaker adversative than the 'but' of the RSV: '*but* they did not understand'.) Throughout the whole of chapter 10 Jesus is addressing the Jews, an audience which never greets Jesus' words with comprehension (γινώσκειν); and indeed Jesus is nowhere represented in this Gospel as addressing 'the Jews' in language they could understand. They exhibit here the same incomprehension that the world shows when confronted by Jesus (1: 10; 17: 25). And it is odd, to say the least, that Jesus' interlocutors, who have just been exposed as unseeing and condemned for that reason, should apparently be expected, a few verses later, to comprehend unaided what the writer himself calls a παροιμία. (The Gospel explains the significance of παροιμία later on, making it clear that even the disciples would not comprehend such sayings as long as Jesus was alive. In that passage (16: 25-9) the contrast between παροιμίαι and speech uttered παρρησίᾳ, 'frankly', shows the proper rendering of παροιμία to be 'riddling discourse'.)

2. The second difficulty is this. However the word παροιμία is translated, as 'figure', 'parable', 'allegory', or 'riddle', we might have expected the next paragraph to offer some elucidation, much in the same way that the story of the sower in Matthew and Mark is followed by a step-by-step explanation. This is not what we get in John. On the contrary, the obscurity, far from being dispelled, is actually deepened:[14] what looks at first sight like an explanation or a series of explanations of the allegorical saying in 10: 1-5 functions rather as a number of variations on a theme, or rather upon two themes, the shepherd and the door, which do not lie comfortably together but keep jostling for a place in the reader's imagination, elbowing one another out of the way. We have to face the simple but bewildering fact that Jesus cannot be the door to the sheepfold and the shepherd of the sheep at one and the same time. Had these images been presented independently, or even successively, then we would have no great problem with

[14] This is why I am left unconvinced by attempts to interpret 10: 7-18 as if it provided readings of a parable, much in the same way as the concluding verses of the wicked husbandmen in Mark 12: 1-11 (a suggestion that has been made to me by Christopher Rowland). Although a synchronic exegesis is forced to take 10: 7-18 after 1-6 (and accordingly to translate παροιμία in v. 6 as 'parable') this reading presents some intractable puzzles.

either of them. As in the other vivid symbol of Jesus' relationship with the Christian community, the so-called allegory of the vine in chapter 15 (also dominated by one of the 'I-am' sayings), we would have been able to make the necessary mental adjustment smoothly and without fuss. In fact we are rapidly jerked to and fro from door to shepherd and back, and the two images refuse to coalesce.

3. There is one further difficulty. Between the end of chapter 9 and the beginning of chapter 10 *the situation has changed*. The story of the blind man reflects a turning-point in the history of the Johannine group—the decision, on the part of the conservative leaders of the synagogue, to expel from their midst any who professed allegiance to Jesus. The following paragraph (and indeed the whole of the subsequent section) points to a radical change of mood on the part of the Johannine Christians. No longer a fringe group (marginalized but maintaining an uneasy relationship with the centre), they now form a new community, self-sufficient enough to justify the appellation ἐκκλησία, 'church'. This has grown in cohesiveness, in independence, in self-awareness; and its enemies are no longer conceived as adversaries within the synagogue but as *coming from outside*. For Ezekiel and Zechariah the danger to Israel comes from within, from evil shepherds whose authority is tacitly acknowledged even as they are accused of abusing it; for John the danger comes from thieves and robbers, threatening the flock from without—and in any case *strangers* (ἀλλοτρίοι), a charge which neither Ezekiel nor Zechariah could conceivably have made.

All this helps to explain the perplexity of Hirsch, Bernard, Bultmann, and Becker, as they tried to come to terms with the evident hiatus between the two chapters. The 'Amen' saying that opens chapter 10 must seem, once our attention has been drawn to it, extraordinarily abrupt, following as it does Jesus' uncompromising denunciation of the Pharisees: 'your sin remains' (9: 41). It is not just that their first reaction is one of incomprehension (10: 6) rather than anger, for incomprehension is a quite proper response to a riddle. When the passage concludes, however, it is surprising that Jesus' allusion to the Father is met not with fury but with dissension (σχίσμα), and the Pharisees who were present at the final episode of the story of the man born blind have now given way to 'the Jews'. If, provisionally, we bracket out 10: 1–21, the sequence is greatly improved, for now one fully narrated story is succeeded by a new episode altogether, signalled by specific indications of time and place.

Such observations as these, though not all of equal force, are surely telling objections against any doctrinaire synchronic approach. They all underline the desirability of a *diachronic* reading as the first line of interpretation. This is what I propose:

At an earlier stage of the history of the Johannine group, shortly after the traumatic rift with the parent community, called here the 'synagogue', the fourth evangelist, using sources whose extent we can now only guess at, wrote the first recognizable version of what we now know as *The Gospel of John*. At this stage, the story of the healing of the man born blind in chapter 9 was followed directly by the scene at the Feast of Dedication, John 10: 22–39. This includes the last of the dramatic dialogues with 'the Jews' which began in chapter 5 and can be categorized collectively as 'the trial of Jesus'.[15]

Towards the beginning of this episode Jesus represents himself, in a strikingly vivid image, as a shepherd. Addressing the Jews assembled round him, he says: 'you do not believe because you do not belong to my sheep. My sheep hear my voice, and I know them, and they follow me; and I give them eternal life, and no one shall snatch them out of my hand . . .' (10: 26–8). The metaphor is a striking one. It is clearly intended to emphasize the gulf that has opened up between the two communities as a consequence of the sentence of excommunication, and also to warn the members of the Johannine group of the likelihood that 'the Jews' may attempt to inveigle back into their own party people who had opted for Jesus. The word ἁρπάζειν ('snatch' or 'seize') is polemical, pejorative, and extreme.[16] Used in conjunction with the sheep metaphor, it implies that individuals within the community can do nothing to protect themselves against would-be marauders.

The sheep/shepherd metaphor was widely used as a means of conveying the strongly paternalistic relationship that was con-

---

[15] See A. E. Harvey, *Jesus on Trial*.

[16] The word is also used of the wolf's activities in 10: 12, and this fact, taken in conjunction with its inappropriateness in the present context, may appear to suggest that its use in 10: 12 was temporally prior. But it is equally possible that the exaggeration in 10: 28 is what *precipitated* the image of the wolf in the first place.

ceived to exist between ruler and subjects throughout the Ancient Near East (and indeed in the Graeco-Roman world as well).[17] It is familiar to modern church-goers (certainly in England) from the beautiful cadences of Crimond's setting of the 23rd Psalm: 'The Lord is my shepherd: I shall not want'. Yet behind the reassuring presence of the good shepherd hovers the threatening shadow of other, less benign figures, people in authority whose concern is to exploit rather than to cherish.

Those who read 10: 26-8 in the light of what has gone before will have no trouble in identifying the threat as emanating from the thief and the robber, the strangers and the hireling who have been mentioned in 10: 1, 5, 8, 10, 12-13. But we are concerned here with the first edition, and on the present hypothesis the *first* occurrence of the metaphor is at 10: 26-8. To appreciate what this entails we must look at 10: 21-39 as a self-contained episode, the last of three furious confrontations that centre on sayings of Jesus that are taken to be blasphemous by 'the Jews'. The question that we now have to consider is whether this passage makes sense if we assume that it followed on directly from the end of chapter 9, and if so how it is to be understood.

Some time has passed. The events recorded in chapters 7-8 took place at the Feast of Tabernacles, which is an autumn feast. It is not clear when the healing of the blind man is thought to have occurred, because nothing is said at the beginning of chapter 9 to suggest a different setting from that of the preceding two chapters. The next precise indication of time comes at 10: 22, which refers to Dedication, a winter festival. In order to preserve the continuity between chapters 9-10 we would have to suppose that the episode in chapter 9 took place just before the Feast of Dedication. Though not impossible, this seems a bit strained.[18] It requires John's readers to do a 'double-take' as they are confronted by the sudden and

---

[17] Apart from the two articles mentioned above in the Beutler–Fortna collection, a good summary of the evidence may be found in the entry 'Sheep, Shepherd' by Jack W. Vancil in *The Anchor Bible Dictionary*.

[18] Bultmann (p. 313) argues that there is a gap of several weeks between the last indication of time in 7: 37 (the Feast of Tabernacles) in September or October and the Feast of the Dedication (10: 22) in December. He puts the healing of the blind man, which is undated, well before this. In his rearrangement 10: 22-6 forms the introduction to the shepherd passage. Raymond Brown's defence of the traditional order (pp. 388-9) is not altogether satisfactory. On the basis of her own lectionary theory Aileen Guilding surmises 'a date at the end of Tishri [i.e. not long after Tabernacles] or, more likely, at the beginning of the eighth month, Cheshvan': *Fourth Gospel*, 121.

surprising information (in 10: 19-21) that chapters 9 and 10 somehow belong together. It is certainly easier to read 10: 22 as the commencement of an entirely separate episode.

On any reading the challenge of 'the Jews' comes as a surprise: 'If you are the Messiah, tell us plainly (παρρησίᾳ)' (10: 24). Why this particular challenge, and why is it made at this particular juncture? The answer is surely easier if we are able to bracket out 10: 1-21, for now 'Messiah' picks up what we know to be the key issue of chapter 9, what 'the Jews' had selected as the touchstone of loyalty to their cause, having 'already agreed that anyone who confessed Jesus to be the Messiah should be expelled from the synagogue' (9: 22). This fresh challenge, then, can have only one aim: to provoke Jesus into condemning himself once again out of his own mouth. For John himself the title 'Messiah' is never a completely satisfactory one,[19] and so, not content with reaffirming his right to this particular title, Jesus goes on to summarize a claim that had triggered the first outburst of Jewish anger: 'The works that I do in my Father's name, they bear witness to me' (10: 25; cf. 5: 17). In chapter 5 'works' referred primarily to the healing of the cripple; here the primary reference is to the healing of the man born blind. The introduction of the shepherd metaphor (now heard, if my thesis is correct, for the first time) marks a new and distinctive twist at this point in the narrative. In picturing Jesus as asserting that the sheep are *his*, and that they follow *him*, the evangelist is stressing the consequences of the fateful break with the synagogue. In Ezekiel the forthright condemnation of 'the shepherds of Israel', who allow the sheep to be 'scattered over all the face of the earth with none to search or seek for them' (34: 6) is followed by God's promise that 'I myself will search for my sheep and will seek them out' (34: 11). Matthew's parable of the lost sheep emphasizes to the point of paradox the shepherd's duty to seek out the solitary stray; but John is prepared to allow Jesus to assume the shepherding role which, according to the prophet, was eventually assumed by God.[20] Having been entrusted by the Father

---

[19] 'Titles like "prophet", "teacher sent by God", "king" or even "Messiah" do not correspond completely with the real status and authority of him to whom they point. The terms are not wrong but insufficient; they may be used in a wrong context and are, therefore, in need of further definition' (M. de Jonge, *Stranger*, 83).

[20] 'I myself will be the shepherd of my sheep' (Ezek. 34: 16). It is true that further on in the same chapter the good shepherd is identified as David ('And I will set over them one shepherd, my servant David' (v. 23)). Is the fourth evangelist

with the task of caring for the sheep, he also takes on, as in the 'hidden parable' in chapter 5,[21] the life-giving function that is one of the prerogatives of the deity. This being so, the claim that infuriates his hearers ('I and the Father are one' (10: 30)) is less abrupt than it might seem—always provided that we bear in mind the Old Testament background.

Accordingly, although the present text of the Gospel invites us to read 10: 26-9 as a resumption of the shepherd/sheep theme of 10: 1-18, these verses would have been perfectly consequential and intelligible as a colourful variant of a familiar theme, quite appropriate in the context of one of the evangelist's controversy stories. However speculative, the diachronic reconstruction required by this reading makes perfect sense. In the Gospel as we know it the whole passage resumes and alludes to the dialogue that has just preceded it. But its intelligibility is not conditional upon this sequence. It may equally well be seen as a particularly vivid expression of the tense and uneasy relationship between the two parties that followed the events cryptically alluded to in the narrative of chapter 9.

3. THE INTERIM

It is necessary to offer some account of what transpired between the publication of the first edition of the Gospel and that of the second. What I propose is this:

1. By the time the first edition had been published the shepherd motif was already part of the evangelist's vocabulary (see 10: 26-9) or rather of his imagery and way of thinking. It was perhaps the first expression, in the newly born Christian community, of what would come to be a fully ecclesial consciousness,[22] and at the same time included a recognition of the presence of outsiders who posed a threat to the integrity of the community. Yet what is emphasized here is the impotence of these, for there are

deliberately fusing two figures (Yahweh/Messiah) placed in succession by the prophet?

[21] See C. H. Dodd, 'Hidden Parable'.

[22] Bultmann restricts the specifically ecclesial content of this passage to v. 16, 'which can only be explained as a secondary gloss inserted by the editor' (p. 383). He wishes to defend the evangelist himself against any possible charge of having ecclesial concerns.

reliable safeguards against the threat from without: the community is assured of eternal life, and the intimate relationship between
shepherd and sheep is a source of hope and confidence.

2. Here, then, is a peaceful picture of a contented flock,
threatened but unafraid. The outlines of this picture are ill defined;
but its various elements are capable of being brought into sharper
focus as the threat, initially somewhat vague, becomes bright and
differentiated: a thief, a robber, a wolf; and the flock (which might
perhaps be browsing on the hillside, as in the parables of Matthew
and Luke) comes to be thought of as confined in a fold or pen with
a gate and a gate-keeper.

3. The potentialities of what was at first little more than a
familiar and not particularly striking metaphor are realized initially
in two concise and challenging assertions: 'I am the shepherd—
I am the door.' Building as they do upon two very different
elements of which only the first is explicit in the original
picture, these two images are not immediately reconcilable, since
the shepherd cannot be a door while he is still thought of as
shepherd—and vice versa. By and large the commentators tend to
opt for construction rather than deconstruction, and so they mostly assert, sometimes quite mechanically, that any contradiction
is more apparent than real;[23] but we are surely entitled to raise
an eyebrow at the suggestion that the juxtaposition of these
two images is first and foremost a brilliant literary trope. *They are
much more likely to have originated from antiphonal voices within a
setting of charismatic prophecy,*[24] with one voice declaring 'I am the

---

[23] In introducing his commentary on this passage, Odeberg argues that
the apparent inconsequence vanishes provided that we recognize the world of
discourse to which these images all belong. He insists that the dual sayings,
far from posing an insoluble problem, cohere admirably with the evangelist's
characteristic vision, and are paralleled by many other sayings: '"Jesus *gives*
the Bread of Life" and "Jesus *is* the Bread of Life". "He *shows* the Way" and "He
is the Way", "He *teachers* [sic] the Truth" and "He *is* the Truth". In fact, so
far from having been able to "melt into a unity" various "foreign" conceptions and
similes, the juxtaposition of the terms "door" and "Shepherd" in self-predicatory
dicta is precisely that intentionally startling feature by which John seeks
to convey the peculiar truths of the Divine-spiritual World and of Jesus' activity and
ministry' (*The Fourth Gospel*, 313). Wayne Meeks compares this 'illogic' with the 'I
am' saying at the beginning of the farewell discourse: 'I am the way, the truth and
the life' ('Man from Heaven', 158). This is an acceptable explanation on the *literary*
level, but does not help us to understand the origin of the various images.

[24] In *Understanding*, ch. 5, I argued that charismatic prophecy is the most likely
Sitz-im-Leben of a whole series of sayings in the Gospel that have a genuinely

shepherd' and a second voice responding 'I am the door'. The first of these sayings is a compressed statement of the basic Near Eastern metaphor of benign authority (according to which, let us not forget, Jesus had already been assigned a role reserved by Ezekiel for God). Connected with this is the life motif, and it is not surprising to hear a third voice at this point, this time with an ἦλθον-saying: 'I have come that they may have life and have it more abundantly' (10: 10).[25]

4. The life here, ζωή, is of course the eternal life (ζωὴ αἰώνιος) of 10: 28. But there is another kind of life, ψυχή, not distinguished in English from the former, which is the life the shepherd lays down (or lays on the line) for his sheep. The nexus between the various motifs is very intricate here; for what had at first been little more than a sort of poaching by one society from another was now seen as a real menace (of seizing and scattering), that could not be averted except by a very drastic intervention on the part of the shepherd. The vague apprehension caused by the proximity of the synagogue and its still powerful leaders had now hardened into a real fear: there was a wolf at large, sinister, dangerous, capable of wreaking havoc in any flock. At the same time the picture is a decidedly odd one. Watching the wolf tearing the shepherd's throat out, the sheep would be alarmed rather than consoled: the hint of self-sacrifice, in the manner of Paul, is very awkward in this context.[26] The relationship between the parent community ('the Jews') and the Johannine group, by this time fully established as an independent community, had now hardened into active opposition; and the situation that forced such an immediate response from the shepherd of the flock, ready to risk his life for his sheep,

prophetic ring and are consequently more likely to have originated as inspired utterances in the kind of prophetic milieu envisaged by 1 Corinthians 14 than as words on a page. We need not suppose that the gift of prophecy in such a setting was confined to a single individual. My proposal of antiphonal voices may be too bold; but it accounts better than any theory of continuous composition for the close proximity of apparently irreconcilable images.

[25] For a full, form-critical discussion of these two groups of sayings and the relationship between them, see J.-A. Bühner, *Gesandte*, 118–66.

[26] Bultmann remarks that 'whereas it is characteristic of a shepherd to risk his life for his sheep it is not characteristic for him to sacrifice it for them' (p. 370 n. 5), and concludes that τιθέναι τὴν ψυχήν in 10: 11 must mean 'to stake one's life, to risk it, to be prepared to lay it down' (unlike vv. 17–18, where the meaning 'lay down one's life' is assured). This may be right, but since the latter passage takes up and builds upon the same phrase, it is in some ways easier to think that it means the same in both places.

was clearly a very grave one. On the second, spiritual level of understanding, the generous and impulsive gesture of the community's leader could be linked with the sacrificial death of the one he represented. There is no evidence that the death of Jesus was interpreted in this way in the first edition of the Gospel; and accordingly we must suppose that here as elsewhere the community's experience of the enmity of 'the Jews' had led to a deepening understanding of the passion and death of the one it knew as its founder and lord. Even the special relationship between Jesus and the Father, long affirmed and proclaimed as the distinctively new feature of their 'Christian' faith, was given a strikingly novel coloration by these reflections: 'No one takes my life from me, but I lay it down of my own accord. I have power ($\dot{\epsilon}\xi o\upsilon\sigma\acute{\iota}a$) to lay it down and I have power to take it up again; this charge I have received from my Father' (10: 17–18).

5. Besides the wolf, and indeed preceding him in the order in which these ideas are presented to the reader, come the thief and the robber. The wolf, as we have seen, represents an immediate danger. The threat from the thief and the robber, on the other hand (10: 1), appears to have receded. One important branch of the manuscript tradition of 10: 8 includes the words $\pi\rho\grave{o}$ $\dot{\epsilon}\mu o\hat{\upsilon}$ after $\mathring{\eta}\lambda\theta o\nu$.[27] But although the words 'before me' may have been added by a puzzled scribe to give guidance to his readers, the past tense of $\mathring{\eta}\lambda\theta o\nu$ is probably enough to justify the inference that what we have here is not a present threat but an attempt to influence the Johannine Christians by destroying any lingering respect for their previous leaders. The identification of these with thieves and robbers is expanded by a gnomic utterance concerning the essential aims of the thief—theft, murder, and destruction. (This statement would have been more defensible if it had been predicated of the $\lambda\eta\sigma\tau\acute{\eta}s$ rather than of the $\kappa\lambda\acute{\epsilon}\pi\tau\eta s$:[28] a thief's job is to steal, and if he kills it is not because he sets out to do so.) The present tense of $\mathring{\epsilon}\rho\chi\epsilon\tau a\iota$ is not meant to imply that the thief is still engaged in his destructive activities: the sentence is added to enhance the contrast between the effective function of the 'good' or 'model' shepherd (which is that the sheep under his charge 'may have life, and have it more abundantly') and the previous

---

[27] The words $\pi\rho\grave{o}$ $\dot{\epsilon}\mu o\hat{\upsilon}$ are omitted by $\mathfrak{P}^{45}$, $\mathfrak{P}^{75}$, $\aleph^*$, and a number of versions, including the Old Latin and the Vulgate.

[28] Especially if $\lambda\eta\sigma\tau\acute{\eta}s$ is taken in the sense, frequent in Josephus, of 'terrorist' or (less tendentiously) 'freedom-fighter'.

rule of those who, whilst no doubt claiming the title of 'shepherds', had brought, not life, but death and destruction. In that case then the accusation of misrule has been replaced by the much graver charge of deliberate murder and mayhem, a charge that only makes sense if the circumstances presupposed by the narrative of chapter 9 have worsened dramatically. Before the break recorded in that chapter the relationship between the two groups may have been marked by bitterness and mistrust; and the violent enmity implied by 10: 1–7 will not have flared up until some time after-wards. Previously the leaders of the synagogue were not outsiders, and certainly not thieves and robbers: only with hindsight will they have come to be regarded in this way.

6. These new ideas are formulated in the Gospel with the succinct urgency that characterizes the *literary* output of the fourth evangelist. As such, they represent a later reflection upon the insights of what was originally a genuinely prophetic vision. This also holds for the interpretation of the second voice: 'I am the door.' From this blindingly intense vision of Jesus in this very different role arose two further conceptions of his relationship with the community. As Odeberg puts it: 'the Door leading to the Flock' and 'the Door for the use of the Flock'.[29] Initially, no doubt, these proceeded from different, independent reflections upon the original prophetic insight, the one expressing a new awareness that entry into the community, depending as it does upon Jesus himself, must be accompanied by a personal commitment to him; the other acknowledging him to be the source of nourishment and therefore of life. (This realization is closely related to another strong 'I-am' saying: 'I am the way, the truth and the life' (14: 6).) Naturally, if they are taken literally these two views of Jesus as 'the door' cannot be harmonized with each other. But the literal is not to be confused with the literary; and on this level, connected within an intricate mosaic that has never ceased to intrigue the commen-tators, the two statements are not contradictory but mutually illuminating.

7. One verse in chapter 10 opens up new vistas: 'And I have other sheep, that are not of this fold; I must bring them also, and they will hear my voice. So there shall be one flock, one shepherd' (10: 16). This saying affords us a glimpse of the larger Christian community, the church outside, to which the Johannine group

---

[29] Odeberg, p. 313.

had not yet become affiliated. This community (or church) is envisaged as on the point of joining their own group (which may well have been much smaller) and of acknowledging the authority of their own spiritual leader. Does this suggest great self-confidence on their part or perhaps a trace of anxiety at the prospect of being swallowed up in a larger whole? We do not have enough information to decide; but in all probability these other Christian communities will have had a different view of themselves from that projected here: they will surely not have seen themselves as presenting a threat to other groups; on the contrary their posture will have been a welcoming one, as they prepared to admit within their ranks strangers from another town or region who, like themselves, owed allegiance to Jesus. In either case, the picture of the Johannine community, as Bultmann, with evident distaste, acknowledges and underlines, is of a *church*—embryonic perhaps, with its organizational structures yet to be fixed and widely recognized, but a church none the less.[10] Those within the fold, recognizing in the voice of the Johannine leader the voice of Jesus himself, had the assurance of being where salvation was to be found. All the rest were outsiders, and only if they agreed to enter into 'the one true fold' could they claim the benefits of church allegiance: life, in abundance and for ever.

8. In what all see to be an interpretative aside, the evangelist qualifies this passage, now fully composed, as a παροιμία, and adds that Jesus' (unnamed) hearers 'did not understand it' (10: 6). Yet it is hard to see why its meaning would not have been perfectly plain to Jesus' interlocutors as long as they were, so to speak, locked inside the narrative in which both he and they were active participants. The real puzzle presented by the riddle is why it was regarded as a riddle in the first place. And the answer, I believe, is that it was not! Originally it was less a riddle than an explanation, or rather exposition, of some of the material contained in the *following* section, 10: 7–18. To understand why it was transposed to its present place we need to observe and acknowledge the imperative requirements of the narrative form—of the story-line of the Gospel. A plausible sequel had to be found for chapter 9; and the 'I-am' sayings that generated these explanations could not provide one: all too obviously they were addressed, not to the Jews/Pharisees who had interrogated Jesus and were in their turn

----

[10] See above, n. 22.

challenged by him in chapter 9, but to the Christian members of the Johannine group. In so far as there was a parable or an allegory, it is to be sought in this series of 'I-am' sayings. Applied, instead, to the *explanation* of the parable, the meaning of παροιμία has shifted from 'parable' or 'allegory' to 'riddle'. In its new position, and with its new meaning, it has, ironically, proved to be a real riddle, and a singularly intractable one, ever since.

4. THE PRESENT TEXT

We should begin by noting that the elements of what we now think of as the shepherd discourse, having been first formulated after the decisive rift with the synagogue, reflect the increasing mistrust and hostility of the two communities. Since the allegory of the vine in chapter 15 exhibits a similar preoccupation with the precarious circumstances of the infant church and the dangers of 'falling away', the evangelist might have thought of placing the shepherd discourse alongside that of the vine; especially so because much of it, as we have seen, was addressed in the first instance, like the farewell discourse, to the members of the Johannine group and insists similarly upon the importance of an intimate personal relationship with Jesus.[11] He chose instead to include it among the series of confrontations with 'the Jews' that occurred on or between the feasts of Tabernacles and Dedication in the last year of Jesus' life. This decision involved some readjustment as well as the addition of three verses, 19–21, to ease the transition between the events of Tabernacles (chapters 7–9) and those of Dedication (10: 22–39):

There was again a division (σχίσμα) among the Jews because of these words. Many of them said, 'He has a demon, and he is mad; why listen to him?' Others said, 'These are not the sayings of one who has a demon. Can a demon open the eyes of the blind?'

These verses are clearly designed as a bridge. The last verse echoes

[11] There is little doubt that if it had been included in the farewell discourse modern exegetes would have had no trouble in arguing that this was its proper place: there are so many conceptual links between the two passages that they cannot be separated without loss. A specious argument, no doubt, but one that serves to remind us that a possible continuity is not a necessary continuity: only in arguing for the existence of God has it ever been seriously maintained that this kind of inference is justified.

the response of the man born blind to the sceptical queries that followed his cure (9: 30-3): the link is clearly intentional, so much so that Bernard places these verses immediately after chapter 9.[12] One can see why: the assertion of repeated dissension (σχίσμα πάλιν ἐγένετο) points back to the earlier division (also σχίσμα) in 9: 16. Both occurrences of the term come in comments on the action interjected by the evangelist. But although the first is quite appropriate, the second (the one that concerns us here) is not, especially if it is placed where Bernard suggests, immediately after Jesus' outright denunciation of the spiritual blindness of the Pharisees in 9: 41. There is nothing in that uncompromising attack to justify or explain the mixed response implied by the word σχίσμα. This can only refer to the dissension following the mysterious utterances in 10: 7-18. Yet σχίσμα, as Bernard sees, does effectively function as a link word, tying the two sections together by signalling the confusion generated by Jesus' words in the ranks of his adversaries.

Next we have to consider the *reordering* of the material of 10: 1-18. As we read this passage today vv. 7-16 appear to offer an explanation for the twin parable in the first five verses; and this is how they are generally interpreted. But the succession of declaratory sayings in this passage ('I am', 'I am', 'I have come', 'I am', 'I am') is a decidedly odd way of explaining a parable, or indeed of elucidating a riddle, which, as I have argued, is probably how the παροιμία of v. 6 is to be translated. I suggest, therefore, that 10: 1-18 has been reorganized in order to make it fit better into its present context: the 'I-am' sayings would look even odder if they were made to follow on directly from the end of chapter 9. What is required here, if the shift of mood is not to seem intolerably harsh, is a saying that can reasonably be applied to the Pharisees. This is what we get. Although the synagogue authorities, the Pharisees, cannot have been regarded as total outsiders at the time the internal squabbles between them and the Johannine Christians were at their height, once the break had been made and the two communities had come to confront one another as distinct and independent entities, this is how, with hindsight, they now appeared: the sheepfold has become the free-standing home of the Johannine community; it has a door and a door-keeper, and anyone who climbs in by another way is a thief and a robber. Difficult as these verses are for a modern reader, we may well wonder why

[12] pp. xxiv-xxv, 341.

it was that the Jews and Pharisees to whom they were ostensibly addressed failed to understand them. There is some irony, moreover, in the valiant efforts of modern 'synchronic' exegesis to give a coherent account of the transition between the two chapters. For the more plausible such readings are, the harder it is for us to comprehend the incomprehension of Jesus' audience.

What has happened, I suggest, is that the parable and the explanation have changed places! What now figures as the explanation, vv. 7–18, is a composition built upon a series of 'I-am' sayings that were addressed in the first place, not to the unbelieving Jews but to the Christian group itself. Rudolf Schnackenburg, spotting the difficulty, gets round it differently: with πάλιν (v. 7), he says, there is 'the beginning of a fresh discourse by Jesus (cf. 8: 12, 21)', directed neither to the Pharisees of 9: 40 nor to the Jews of 10: 19, but to the believing readers.[13] In fact the whole Gospel, as Painter points out, is directed to the believing readers![14] Yet Schnackenburg is surely right to detect a shift of focus at this point: like the other 'I-am' sayings of the Gospel, the shepherd saying is primarily consolatory in tone: so too, essentially, is the door saying. The difficulty is resolved, however, once we recognize that in placing the passage in a new setting, the evangelist has altered its function, so that it now works as an *explanation* of 'the difficult saying' of 10: 1–5.

The continuity of chapters 9 and 10 is more commonly asserted than argued, though sometimes with a tentativeness that detracts from the force of the assertion. Thus C. H. Dodd: 'It would in fact be quite possible to read ix. 41–x. 5 as what it formally is, a single speech of Jesus, directly motivated by the situation depicted in ch. ix.'[15] More often than not the connection is established by appeal-

---

[13] ii. 288.

[14] 'Tradition', 60. Although I disagree with Painter's view that verses 11–18 are a later stratum of interpretation that does not fit the παροιμία, it must be admitted that we are all guessing at this point.

[15] *Interpretation*, 359. A few pages earlier Dodd had admitted that 'if we were enquiring into the history of the composition of the work, it might plausibly be argued that ch. ix . . . once existed as a separate unit, and that the discourse about the shepherd and the flock, x. 1–18, similarly may have had a separate existence' (p. 355). Ulrich Busse, having discovered a satisfactory continuity between chapters 9 and 10, goes on to assert: 'Therefore 10: 1ff. cannot be separated from chapter 9, and notably 9: 39–41, without difficulty' ('Open Questions', 8). Johannes Beutler comes to a similar conclusion: the 'polemical character of the shepherd discourse is most plausibly accounted for by its polemical context' ('Hintergrund', 20). As an *argumentum ad hominem* it is worth remembering that Busse and Beutler adopt

ing to Ezekiel 34, and there can be little doubt that this chapter does indeed lie behind John 10. Yet we have seen that the *timing* is a problem. In chapter 9 the Pharisees are still very much present, and in control, unlike Jesus' 'predecessors' in the next chapter, upon whom one insult is heaped after another: not merely are these implicitly identified as thieves and robbers, but they are relegated to the past of the Johannine community. Yet if we are to look for and insist upon a synchronic interpretation and read the two chapters continuously, then Dodd is surely right, both in his identification and in the cautious way in which it is phrased. In this way the present of the Johannine community (at the time that the second edition was about to be published) can be read back into the story of Jesus' confrontations with Jews and Pharisees, as it had always been, by Mark and Matthew as well as by John. As it stands the shepherd discourse serves rather, as C. K. Barrett observes, as 'a comment upon ch. 9 than a continuation of it. A signal instance of the failure of hireling shepherds has been given; instead of properly caring for the blind man, the Pharisees have cast him out (9. 34). Jesus, on the other hand, as the good shepherd, found him (9. 35, εὑρὼν αὐτόν) and so brought him into the true fold.'[36] Similarly, the man born blind may be seen as a prototype and exemplar for the sheep of the next chapter, who turn aside from strangers and false prophets to listen to the voice of Jesus. The welcome Jesus gives to new disciples contrasts favourably with the expulsion from the synagogue of those who had previously professed allegiance to him.

If we were to attempt to establish a closer relationship than this between the two passages, we should find it hard to do so without arguing at the same time that the evangelist had designed one to follow the other from the very beginning, and consequently that any attempt to demonstrate a diachronic relationship would be both otiose and misguided. For the reasons I have already given this view seems wrong to me; but we shall see in the next section that alternative views of the nature of the material lend it rather more plausibility.

---

different readings of 10: 7, the former selecting θύρα, the latter ποιμήν, yet each insisting that any proper construing of the passage depends upon the reading he prefers. Cf. n. 11.

[36] p. 367.

5. THE WORLD OF DISCOURSE

Up to this point I have assumed, along with most commentators, that the shepherd discourse is a particularly vivid example of the ideological and social opposition between Jesus and the religious leaders of his day (and thus, not incidentally, between the Johannine community and 'the Jews'). This entails another common assumption: that the allegory of Ezekiel 34, at least as it was read in the first century AD, is built upon the shepherd/ruler metaphor known to be widespread throughout the Ancient Near East. In aligning the Pharisees of his own day with the wicked shepherds of Ezekiel's allegory, the fourth evangelist is at the same time undermining their authority and making on Jesus' behalf the claim to 'equality with God' which was what finally put paid to any possibility of the peaceful coexistence of the two communities. The sheep are the Johannine Christians and the sheepfold is the church.

This picture resembles and is much indebted to that found in one of J. Louis Martyn's programmatic essays.[17] The details must remain uncertain. I still believe that this is the kind of interpretation that best helps us to *understand* the Gospel; but it is far from being the only possible interpretation; and we must not forget that it is only a hypothesis. Its strength and consistency tempt me to avert my gaze from alternative views. This is a frequent experience of scholars: their own theory acts as a kind of siren-song, in that it appears immeasurably more attractive and compelling than any competing theories and makes it hard to regard these with due attention. Here is Hoskyns, who has looked at a theory different from his own and looked away again:

The background of the parable is the Old Testament of metaphor as that heritage has been transformed by Christian truth. . . . Some commentators (e.g. Bauer) have endeavoured to disturb this precise heritage by placing the parable upon the background of general Hellenistic and Oriental mysticism. . . . [This] is to obscure the delicate allusions to the Old Testament and to destroy that vigorous sense for history which it is the main purpose of the Evangelist to expose as the ground of Christian truth.[38]

Bauer, of course, cites all the relevant Old Testament texts as

[17] 'Glimpses', 115–21.   [38] *The Fourth Gospel*, 368.

well, and many of his other references, including some striking
quotations from the Mandaean writings, are quite conceivably
indebted to the Fourth Gospel rather than the other way round.
Yet one feels that the mysticism of which Hoskyns so strongly dis-
approves is not far away.

Accordingly I propose at this point to put forward a completely
different interpretation from the one defended up to this point.
The purpose of this sudden shift is to emphasize the importance
of identifying what, at the beginning, I called the *content*. Like
all exegetical assumptions, the assumption that the most important allusion in Jesus' claim to be the Good Shepherd is to be
sought in Ezekiel's famous denunciation of the shepherds of Israel,
remains open to challenge. The allegory it both relies upon and
reinforces is a strong one, but we shall see that if we seek enlightenment elsewhere (*1 Enoch*), an alternative allegory presents
itself.

We may start, however, with some suggestions of Hugo
Odeberg. In common with all commentators except the narratologists of the 1980s, Odeberg assumes that the text gives us access
to a world outside and beyond itself, but he is unusual in that his
window is a skylight. Rejecting the ordinary understanding of the
sheepfold as the church, he sees it instead as 'the Divine-spiritual
world into which J[esus] seeks to lead men through his coming
into the "world", his "work", his "love unto death". The sheep
are those who "listen to his voice", recognize him, and hence
"enter through him" into the Divine reality. Already at this point
it will be clear, that with this interpretation there is no difficulty in
the dual dicta: "I am the Shepherd" and "I am the Door".'[39]
Odeberg continues by referring to a text from the *Mekilta* which
asserts that to oppose 'a faithful shepherd' is equivalent to opposing God himself: מי שמדבר ברועה נאמן כאלו מדבר במי שאמר והיה העולם
(*Mekilta* 13d). He adds that this very passage is remarkable for 'its
successive introduction of both the present terms, viz. the
"Shepherd" and the "Door" or "Gate"'; and it is true that it proceeds by quoting Psalm 118: 20: 'This is the gate of Yahweh; and
the righteous shall enter through it'; and Isaiah 26: 2: 'Open the
gates, that the righteous nation which keeps faith may enter in.'

These suggestions of Odeberg (and he has more) deserve to be
taken seriously. The parallels he adduces (like those of Bauer, so

[39] pp. 313–14.

summarily dismissed by Hoskyns) are inexact and taken out of context. There is no possibility that the evangelist actually drew upon these sources (all of them are later than the Fourth Gospel). But the resemblances are none the less striking, and we would be wrong to reject out of hand the possibility that the *world of discourse* is the same or at least similar.

We may now turn to an argument put forward by A. J. Simonis in a full-length book (originally a doctoral thesis) devoted to the shepherd discourse.[40] One of his most important proposals concerns the connection between chapters 9 and 10. He finds this, surprisingly, in the Book of Dreams (chs. 83–90 of *1 Enoch*), especially the last three chapters. The key to the understanding of this, a mini-apocalypse, is that it is a dream-vision, first of the pre-history then of the history of the world. What interests the writer most about human history is Israel and the calamities that have befallen her. He finds the explanation in the wicked deeds of the seventy shepherds to whom God had entrusted the task of tending and protecting Israel. In keeping with the symbolism of the whole of this section, in which men are portrayed as beasts and angels as men, the shepherds are angels[41] and the sheep are the people of Israel.[42]

Fleeing from Egypt (not actually named), the sheep are pursued by blind wolves, but once across the sea they soon become blind themselves. The period of the Judges is told with striking brevity: 'And sometimes their eyes were opened, and sometimes blinded, till another sheep [Samuel] arose and led them, and brought them all back' (89: 41). Subsequently the sheep are entrusted to seventy shepherds, who turn out to be untrustworthy and wicked. Later still, 'the eyes of these sheep were blinded so that they saw not, and the eyes of their shepherds likewise; and they were delivered in large numbers to their shepherds for destruction, and they trampled the sheep with their feet and destroyed them' (89: 74). As the story moves, almost imperceptibly, from prophecy into history, the wicked shepherds are judged, found guilty, and cast into the fiery abyss (90: 25). The sheep are then 'invited into

---

[40] *Hirtenrede.* Simonis's reading is supported by de la Potterie ('Bon Pasteur') and (independently, in a private communication) by Margaret Barker.

[41] As is argued by R. H. Charles, *The Book of Enoch*, 242–4. I quote from Charles's version here.

[42] From Isaac onwards: his father Abraham was a white bull! (We must remember that this is a dream.)

that house [i.e. the Temple];[43] but it held them not. And the eyes of them all were opened to see the good, and there was not one amongst them that did not see' (90: 34–6).

According to Simonis, we need look no further for the association of ideas that prompted the evangelist to follow up a section on the healing of a blind man (a blinded sheep, that has had its sight restored)[44] by a discourse on Jesus' predecessors: no true shepherds these, but thieves and robbers. He goes on to argue that the continuity between the two chapters is established by the fact that the events of both are conceived to take place against the background of the Feast of Tabernacles: 'In connection with the Zealots the paroimia represents a concrete event set within the historical framework of the Feast of Tabernacles: the αὐλή is primarily the forecourt of the Jews in the Temple, the θύρα the entrance to the Temple, the θυρωρός the temple guards, the thief and robber the Zealots.'[45]

Neither the subsequent commentators nor the contributors to the Beutler–Fortna volume appear aware of Simonis's thesis. Yet for those who insist upon a synchronic reading of the Gospel it must carry a certain attraction; for the allusion to blind sheep and blind shepherds, which we may assume would have been more obvious to John's readers than it is to us, helps to ease the passage from chapter 9 to chapter 10.

Here, then, is an alternative reading that should not be dismissed out of hand: a combination of the original insights of Odeberg and Simonis that serves to underline the distinctive flavour of the prophetic sayings in John 10, resembling as they do much else in this Gospel (especially the allegory of the vine in chapter 15) but at the same time so different from, say, the parables of the kingdom in the Synoptic Gospels. The parallels from the *Mekilta*, from the *Odes of Solomon*, from the Mandaean

[43] The term αὐλή is sometimes used to refer to the temple courtyard; and it is possible that there is another link here, especially if the writer is still being influenced by the imagery of the Feast of Tabernacles. De la Potterie ('Bon Pasteur', 938–9) insists on this interpretation, arguing that αὐλή occurs 177 times in LXX but never with reference to a sheep-pen. But if the writer is thinking of sheep then the only reason for bringing them into the courtyard of the Temple would be for purposes of ritual slaughter!

[44] Cf. C. K. Barrett, p. 367. Barrett seeks to establish a similar link between the two chapters by stating that it was as the true shepherd that Jesus found the man (εὑρὼν αὐτὸν 9: 35), 'and so brought him into the fold'.

[45] p. 160.

writings, are surely not without force. If, to take but one example, we consider the sense of mystical union between God and the Shepherd in the *Mekilta*, then we are surely not so very far from the claims of Jesus that provoked righteous indignation among 'the Jews' in the conclusion of John 10. The fact that for the writer of the *Mekilta* the Shepherd is Moses (see too Isa. 63: 11; *T. Mos.* 11: 9) tells for rather than against this suggestion once we recall how frequently Jesus takes the place of Moses in this Gospel. Moreover, even if we reject Simonis's main (strong) thesis, there may be something to be said for the weaker suggestion that the shepherd discourse in John 10 picks up themes that had, so to speak, gone underground after Enoch but were now resurfacing as traditions suppressed by the self-appointed guardians of the Torah (the deuteronomists) were now coming to be championed once again by Jesus and his successors? Could it be that Enoch's apocalyptic account of Israel's demise, according to which the true villains were not kings and politicians but wicked angels (shepherds, watchers), is the real key to Jesus' claim to be the *good* shepherd— not so much another king as another angel? If this were the true explanation of the shepherd saying it would admirably account for the sequence of thought in chapter 10 itself, which culminates in an outburst of anger at the implication, otherwise hard to pin down, that Jesus was pretending to equality with God.

6. CONCLUSION

Despite the initial attractiveness of these suggestions, there are two important reasons for hesitating to accept them.

In the first place, if this alternative interpretation of John 10 is to be taken seriously *the whole Gospel* must be interpreted in the same way. This is a formidable task. Odeberg has made a start, but he has had no followers; and in my view the characteristic Johannine mysticism is to be located not in the cloudy regions of *merkabah* tradition, which is where Odeberg would place it, but rather in the atmosphere of charismatic prophecy discernible in the Johannine community. This will have arisen from, or at least been nourished and fostered by, a powerful sense of intimate union with Jesus which was itself harmonically reinforced (Meeks's phrase) by the opposition of the leaders of the synagogue we find so strongly reflected in John 9.

In the second place, like all other purely synchronic readings, the proposals of Odeberg and Simonis fail to surmount the hurdle of the original aporia: the abrupt shift in theme and mood between chapters 9 and 10. At the same time it must be said that the majority of modern scholars appear to be unimpressed by the arguments against continuity; and in the face of so much disagreement all one can do is to urge readers of the Gospel to judge the matter for themselves. For my part, I remain unable to see the transition as smooth, still less as natural and obvious. There is a real hiatus here. Even Simonis, with Enoch to aid him, describes the appearance of the shepherd theme as sudden (*plötzlich*), and few, I suspect, will be convinced by his appeal to Enoch's dream.

Narrative Criticism

Fashions in scholarship, including those in gospel studies, have at least one feature in common with architecture, dress, cuisine, religion, and most other human institutions: they change. In the nineteenth century, which was when historical criticism in the broad sense established itself, the Gospels were studied with two primary ends in view: first to determine their relative dates and the literary relationships between them (source criticism) and secondly for what they can tell us about Jesus, his mission, and his consciousness of his mission (the quest for the historical Jesus). Though never entirely abandoned, these two approaches gave way early in this century first to form criticism, the study of the form and projected background (*Sitz-im-Leben*) of individual gospel passages, and then to redaction criticism, the attempt to determine the particular preoccupations of the evangelists, especially the Synoptists. One does not hear very much about form criticism these days, but numerous recent books and articles go to prove that the historical critical method itself, its muscles now hardened by occasional injections of sociological theory, is still alive and running strongly. In the last decade or so, however, it has had to compete with a new and very different kind of approach. Though this has a variety of emphases and a corresponding variety of names, I shall use the label 'narrative criticism': it is distinguished from earlier fashions by a consistent vision of the Gospels as, above all, *stories* and the desire to reach a better understanding of how these stories are told.[1] I shall argue that narrative criticism is more of a fad than a fashion, and that since it misconceives the true nature of the Gospels the results it yields are trifling, if not altogether illusory. Since my central concern here is with the Gospel of John I shall concentrate mainly upon three books[2] and

---

[1] Stephen Moore quotes the programmatic statement of one of the earliest examples of the genre: 'Narrative criticism . . . brackets historical questions and looks at the closed universe of the story-world' (*Literary Criticism*, 8).

[2] R. A. Culpepper, *Anatomy*; J. L. Staley, *First Kiss*; G. Mlakuzhyil, *Christocentric*

the first of a collection of articles in an issue of the periodical *Semeia*.[3]

I. ROUGH VERSUS SMOOTH

Narrative criticism relies for its initial appeal and plausibility upon a number of key principles, one of which I wish to call into question in the present section. This is the priority and superiority of what may be called smooth readings of the Gospels: smooth as opposed to rough.

'Smooth' is a shorthand term for synchronic; 'rough', in the same context, is equivalent to diachronic. I have explained these terms elsewhere as follows:

> The term 'diachronic' was used by Ferdinand de Saussure in his famous *Cours de linguistique générale* (117-40) to refer to the approach of linguistic theorists chiefly interested in the *history* of languages. The alternative approach is 'synchronic': the study of the interlocking relationships that go to make up a language at a particular point in time, ignoring the problem of how it reached that state in the first place. The two approaches, then, though quite distinct, are not mutually exclusive. In the study of individual texts, however, although the partisans of the synchronic method can certainly acknowledge the possibility that the text had a pre-history, they cannot take this into account in practice. Consequently they tend to emphasize both the extreme difficulty of getting back behind the received text and the nugatory nature of anything likely to be learned by doing so.[4]

The initial attractiveness of smooth readings is to be explained by the fact that the most important task of exegetes is to enable their own readers to understand the text in its final state, as it lies before them. The starting-point and the finishing-point are the same: the text of the Old and New Testaments as it has come

Structure. Mlakuzhyil's book is singled out here because it is the most fully worked-out of a number of recent proposals concerning the structure of the Gospel. These are very varied and, of course, mutually incompatible, but they are all put forward with great assurance. Besides Rissi (1983) and Staley (1988), see P. F. Ellis (1984) (a commentary), Wyller (1988), Giblin (1990), and Østenstad (1991).

[3] F. F. Segovia, 'Journey(s)', *Semeia*, 53 (1991), 23–54. This issue contains a number of other articles by a variety of different scholars, including Culpepper, Staley, and Segovia himself. But to deal with these studies, and others like them, would defeat the purpose of this chapter, which is critical rather than expository.

[4] *Interpretation*, 11.

down to us. In *Understanding* I offered an analysis and critique of C. H. Dodd's important apologia for the smooth approach, concluding with the query 'whether his decision to ignore questions of redaction was not motivated to some extent by convenience as well as conviction'.[5] For there can be no doubt that in most respects the smooth approach is much *easier* than the alternative, which in the nature of the case promises a very bumpy ride.

In 1986 the German review *Theologische Rundschau* included an extended survey by Jürgen Becker of Johannine scholarship in the five years 1980-4.[6] The section dealing with works that begin by assuming the literary unity of the Gospel (*Der Ansatz beim Text als literarischer Einheit*) is fourteen pages long and includes what are to my mind a number of devastating criticisms of the smooth approach. It deserves a wider distribution. Yet it can scarcely be said to have won the day.

Becker starts by pointing out that the debate between rough and smooth (to retain the same terminology) has dominated Johannine exegesis for generations, as can be easily verified by a glance at the articles on the Gospel in the three successive editions of *Religion in Geschichte und Gegenwart* (1912, 1927, 1959). What is new is the deployment of arguments of a structural or literary-theoretical kind in the debate. These, he points out, tend to slide all too quickly and easily from the obvious point that we have to begin with the text as we have it (*die Texteinheit*) to an assumption of its integrity (*die Texteinheitlichkeit*), an assumption which predetermines the outcome of any inquiry. The new approaches, themselves anything but theory-free, are frequently based upon an arbitrary dismissal of the old questions as insignificant or else upon a systematic refusal to allow them a hearing. Becker himself appeals, with every justification, for properly exegetical arguments concerning these issues. I single out a few sentences of an extended extract from G. C. Nicholson's *Death as Departure* (1983): 'We would agree that the text [of the Fourth Gospel] appears to have had a long pre-history . . . However, the meaning of the present text is not dependent upon the recovery of these sources. It does not matter where this earlier material came from . . . Even if the sources were recovered, focusing attention on them would only serve to distract us from our task of reading the Evangelist's text.'[7]

How many genuine literary critics, one wonders, would react

with anything but bemused astonishment to these remarks? What student of *The Waste Land*, for example, would wish to dispense with the facsimile of the manuscript, with all the passages that Eliot was persuaded by Ezra Pound to alter or elide? What scholar would dismiss as irrelevant for the understanding of Goethe's *Faust* all the poet's preliminary sketches? Yet we find identical sentiments repeated in a study of narrative criticism published nearly ten years after Nicholson's work: 'Ultimately, it makes no difference for a literary interpretation whether certain portions of the text once existed elsewhere in some other form.'[8]

One must conclude, I think, that this writer is not thinking in general terms of literary criticism as it is actually practised (unless he happens to be an adherent of the tenets of New Criticism, a school that went out of fashion more than thirty years ago); rather he is thinking very narrowly of the exclusively *biblical* understanding of narrative criticism. And this is based, as Becker pointed out years earlier, not upon conclusions reached by argument but upon a priori principles which, to a critical eye, look especially wobbly and insecure, based on nothing stronger than the unexamined efforts of a handful of like-minded enthusiasts.

There are strong reasons for believing that the Fourth Gospel was not composed at a sitting, nor yet in a matter of weeks or even months. Some chapters, e.g. 6, 15-16, 17, appear to have been inserted later. The final chapter, 21, is widely regarded as an appendix and an afterthought. It is a plausible hypothesis that the story of the raising of Lazarus in chapter 11 displaced the temple episode (now in chapter 2) as the immediate occasion of the decision to have Jesus killed. Further, smaller additions are also likely. These are not trivial suggestions.[9] On the contrary, they proceed from a hundred years and more of meticulous research (which still goes on) into the history of the Gospel, from its earliest beginnings up to the form in which it has come down to us. Yet sound as the reasons are for rejecting the hypothesis of an integrally conceived, unitary Gospel, it has to be said that no consensus has been reached or is ever likely to be reached concerning the genesis of the present text. Scholars who attempt any close and detailed analysis of the Gospel's structure or its plot (a rough outline may still be possible) find themselves in a trackless waste, and

---

[8] Mark Alan Powell, *Narrative Criticism*, 7.
[9] For a brief discussion of these suggestions see *Understanding*, 199-204.

seem condemned to trudge on doggedly through its shifting sands, covering a lot of ground but getting nowhere. This pathetic vision of the aimlessly wandering exegete is no doubt more likely to elicit scorn than sympathy; but in fact narrative critics see themselves in a very different light: not as victims but as heroes, champions of a new and noble cause. Undaunted by the so-called aporias of the Fourth Gospel, and throwing a pair of enormous brackets around the historical hypotheses of their colleagues, they proceed *as if* the Gospel was designed from the outset in its present form. (The story of the woman taken in adultery forms the solitary exception; not found in any of the best and earliest manuscripts, this is relegated to small print at the bottom of the page in most modern editions.) To scholars who refuse to turn a blind eye to the aporias of the Gospel such a procedure seems foolhardy in the extreme. These, convinced that the Gospel was *not* originally designed as we have it now, are astonished by the pretence or assumption that the plan, plot, or trajectory of the Gospel should be viewed in its entirety as a unified whole. To rely upon this assumption is, in their view, to put out to sea in a very leaky vessel indeed, one that is likely to founder as soon as the winds of criticism begin to blow. How do the champions of narrative criticism cope with this difficulty, surely a very serious one? Interestingly, in very different ways.

Staley is perhaps the boldest: in what he calls narrative critical analysis 'questions of multi-layered editorial interpolation . . . have no place . . . no more than do questions of "the author's intentions," for the assumption of unity endows the entire text with intentionality'.[10] 'Intentionality' here is left conveniently undefined, but it is surely a strange kind of intentionality that debars all consideration of the author's intentions and is somehow conjured into existence by an assumption of unity whose only basis is the printed text.[11] The Book of Isaiah too appears in print as a

---

[10] *First Kiss*, 29–30.

[11] The concept of intentionality, it seems, had its origins in the philosophy of Husserl (who took it over from Brentano), whence it has passed into literary theory via Roman Ingarden and Wolfgang Iser. Ingarden, the philosopher on whom Iser most relies, explicitly includes the author's aims in his concept of intentionality. He is concerned with works of the artistic imagination that take on a life of their own 'precisely as a result of the creative acts producing them'. He asserts that 'once the creative intentionality has been actualized, it becomes to a certain degree binding for us' (*Cognition*, 40). True, he continues by speaking of the reader as 'to some extent . . . the cocreator of the literary work of art': but this is a real reader,

single text: does this mean that the arguments of Duhm and his successors must crumble to dust when confronted by a modern reader's 'assumption of unity'? In any particular case the decision to treat a document as a unitary whole may be defensible; but the fact that it has been transmitted as such is not in itself an adequate defence.

Segovia, on the face of it, is more conciliatory. He proposes 'an initial reading of the plot of the Fourth Gospel as it presently stands, . . . as a unified and coherent work, thus bypassing altogether any discussion of literary strata underlying the present Gospel, no matter how complete or extensive such literary strata may be . . . or of the process of redaction and accretion resulting in the present text of the Gospel. While such excavative concerns are certainly justified and worth pursuing, they are not at all relevant to the main thrust of this study.'[12] But hold on a minute! *Why* are they not relevant? Why should we accept these bland assurances without argument, especially when what lies behind them is a covert plot to exclude the author or authors of the text from any say in the matter? 'Narrative unity', we are informed in a recent book, 'is not something that must be proved from an analysis of the material. Rather, it is something that can be assumed. It is the form of the narrative itself that grants coherence to the material, no matter how disparate the material might be.'[13] But there is surely some evasiveness here, for there is no explanation of how the act of granting coherence is to be conceived. Is it like granting citizenship, or a driving licence, or a degree?

Culpepper defends his approach with a statement which, seemingly, he regards as self-evident: 'the gospel claims that its world is, or at least reflects something that is more "real" than the world the reader has encountered previously'. In accordance with this 'mirror' model, he continues, 'dissection and stratification have no place in the study of the gospel and may confuse one's view of the text'. The question, 'What text?', he answers by saying that '"text" here means simply the words or signifiers of the story as recorded in the 26th edition of the Nestle-Aland *Novum*

not an implied reader, and his/her collaborator in this joint enterprise is evidently not the implied author but the real one. Intratextuality, which leaves the real authors and readers outside, is not given any philosophical or speculative justification here.

[12] 'Journey(s)', 24.
[13] Powell, *Narrative Criticism*, 92.

Testamentum Graece.'[14] Thus the anatomy of the Gospel he proposes (which can scarcely be said to have been achieved without dissection) evokes the image of a pathologist who, after a close inspection of a corpse that has earlier undergone major surgery, makes no reference to this in his report, and is even reluctant to mention the fact that the body has recently been fitted with a sizeable prosthesis. Much further on in his book Culpepper does actually go on to speak of John 21 as an epilogue 'apparently added shortly after the Gospel was completed', but even here he hedges his bets with the assertion that it is 'the necessary ending of the gospel'.[15] One wants to ask: what kind of necessity is envisaged here? Should the final chapter be included in a consideration of the Gospel's structure or not?

Mlakuzhyil, unlike the others, recognizes that if the arguments against unity were valid they would scupper his own project before it had got under way. But so confident is he of their fundamental weakness that it takes him barely a page to dispose of them.[16]

In sum, Staley sidesteps the objections; Segovia declares them irrelevant; Culpepper ignores them; and Mlakuzhyil airily dismisses them as without force. This cannot be right. Strong reasons may be adduced for allowing the synchronic approach they all favour, but not at the expense of a deliberate disregard of the obstacles that stand in the way.

The arguments for reading the Gospel as it stands are partly historical (this is the book that has left its mark on earlier generations and continues to be read today); partly internal: the consistency of style and tone, which led Strauss to see the Gospel as a seamless garment, the sustained self-allusiveness, the frequent authorial interjections—all these suggesting that at a stage of the Gospel's history preceding all the manuscript versions a successful attempt has been made to produce an integrated narrative, one that can be read uninterruptedly from beginning to end. (Note that the same is *not* true of the Book of Isaiah.) Just as present-day readers of the *Iliad* may well fail to notice the marked stylistic shift in Book 9, so only hypersensitive exegetes are likely to stumble over the so-called 'aporias' of the Gospel; and even they may wish to offer a synchronic reading, if only because with the possible exception of chapter 21 there are strong reasons for seeing the whole Gospel as carrying the authoritative stamp of the evangelist.

---

[14] All quotations from p. 5.   [15] p. 96.   [16] pp. 8–9.

At the same time, any acknowledgement of the probability, to put it no more strongly, that the Gospel was not conceived from the outset in its present form would make it hard to accept some of the very detailed and intricate structural proposals that we are about to consider. Sharing as they do so many presuppositions, the extent to which the four scholars disagree may surprise the unwary.

2. STRUCTURAL CRITICISM

In this section we shall be concerned with formalist approaches (not to be confused with structuralism in the strict sense) that meld easily with narrative criticism because they can be regarded simply as ways of analysing the plot; but for the narrative critic these are means, not ends, and Culpepper for one manages perfectly well without them. From the formalist point of view the most interesting of our four authors is Mlakuzhyil, in spite of, or perhaps because of, the fact that he is unaffected by the theoretical concerns of narrative criticism. Staley integrates a detailed and strikingly individual analysis with a subtle and intriguing theory of the 'implied reader' which will have to await further discussion. Segovia's approach resembles that of Staley, whose work he respects, but he lacks the latter's theoretical sophistication.

Bracketing out all considerations of diachronic development carries with it obvious benefits for the structuralist critic. And although the proposal to restrict our study to 'the text that has come down to us' is unacceptable if it is intended to exclude what Segovia calls disparagingly 'excavative procedures', a synchronic reading of the Gospel remains, as I have argued, a perfectly legitimate option. Even if the final version turns out to be the work of a redactor rather than an author, we may reasonably expect one of this person's concerns to have been to piece together narrative and discourse in a readable and coherent form. Such breaks and blemishes as continue to alert the critic to the presence of strata of tradition need not deter the ordinary reader from instinctively seeking a patterned development.

At another level of critical awareness, however, the suggestion that the Gospel has undergone some restructuring may assist rather than hinder an understanding of its present state; and I will elaborate upon this idea at the end of the discussion.

Any comprehensive treatment of the structure of the Gospel would be indescribably tedious, and is in any case outwith my present brief. I will confine myself here, therefore, to a few illustrative probes, selecting examples that illuminate the principles as well as the practice of this kind of criticism.

(a) Chapter 13

Almost all the major commentators agree that there is a significant break at the end of chapter 12. Whatever other minor divisions are discernible, here at least, one might suppose, the shift of scene and focus must be obvious to any reader, even the least responsive. There are four simple but strong reasons for retaining the break at the end of chapter 12: (1) that chapter's particularly solemn conclusion, which rounds off what Jesus has to say to the world; (2) the exceptionally weighty and measured introduction to chapter 13;[17] (3) the change of audience from 'the Jews' to Jesus' disciples, to which corresponds a shift in *mood* from confrontation to consolation and encouragement; (4) the sense of finality signalled by the word τέλος (not found elsewhere, but echoed in Jesus' dying τετέλεσται—'it is accomplished' (19: 30)).

Accepted by both Culpepper and (with reservations) by Mlakuzhyil, this seemingly natural division is challenged by Staley in the name of narrative critical analysis: 'While chapter 13 begins with the narrator's meta-historical summary of the story, it cannot represent a major turning-point of the plot, since Jesus' subsequent actions and words have no meaning apart from the significant turn of events which began with 11: 1 ff. . . . . On a story level,' he concludes, 'the interconnections between chapter 13 and the preceding scenes do not allow for the kind of major division that scholars frequently foist upon the text there.'[18] The first scholar I know to have cast doubt on the division of the Gospel at the end of chapter 12 is Matthias Rissi, in an article published in 1983.[19] Since Staley is confessedly indebted to Rissi, and since Segovia has

---

[17] All commentators (with the solitary exception of Boismard) point this out. Bultmann is especially perceptive, but does not connect the break with his dislocation theory and so fails to remark upon the happenstance (happy chance?) that prevented pages from the first half of the Gospel from straying into the second, and vice versa.

[18] *First Kiss*, 67.

[19] 'Aufbau.'

subsequently joined his two predecessors in galloping roughshod
over this apparently obvious break in the interests of promoting an
alternative approach to the narrative structure of the Gospel, a
word of explanation is in order. For Rissi the key to the structure
of the Gospel is to be found in Jesus' journeys to Jerusalem. There
are four of these, three in the first half of the Gospel (1: 19–3: 36;
4: 1–5: 47; 6: 1–10: 39), and one in the second (10: 40–12:
41).[20] Rissi argues that Jesus' 'hour' (the hour of his passion)
begins at 12: 23 ff.; that he is sentenced to death by the Sanhedrin
in absentia in 11: 47–57; that this sentence is bound up with the
story of the resurrection of Lazarus, which starts at Bethany, the
endpoint of Jesus' first journeys; and that the symbolic portrayal of
Jesus as the Paschal Lamb is already foreshadowed in 12: 1 and
11: 55. Moreover, Jesus' dealings with 'the world' are not finished
at chapter 12, as is often alleged, but are continued in the passion
story. Many of Rissi's observations are correct (though by omitting
the conclusion of chapter 12 he neatly eliminates one of the main
objections to his position—a move that is not open to Staley or
Segovia). But one-sided as they are, not only do Rissi's arguments
fail to outweigh the observations of the scholars he criticizes: they
have to be buttressed by an emphasis on the structural significance
of Jesus' journeys, and this is an emphasis that he cannot expect
all to share. Even if he is right, he is not *obviously* right: the data
he uses are not self-interpreting.

(b) Chapter 5

Chapter 5 marks the beginning of the series of great debates with
'the Jews' that punctuate the next six chapters. Most of those
who acknowledge the structural significance of Jesus' journeys
(especially of his journeys to Jerusalem) recognize a break here.
This, the second of Jesus' journeys to Jerusalem (to an unnamed
feast), is marked by a noticeable change of mood and above all by
an increase in tension. It is true that the long debate section that
begins here is foreshadowed by the brief confrontation that takes
place on the occasion of Jesus' first trip, recorded in 2: 13–25.[21]
But in spite of the μᾶλλον ('the Jews sought all the more to kill him'
(5: 18)), the story of the healing of the cripple and the angry scene

---

[20] Rissi thinks that 12: 42–50 has been interpolated; likewise 15–17 and 21.

[21] Note too the suggestion that Jesus felt unwelcome in Judaea (4: 3), 'his own
country' (4: 44).

that ensues mark a real turning-point in the story and compel any perceptive reader to recognize that the Jews' incomprehension of Jesus' message will persist until they eventually succeed in their determination to see him dead.

Once again Staley, who has his own views about the way Jesus' journeys function in the plot, challenges the broad agreement that there is a significant heightening of tension at this point of the Gospel. After a Prologue in which the implied reader is instructed how to read what follows, the Gospel, in Staley's view, is composed of a series of four journeys (Ministry Tours), each of which is structured chiastically or concentrically, containing two visits to Judaea, with a trip to Galilee sandwiched between each pair. Chapters 4–6 make up 'the Second Ministry Tour', and so there is no place in this analysis for a new beginning at chapter 5. The continuity of the section, argues Staley, 'can be seen when taking into account the conventions of Leitwörter [key-words], symmetry, and narration/direct speech'.[22]

Staley's method of proceeding may be illustrated by an example of how he argues from key-words. With the aid of a friendly concordance it is possible to determine that 12 out of the 16 occurrences of the word ζᾶν in the Fourth Gospel are used in chapters 4–6; 21 out of 38 occurrences of ζωή; all 3 occurrences of ζωοποιεῖν; besides nearly all the words associated with eating and drinking—ἄρτος, 21 out of 24; ἐσθίειν, 14 out of 15; πίνειν, 9 out of 11; and the list goes on. Staley, to whom I am indebted for these figures, uses them to build up a case that chapters 4–6 constitute one of the Gospel's four main concentric sections;[23] but he is alone, as far as I know, in interpreting the figures in this way, and one can no more imagine the discourse on the bread of life dispensing with 'words associated with eating' than one can imagine the discourse on the Good Shepherd doing without the word 'sheep'. Data concerning the distribution of words, like all other data, have to be interpreted: they are not like car registration numbers, whose significance can readily be ascertained by anyone with access to the relevant records. The fact that Staley's proposals differ widely from those of the vast majority of his predecessors evidently worries him not a jot. But perhaps it should.

---

[22] *First Kiss*, 61.   [23] Ibid. 64.

(c) Chapter 2

My next example is more contentious, and although the exegetical
options involved are apparently more clear-cut, they are not really
so. Does the Cana episode belong with what precedes or with what
follows? If taken with what follows it provides a neat inclusion
with the second Cana miracle at the end of chapter 4, the healing
of the nobleman's son. But a perception of this pattern does not
entitle us to ignore the arguments that favour a different reading,
which sees Jesus' first sign as the culmination of the story of the
discovery of Jesus and the initial revelation of his glory: the opening phrase of chapter 2, 'on the third day', strongly suggests a link
with what precedes.[24] Should we perhaps see this episode *both* as
the triumphant conclusion of the opening sequence *and* as the start
of a new phase of Jesus' career—the end of the beginning but
equally the beginning of the end?

(d) Chapter 11

My final example is another illustration of the same dilemma. The
last verses of chapter 10 constitute a very evident conclusion, and
yet at the same time they do not, for the story of Jesus' public
career carries on for a further two chapters. We may be tempted to
wield our structural cleaver either at 10: 39 ('Again they tried to
arrest him, but he escaped from their hands') or at 10: 42, following a tiny, three-verse pericope centring on the phrase, 'And John
did no sign'. At the same time, as I have already argued, the break
at the end of chapter 12 is too obvious to be ignored. Here again
there are sound reasons for retaining both proposals; but this
cannot be done without complicating the structural analysis more
than most scholars would be prepared to allow.

This is where Mlakuzhyil comes into his own. Availing himself
of all the drills, needles, and probes that he can find in the literary
critic's surgery, he finds himself forced, at two significant points, to
break away from the familiar, one-dimensional structure. He
acknowledges that with chapter 13 there commences a major new
section, 'Jesus' farewell of the hour'. But at the same time he
recognizes its links with the preceding two chapters. For him, then,

[24] On this see *Understanding*, 266, 290–1.

these represent what he calls a bridge-passage, and he names this 'the climactic sign and the coming of Jesus' hour'. The other bridge-passage is the wedding-feast of Cana (2: 1-11), which belongs both to what he calls the 'Christocentric introduction' (1: 1-2: 11) and to a section entitled 'Jesus' works, signs and discussions' (2: 1-4: 54).

Mlakuzhyil, unlike most other scholars who have busied themselves with dissecting the Gospel in order to disclose its anatomical structure, does his best to present the data as exhaustively as possible. Though he is able to account for the two 'bridge-passages' synchronically, his findings tally remarkably well with a very different view of the Gospel. If, as I believe to be probable, the wedding-feast of Cana was the third panel of a triptych that opened the so-called Signs Source, then one can understand how the evangelist may have used it to introduce his own story of Jesus' public career. Similarly, when inserting the Lazarus episode into the second edition of his Gospel, he will have seen it both as the culmination of Jesus' dealings with 'the Jews' and as the occasion of the fateful decision to bring about his death, and consequently as a new start for the passion narrative (which up till then, we may suppose, had begun with the story of the Last Supper). Mlakuzhyil's data, so carefully assembled, are best accounted for on the hypothesis of a step-by-step *re*structuring of the Gospel. At the very least such a hypothesis fits the data quite as well as his own. Indeed, these two explanations are not mutually exclusive, and may even be said to reinforce one another.

The great weakness of Mlakuzhyil's work is his gargantuan appetite for chiasms. Each of the five major sections of his overall plan displays a chiastic pattern that no one else had succeeded in spotting before. Chapter 6, for instance, is balanced by 10: 1-21, the Good Shepherd. True, the word ἀκολουθεῖν occurs in both passages. But is this enough? (The word is found in eight other chapters besides.) And is the story of doubting Thomas a satisfactory match for the episode of Jesus' arrest? The trouble is that if you are interested in structure to the exclusion of practically everything else, then you are bound to want to find as much of it as you can. But perhaps the most damning criticism of Mlakuzhyil is that even if he were right, it is hard to see how his findings would affect our understanding of the Gospel to any significant extent.[25]

Whether in science or mathematics or in art and literature human beings have an incurable propensity for devising patterns. When not engaged in inventing these, they may be concerned in discovering them. Invention is a creative occupation; discovery (at least in the arts) pertains to criticism. Finding patterns in the natural universe and reducing them to formulae and equations is probably the peak of scientific achievement. The structures planned by the creators of works of art, music, and literature are generally more obvious: in a painting by Michelangelo or Piero della Francesca, for example, or in a sonnet by Petrarch or Michelangelo, such patterns often leap to the eye and do not need to be pointed out except to the dullest or least-informed critical intelligence. 'Ars est celare artem,' said Horace; but the imagination can often be seized and delighted by sheer bravura and technical display, whether in a massive novel like *Ulysses* or in a brilliant sestina by Elizabeth Bishop or Amy Clampitt. In works such as these the structure is unproblematic; but where an author has no interest in underlining the structure, it is largely left to the reader to pick out the emphases and make the necessary connections, and here there is inevitably a large element of subjectivity. The Fourth Gospel is a case in point. I stress the word inevitably, because when a number of experienced critics fail to reach agreement on structural issues, it is surely futile to keep underlining the same facts and labouring the same arguments over and over again, much as Margaret Thatcher used to do, in the conviction that no one who actually understood what she was saying could possibly disagree with her. Simply listing data, whether of vocabulary, syntax or style, narrative development or physical action, will never be enough to persuade everybody else that your *interpretation* of these data is the only correct one.

Since neither the Gospels nor indeed any other writings of the New Testament were originally furnished with chapter or verse numbers, we must acknowledge that in providing these, or in

---

[25] This is Mlakuzhyil's conclusion: 'We have shown how the *major Johannine themes* such as the Messiahship and the *divine Sonship* of Jesus, his *signs (and works)*, *discipleship, faith* and *eternal life* are *Christocentric* in character', and that 'there is a *progressive revelation of Jesus, the Christ, the son of God and the life-giver* in the dramatic and organic development of the Gospel' (p. 350). Any attentive reader will agree; and at least one can say of Mlakuzhyil's laborious argument that it does not occlude the obvious.

making any other suggestions concerning structure, we have already begun the work of interpretation. Structural analysis, in other words, is part of exegesis.

Of our four authors it is Culpepper whose structural proposals are the least idiosyncratic, and that is no doubt because questions of structure absorb him less than they do the other three. In the fourth chapter of his book ('Plot'), once he has shrugged himself free from his theoretical strait-jacket, he demonstrates that it is possible to give a perfectly adequate account of the plot with a minimum of structural comment. When it comes to narrative criticism, however, it is a different matter.

3. NARRATIVE CRITICISM

With the passage of time all literary texts, even the most ancient and well-studied, confront scholars and critics with new questions, and they generally respond to the challenge by elaborating new methods. Sometimes the necessary tools have been developed previously in allied disciplines and lie ready to hand; it can even happen that the very availability of these is partly responsible for generating new questions. Sometimes the questions knocking at the door have arrived carrying a knapsack on their backs with the appropriate tools inside. Such was the case in the second decade of the century, when Bultmann and Dibelius began to apply to the Gospels methods of study that had been developed in the early days of form criticism to solve puzzles in the Hebrew Bible. Such, too, it may seem, was the case some sixty years later, when some of their successors, stimulated by the sight of a bag of gleaming new tools, began to look for ways of applying these to the Gospels. This, however, is at best a partial explanation of the truly remarkable change of direction that was taken by a number of scholars, now called narrative critics, in the wake of redaction criticism. The most important reason, as we shall see, belongs in the order of theology or philosophy, and can be properly called hermeneutical. (I propose to defer the consideration of this until the concluding paragraphs of this section.)

Meanwhile, there is another curious factor, one that has generally, I believe, been overlooked. The new tools seized on by the narrative critics had really been designed to do very different jobs. Many of the tasks eagerly undertaken by the new critics had already been quite competently performed by scholars with a much less spectacular array of tools at their disposal. This can be seen from a glance at Hans Windisch's 'Der johanneische Erzählungs-stil' (1922) or Dodd's *Interpretation of the Fourth Gospel* (1953). Both of these scholars, the keenness of whose literary sensibility is beyond question, had offered good and often brilliant analyses of a variety of episodes in the Gospel, analyses specifically intended to draw attention to the narrative skills of the evangelist. Taking a rather different tack, Herbert Leroy's *Rätsel und Missverständnis* (1968) and David W. Wead's dissertation on *The Literary Devices in John's Gospel* (1970) had ably dealt with the evangelist's use of riddle and irony.[26] So in order to find something new to say different models of interpretation had to be sought.

Culpepper found his models in the work of contemporary literary theorists: Murray Krieger, Wolfgang Iser, Seymour Chatman, and Gérard Genette, all highly sophisticated critics, dealing mainly with rather complex works of literature, and, in Chatman's case, of cinema also. But when we examine *how* Culpepper uses his models, we are in for a surprise. He begins, for instance, by criticizing the inadequacy of the 'window' model of the Fourth Gospel, that is to say as a way of looking into—or out upon—the world of the Johannine community. He proposes to replace this by the model of the 'mirror', derived, he tells us, from Murray Krieger: 'This model assumes that the meaning of the text lies on this side of it, between mirror and observer, text and reader.'[27] The proposal to employ John's Gospel (or indeed any other text) as a mirror may seem strange to the point of incomprehensibility; but Krieger's concept of the mirror, introduced right at the outset, is actually much more complex than (and very different from) Culpepper's version of it. Krieger speaks of a view of poetic language as functioning 'as an enclosed set of endlessly faceted mirrors ever multiplying its maze of reflections but finally shut up within itself'. In fact, Krieger's declared aim is to transcend the opposition between window and mirror: 'to see the poem as both trapping us in the looking glass and taking us *through*

---

[26] Mention should be made at this point of the work of Birger Olsson, the first Johannine scholar, as far as I am aware, to apply sophisticated literary critical methods to the study of the Gospel. See *Structure and Meaning*.

[27] *Anatomy*, 6. It is actually rather hard to see the purpose of placing a mirror on the other side of an object one wishes to examine.

it'.[28]

Since Culpepper treats the theorists to whom he appeals as authorities, and never calls the correctness of their views into question, it comes as something of a shock to find how loosely, carelessly even, he applies the categories he has taken over from them. His 'mirror' model, as we have seen, bears little resemblance to Krieger's; his 'implied reader' lives in a different world, speaks a different language from Iser's;[29] and the crucial distinction implicit in the title *Story and Discourse* is quietly dropped when Culpepper introduces his own modifications of Chatman's programme.[30] The most important difference between Culpepper and the theorists whom he cites as authorities has been well observed by Stephen Moore: 'Narratology is about theory, narrative criticism is about exegesis. Narratologists analyze texts mainly to develop theories. Narrative critics utilize theory mainly to explicate texts.'[31] Culpepper himself forestalls a possible objection on the grounds 'that perspectives and methods drawn from the study of fiction are inappropriate for the study of scripture'.[32] Such an objection, he rightly argues, would be misplaced. There is nothing wrong in itself in treating the Gospels as stories. But (and this is my first

[28] Krieger observes that such a procedure involves moving beyond the New Criticism: 'to get through the poem's closed context back to history and existence in a way which I hope criticism will increasingly be doing' (*Window to Criticism*, 3). There is in any case something odd about Culpepper's use of the metaphor of the mirror to suggest that art or literature does something other than reflect life or nature, especially if it is used instead as a metaphor for self-expression. This effectively reverses the traditional use of mirror to suggest a mimetic approach to literature, as this is expounded in M. H. Abrams's famous study, *The Mirror and the Lamp*. In the nineteenth century Stendahl (or rather the narrator of *Le rouge et le noir*) was able to describe a novel as a walking mirror: 'un miroir qui se promène sur une grande route'. Balzac and Zola would certainly have agreed, and no doubt Flaubert too. That the metaphor retains its force even today is proved by a remark made by Brian Keenan, introducing his powerful and disturbing account of his imprisonment in Lebanon: 'Stories should be a mirror held up to life.'

[29] Who, as he notes, 'will vary historically from one age to another' (*The Implied Reader*, p. xii), a characteristic of 'the implied reader' that Culpepper does not bother to take into account. Iser bases his study on the work of English-language novelists ranging from Bunyan to Beckett, observing that the novel is 'the genre in which reader involvement coincides with meaning production' (p. xi).

[30] In this instance the omission is certainly prudent, for Chatman's division of narrative into two 'parts' (story on the one hand and 'discourse' or expression on the other) betrays a breathtaking philosophical naïvety and offers easy access to the skilful sappers of deconstruction.

[31] *Literary Criticism*, 51.

[32] *Anatomy*, 9.

main criticism of Culpepper's procedures) they are very much *simpler* stories than the majority of those studied by narratologists; and consequently the benefits of the new methods are seriously open to question.

In much of Culpepper's work the theoretical scaffolding which he erects in its support is simply an encumbrance; and in the remainder its actual contribution to scholarship is quite small. Two longish chapters (those concerned with 'plot' and 'character') follow the model closely, but the fact is that the plot of the Fourth Gospel is episodic and the characters one-dimensional. Culpepper is perfectly well aware of this: 'each episode has essentially the same plot as the story as a whole. . . . The story is repeated over and over. No one can miss it.'[13] (So why spend twenty pages analysing it?) 'The character of Jesus is static; it does not change. He only emerges more clearly as what he was from the beginning.'[14] In so far as the minor characters change (and only a few of them do), it is to serve the plot: will they or will they not accept the revelation of Jesus? In short, one has to say that although certain episodes (the healing of the man born blind, for instance, and the passion narrative) are very well crafted, from the point of view of narrative technique the Fourth Gospel as a whole is unremarkable. What distinguishes the Gospel is not what Chatman would call its *discourse*,[15] but the content of what Jesus reveals, in word and deed; and this is something which slips through the net of narrative criticism.

In the chapter headed 'Implicit Commentary' Culpepper deals with misunderstandings in John, and also with irony and symbolism. His treatment is both competent and thorough: these are all important issues, but they are all guests in the household of narrative criticism, not part of the family, and in any case, as we have seen, can easily be entertained elsewhere. The category of implicit commentary is not found in Chatman's model, and his discussion of covert narration has a very different focus. As Culpepper himself admits, Johannine scholars were interested in irony and kindred topics long before narrative criticism joined in the fray.

Culpepper's most significant contribution is to be found in his

---

[13] Ibid. 89.   [14] Ibid. 103.
[15] A better translation of the French *discours*, which Chatman elsewhere renders 'expression', would be 'rhetoric'.

introduction and in the chapter that follows, 'Narrator and Point of View'. Even here the facts to which he draws our attention are not new. Bultmann, for one, was always alert to the comments and observations of 'the evangelist', a personage that Culpepper does not always distinguish clearly from the implied author.[16] Nevertheless, the distinction is a useful one, and Culpepper deserves credit for introducing it. The following chapter, 'Narrative Time', is less important simply because the analepses and prolepses which form its subject are not complex enough to require detailed analysis. Culpepper refers here to the work of Gérard Genette, *Narrative Discourse*, an elaborate and difficult study of Marcel Proust's masterpiece, *A la recherche du temps perdu*. This is a work whose convoluted intricacy more than justifies the attention it has received from narratologists (such as Genette) and from literary critics. To apply the same technique to the Gospels (any of them) is like using a combine harvester to mow the garden lawn.[37]

Staley applies the narratological distinctions between real and implied author/reader and narrator/narratee with considerable rigour. His purpose in doing so is to throw a fence around the domain of the text and then to lower himself carefully down inside this, sticking religiously to the principle of what he calls intra-textuality and availing himself of the protection afforded by its magic circle. He displays none of the insouciance with which Culpepper oscillates between author and implied author or between real and implied reader. For him the text is sacred, and he is not even prepared to treat chapter 21 as an appendix: every word on every page has to be included. In theory, of course (to

---

[16] He speaks at one point, for instance, of the evangelist as 'the author of the gospel's ironies' (p. 178), and shortly afterwards of 'the implied author's irony' (p. 180). See Staley's criticisms of Culpepper, *First Kiss*, 11-15.

[37] Moore (*Literary Criticism*, 52-3) comments sardonically on the use made by gospel critics of *Narrative Discourse*. Genette's views, he observes, 'are calculated more to unsettle than to reassure'. Mary Ann Tolbert makes an equally telling objection against narrative-critical studies of single chapters or even, in some cases, a couple of paragraphs: 'Especially for reader-response critics, who must acknowledge that a reader's understanding of any section of a text is built upon what the reader has learned up to that point, studying only isolated sections of longer stories is extremely problematical. Actually, the books in the New Testament and even in the Hebrew Bible are hardly longer than brief to moderate short stories. Yet, what literary critic would characteristically write essays on only one or two pages of a short story, much less one or two paragraphs? Indeed, in the world of English literature, one essay might well analyze the plots of several novels, covering considerably more material than is found in the entire Bible' (*Semeia*, 53 (1991), 206). This particular objection does not apply, of course, to the works considered here.

employ this phrase somewhat ironically), his rigour is thoroughly commendable, and there is some intellectual satisfaction in following his step-by-step construction of the complex narrative pattern he detects in the Gospel and attributes, not of course to the author (who is out of sight), but to the implied author.

Staley's distinctive contribution lies in the picture he builds up of the implied reader. Like his creator, the implied author, the implied reader resides entirely inside the text, and has no life, knowledge, or interest outside it. Moreover, once the critic has succeeded in stepping inside the magic circle of the text, there is no limit to his understanding of the strategies of the implied author, who starts 'by subtly prestructuring the implied reader's responses to subsequent concentric repetitions' and continues by manipulating other 'levels of discourse, focalization, and discourse and story order to develop further the narrative's implied reader'.[18] The implied reader of *The Print's First Kiss*, I think, is one who has been gulled by the implied author of that work (and of course there is no way of knowing how closely this personage resembles Staley himself) into believing that in the picture offered of the implied reader of John's Gospel we have a totally objective, carefully delineated, outline of the way the Gospel should be read. The fact that, to take just one example, the concentric structure of the Prologue might easily escape the notice of any *real* reader is hugely irrelevant to the picture of John's implied reader, who, of course, sees the Gospel exactly as Staley's implied reader does. Real readers, too, or any who are ready to sip the enchanted potion held out invitingly towards them, are liable to be bewitched by this clever rhetoric. But what Staley calls the implied reader of the Gospel is really a surrogate exegete, and those who manage to pierce his clever disguise will continue to respond critically to every stage of the presentation.

If we were to ask how narrative criticism assists our understanding of the Gospel, the answer is, I think, not that it adds anything of substance to what trained and educated readers can pick up for themselves, but rather that, properly conducted, it can help us to appreciate reflectively just how our first, quasi-instinctive response, has enabled, in the strong sense of this term, our understanding; help us, in other words, to appropriate our knowledge, to grasp it more closely. Like musical analysis, narrative criticism is not in

[18] *First Kiss*, 74.

everyone's power to perform, but it is similarly limited in its capacity to enlighten the mind. 'I conceive historical and analytical criticism,' writes Charles Rosen, 'not as the attempt to find new and ingenious things to say about the music of the past, but to account for the way music has been experienced, understood and misunderstood.'[39] With one significant exception this is equally true of the narrative criticism of the Gospels. The exception is this: the latter, as we have seen, shackles itself by limiting its concern to the Gospels as stories. Why are they so anxious to seek asylum in the house of textuality and why do they refuse to step outside its protective walls?

There are three reasons, all concealed in the tangled thickets of twentieth-century theological debate. Historically speaking, the first of these is an understandable impatience with an over-simplistic view of the Gospels as little more than biographies. Such a view, one might have thought, should have been permanently banished from the realms of New Testament scholarship as long ago as 1901 by Wrede's *Messianic Secret*. But, as is well known, even Albert Schweitzer, who admired Wrede and would have liked to have had him on his side, was not persuaded by him to abandon the attempt to treat the Gospels (particularly, in his case, the Gospel of Matthew) as immediate sources for writing a life of Jesus, with the result that in the last chapter of Schweitzer's book the old quest emerges, brushing itself down, from the grave to which he had thought to consign it.[40] Later in the century, despite the reiterated warnings of Rudolf Bultmann, the so-called New Quest received the backing of a number of prominent German theologians (most of them pupils of Bultmann), and though this soon petered out the quest itself still goes on, mostly in a form that Schweitzer would have had no difficulty in recognizing. Even if Wrede's strictures did not go entirely unheeded, they have been largely counterbalanced by a growing tendency among modern scholars to see the Gospels as examples of the Hellenistic genre of idealized biography. Whatever the literary merits of this comparison, it has the disadvantage of promoting a return to a pre-Wredean perception of the Gospels as containing directly usable materials for reconstructing the life of Jesus. The very term

---

[39] In a letter in the *New York Review of Books*, 39/7 (9 April 1992), 54.

[40] It is worth recalling that the original title of Schweitzer's *Quest of the Historical Jesus* (ET 1910) was *Von Reimarus zu Wrede* (1906).

'biography' carries with it important historical implications. Consequently, narrative critics have good reason for congratulating themselves on having got rid of the embarrassing and intractable truth-claims inseparable from this genre. By proposing to treat the Gospels simply as stories, they have shut out the sight and sound of the sirens who tirelessly beckon unwary voyagers towards rocks already strewn with the wreckage of earlier lives of Jesus.

The second reason for the decision to treat the Gospels simply as stories is a natural dissatisfaction with the one-sided tendency of redaction criticism to regard the Gospels as vehicles fashioned to carry theological messages. This has certainly fuelled the enthusiasm for narrative criticism. Here too a renewed emphasis upon the story element of the Gospels is a pardonable reaction to the grandiose claims of theology. For whatever else they may be the Gospels are not theological treatises. It seems reasonable to insist that exegetes should pay proper attention to the narrative form that the Gospels share with a wide variety of contemporary genres. What is less reasonable is the way in which many of these critics set about a task that could be accomplished, one would think, with relatively little fuss and strain. By invoking the names of eminent literary theorists whose work is unlikely to be known at first hand by more than a tiny handful of their own readers, the narrative critics exaggerate the difficulty of their enterprise and in doing so develop a rhetoric of their own, built upon the frequently unexamined assumption that the Gospels justify, indeed demand, the same kind of convoluted analysis that they find in the writings of their mentors. The resulting misfit (for the sophisticated tools they are now wielding have been designed for the dissection of works of a very different kind) can only be perceived by those with enough time and energy to investigate the original dissertations for themselves. The highly rhetorical style of narrative criticism, with its needlessly bewildering complexity, resembles that of the ancient Greek sophists criticized by Socrates, who would have found the obfuscating pretentiousness of much modern scholarship depressingly familiar.

Behind these two reasons lies a third, deeper, reason, this time hermeneutical as well as theological. This is the fundamental change in the understanding of scriptural narrative texts that took place towards the close of the eighteenth century and has been

impressively charted by Hans Frei.[41] Frei's name is invoked both at
the beginning[42] and at the end of Culpepper's book,[43] so that his
influence here is a matter of record. Before the Enlightenment had
forced biblical scholars to rethink the nature of the truth-claims of
scripture, the narrative sections of the Bible (even those of Genesis,
Job, and Jonah) were for the most part assumed without question
to be historical, and what is more, historically reliable. Once this
historical reliability had been called into question, scholars tended
to locate the truth-values of these parts of the Bible *outside* the
narrative, and to treat the stories themselves as of little value or
significance. 'Neither religious apologists nor historical critics',
argues Frei, 'were finally able to take proper and serious account
of the narrative feature of the biblical stories.'[44] Although he
continues to observe a notional distinction between history writing
and what he calls 'history-like writing' (which would presumably
include most of nineteenth and twentieth-century novelistic
fiction), he insists that in both cases the meaning is '*constituted*
through the mutual, specific determination of agents, speech,
social context, and circumstances that form the indispensable
narrative web'.[45]

Underlying Frei's argument is his awareness of the extraordinary
difficulty of using the biblical narratives, even those which are
broadly speaking historical accounts, to reconstruct the past, in
von Ranke's words, 'as it actually happened'. By diverting the
attention of biblical scholars to the narratives themselves, he hopes
to evade this difficulty. Perhaps he does, but in doing so he plunges
them, or at least the less cautious among them, into new
problems. For many of the biblical narratives, and the Gospels in
particular, are not just stories, and to ignore this fact is both
unwise and disingenuous. This point is important enough to be
developed further.

By plumping for intratextuality and thus refusing to consider
any possible reference to a world outside or beyond the text, narrative critics spare themselves the obligation of answering awkward
questions concerning the historicity of the events recorded in the
Gospel and the accuracy of the words assigned to Jesus. They do

---

[41] Hans W. Frei, *Eclipse*.
[42] *Anatomy*, 3.
[43] Ibid. 235.
[44] *Eclipse*, 136.
[45] Ibid. 280.

not even have to determine whether characters like Nicodemus, Lazarus, and the beloved disciple ever actually existed. But if they continue to make truth-claims for the Gospel, the truth in question cannot be different in kind from other stories which recount high ideals and noble deeds, endurance in adversity, patience, strength of purpose, generosity, steadfastness, and so on. 'By understanding more clearly the nature and functions of a gospel,' writes Culpepper, 'avenues may be opened for a more precise definition of the genre.'[46] Yes indeed, but Culpepper rather assumes that such understanding is available for the asking, without any need to work for it, and as a result the purpose he assigns to John is curiously vague: 'The gospel claims that its world is, or at least reflects something that is more "real" than the world the reader has encountered previously.'[47] How does he, or any other reader, know this? And indeed, who is this reader, previously unacquainted with the 'world' of the Gospel? Not, evidently, a member of the evangelist's community. No, it must be someone, Christian or not, *who has not yet read the Gospel*, for according to the principle of intratextuality the Gospel is the only world which counts. If Culpepper is to be believed, the rhetorical structures of the Gospel 'focus the affective power of its conflicts, characters, and comments. The effect is a profound challenge to accept the literary world as representative of reality, to see Jesus as the narrator sees him, and to see the world in which we live as a mere appearance concealing and revealing the reality of a higher plane of life which can only be experienced by accepting the perspectives affirmed by the gospel.'[48]

What the evangelist really wants to convey and to persuade his readers to accept may be concisely summed up as *the revelation of God in Jesus*. But this Jesus is a real historical figure, 'the son of Joseph' (1: 45; 6: 42), and to ignore this (as the narrative critic must) is not just to apply to the study of the Gospels methods devised for analysing fiction: it is to forbid oneself to consider them in any other light. Certain kinds of fiction, no doubt, can and do have a profound effect on responsive readers. But how is one to distinguish the impact of the Gospels from that of other stories, Tolstoy's *Ivan Ilyich*, say, or Eliot's *Daniel Deronda* or Dickens's *Tale of Two Cities*? Such tales as these may radically alter our way of looking at the world, even if they do not reduce it, in Culpepper's

---

[46] *Anatomy*, 5.   [47] Ibid.   [48] Ibid. 234.

phrase, to 'a mere appearance'; and the same is true of dozens of other great works of literature. Since, as stories, the Gospels make their effect in the same way, they must be placed on the same shelf. If this seems an unsatisfactory conclusion, then one is forced to acknowledge that 'the perspectives affirmed by the gospel' direct our gaze to a world which, though conveyed in a story, cannot be confined to it. Far from being a mirror, the Fourth Gospel, like the others, directs our attention to the historical character who is its protagonist. It surrounds him, unquestionably, with the aura of myth. But as someone who has left his mark on the real world, he resembles Caesar and Napoleon, Kennedy and de Gaulle (also mythical as well as historical figures) more than he does Heracles or Lemminkainen. However difficult it may be to tease out the history from the legend, to close our eyes to the difference between fiction and reality is sheer obscurantism.

4. CONCLUSION

I have called into question the value of narrative criticism on a number of grounds. In the first place, it systematically ignores the strong likelihood, to say the least, that the text of the Fourth Gospel, like that of the other three, had a history, and therefore should not be assumed without further ado to be a single, fully integrated, composition.[49] Secondly, it throws a highly questionable theoretical net over all aspects of the narrative, most of which are more easily dealt with by other, simpler methods. Thirdly, in emphasizing the story element, it neglects the difference between fictional and non-fictional texts. My own belief is that the Gospels are best compared with composite genres such as that of Aeschylus' *Persae* or Shakespeare's history plays, where the historical reference is crucial for understanding what is going on but the dramatist is not afraid to adjust his materials in order to convey the desired impression (dare one say, his intended meaning?). But this case cannot be argued here.

[49] For a perceptive critique of narrative criticism along similar lines, see M. C. de Boer, 'Narrative Criticism'. The present chapter was completed before de Boer's article reached me. I agree with everything except his conclusion: 'For the historical critic . . . the real work of interpretation has only begun when the work of the narrative critic is finished' (p. 48). I should be inclined to reverse this dictum.

7

The Discovery of Wisdom

I. INTRODUCTION: METHODOLOGICAL REFLECTIONS

'What a strange-looking caribou!' an Eskimo is reported to have exclaimed on first venturing south of the Arctic circle and catching sight of a cow. I have a similar reaction on meeting claims that if only we were to inspect John's Gospel a little more carefully we would recognize that it is really a tragedy or indeed a comedy.[1] To expect to be able to slot anything we read into the ingenious grid devised by Northrop Frye is surely to be naïvely over-optimistic. Despite an impressively broad range of learning, the claims he makes in *The Anatomy of Criticism* are based, not upon exhaustive research, but upon a sweeping hypothesis that should not be allowed to go unchallenged.[2] In any case, the category that best fits John's Gospel is, I suspect, not tragedy and certainly not comedy, but romance. This is not a case that can be argued here, but it may be admitted in passing that one of the themes with which we are most concerned, that of the quest, has evident affinities with the medieval romance.[3]

When we turn to genres with more obvious resemblances to the Gospels, and more likely to have been accessible to their authors—genres such as biography, aretalogy, apocalypse—we are better placed to see how they touch upon contemporary writings and where they diverge from these. But in spite of the real likenesses (and I have myself argued for the prima-facie improbable affinity of John's Gospel with apocalyptic literature) the differences, too, are

[1] Or that the best way of regarding Mark's Gospel is, *sit venia verbo*, as an erotic fiction. See Mary Ann Tolbert, *Sowing the Gospel*, 59–79.

[2] In lifting the ancient genres out of their proper context and carrying them into modern times, Frye may be said, as Terence Cave points out, 'to construct classes hermeneutically, rather than simply to uncover or recognize them' (*Recognitions*, 237).

[3] As is acknowledged by Alan Culpepper, *Anatomy*, 83. The approach taken in this chapter resembles that taken by two other recent works of Johannine scholarship: John Painter, *Quest*; Mark W. G. Stibbe, 'Elusive Christ'. But there are differences too.

manifest, and we are consequently forced back upon the recognition that where genre is concerned the four Gospels must be assigned a pigeon-hole of their own.

But where does this leave us if we want to reach an understanding of John's Gospel as a narrative (which it certainly is) or a story? We can of course, if we wish, follow Alan Culpepper in using the techniques of literary criticism to inquire into such matters as plot, character, and authorial viewpoint. But there are a number of objections to be made against this procedure.

The first is that narrative critics, operating, as they always do, from a synchronic rather than a diachronic viewpoint, are hampered by their inability to take proper account of a truth about the Gospel now acknowledged by most serious scholars: that having been composed over a number of years, it does not now appear in the shape that was first planned. Major insertions, notably the Lazarus episode, radically disrupt the original story-line, and render the kind of detailed analysis required by narrative criticism extraordinarily difficult, possibly futile.

What is more, to take one further example, the kind of fault-lines in the narrative that led critics as early as the fourteenth century[4] to suggest that chapter 5 may have been displaced shows that whoever was responsible for the final edition of chapters 1–20 (probably the evangelist himself) did not attach any great significance to a peculiarity that has continued to perplex many of his readers. The plot that really interested him moves serenely on, unaffected by such obvious interruptions. Even the raising of Lazarus, the episode that provides a new motivation for the fateful decision to have Jesus killed, leaves the broad outline of the narrative unchanged. Preoccupied as they are with the surface structure of the Gospel, modern narratologists are usually oblivious to the more important current of ideas running beneath.

We can attempt to overcome this objection either by restricting our attention to individual episodes or by conducting our inquiry into the plot on much more general lines. But the study of single episodes, such as the stories of the Samaritan woman and the man born blind, is beset by the same kind of problems as any more large-scale inquiry; and the kind of rough outline that may result from a deliberate blurring of the focus is likely to be of as much use to a serious student as, say, a floor-plan of the British Museum

---

[4] Ludolph of Saxony. See J. H. Bernard, p. xvii n. 1.

would be to an archaeologist. In fact the structure of the first half of the Gospel is quite loose, so loose that a close analysis is neither necessary nor really desirable. It may be compared in this respect with the *Odyssey* or *Don Quixote*, where a microscopic scrutiny of the details of the plot is unlikely to yield many dividends to the interpreter.

An alternative way of circumventing the difficulty is the route taken by C. H. Dodd in *The Interpretation of the Fourth Gospel*. After completing the brilliant series of thematic studies that forms the second part of the book, Dodd remarks that 'the structure of the gospel as we have it has been shaped in most of its details by the ideas which seem to dominate the author's thought'.[5] The advantage of this approach lies first in the recognition that the purpose of the Gospel is not just to tell a story but to convey a message, and secondly in the freedom it allows the commentator to roam around the Gospel, selecting for close examination whatever material he finds most helpful. The rich and complex texture of Dodd's thematic analyses shows up the threadbare nature of present-day narratological fashions.

Nevertheless, I confess that I have always been puzzled by the suggestion that the structure of the Gospel has been shaped by its *ideas*. The structure of any narrative is determined, quite simply, not by its ideas but by its plot. One can well understand why Aristotle, who had before him a wide variety of elaborately constructed Greek tragedies, concluded that of the three key elements that go to make up the material of tragedy—plot ($\mu\hat{\upsilon}\theta os$), character ($\mathring{\eta}\theta os$), and thought ($\delta\iota\acute{a}\nu o\iota a$)—plot, or 'the arrangement of the incidents', is easily the most important.[6]

All these considerations leave anyone anxious to do justice to the story element of the Gospel in an apparently insoluble dilemma. If we follow the narrative critics we are proceeding along a path full of pitfalls, with no sure footing; if we adopt Dodd's alternative, thematic, approach, we must, it seems, abandon any pretence that we are taking the story seriously.

Before going any further, I want to propose a way round this dilemma, starting with some reflections upon a theme that Dodd does not discuss in his book. This is the theme of revelation, the *Grundkonzeption* of the Gospel. Its importance for my argument is considerable, not least because of the curious, but hitherto dis-

---

[5] *Interpretation*, 290.   [6] *Poetics*, 6. 5–28.

regarded fact that revelation, like a number of other key concepts upon which plays or fictions have been constructed (e.g. jealousy, ambition, revenge), comes already equipped with a pattern or structure, and already projecting, implicitly at least, a *story*.

The story of revelation (called Logos in the Prologue, Jesus elsewhere) fits in readily with the general outlines of Jesus' career as these emerge in the Synoptic Gospels. This has an unfortunate consequence: it may escape our notice that the plot of the Gospel derives its dynamic thrust more from the fate of revelation, as this is summarized in the Prologue, than from reminiscences of Jesus' career. The fusion of these—career and revelation—makes it necessary to give a double version of the plot. Taken separately, neither the straightforward recital of Jesus' words and deeds nor the subtle story of the ups and downs of revelation can pretend to give an adequate account of the plot. But though the two intermesh so successfully, the controlling cycle, the one that gives the Gospel its purpose and direction, is that of revelation.

With these considerations in mind, it is instructive to turn to Bultmann's seductive thesis that the evangelist, having before him a mythological account of the descent and subsequent ascent of a redeemer figure, set about ridding this account of its dominant myth. The truth is almost the opposite. Far from relieving the story of its mythological elements, the evangelist has *injected* his own myth (which we have already identified as revelation) into a recital broadly similar to that of the Synoptic Gospels.[7] Or perhaps it might be better to say that he has *read off the myth from the story*— prompted no doubt by the same startling insight that is displayed in the Prologue, namely the realization that Jesus, the hero of the gospel story, somehow re-enacted on earth the chequered career of heavenly Wisdom (Logos/revelation) and thus may be said to have incarnated the wisdom tradition, to have given it flesh.

Furthermore, the evangelist has been able to integrate his narrative with the content of the words uttered by the protagonist— what Aristotle would call διάνοια. This is an important observation,

[7] Such tension as remains between the tradition of Jesus' life and the myth that has been superimposed upon it may be compared with the composition of a work of fiction, which is something other than a reproduction or mimesis of the real world. The novelist Ivy Compton-Burnett, rejecting a suggestion that 'the mere act of devising a plot involves a degree of distortion of reality', replied: 'I think the reality and the plot have to be adapted a little to each other, not distorted' (*The Novelist Today*, ed. M. Bradbury, p. 130). In the case of the Gospel the plot (Aristotle's μῦθος) coincides at this point with the myth.

one which, to the best of my knowledge, has not been made elsewhere. The text of Aristotle's *Poetics* is far from being a well-lit
path along which commentators and critics can stride confidently,
hand-in-hand, towards a common goal. It is rather a rich mix of
suggestive ambiguities which allows and indeed encourages strong
but conflicting growths to spring up alongside one another.[8] Of the
many categories that Aristotle has assembled for constructing
his argument—μῦθος (plot), ἦθος (character), ἁμαρτία, κάθαρσις,
περιπετεία, ἀναγνώρισις—the one that has received least attention is
certainly διάνοια. This is generally translated 'thought', but it also
refers to the characters' power to put their thoughts into words,[9]
and is related, as Aristotle insists more than once, to rhetoric. Of
those commentators on the *Poetics* that I have consulted, Northrop
Frye is the only one to suggest that διάνοια is worthy to flourish
alongside the other categories in his luxuriant and boldly patterned
garden of ideas. This is what Frye says:

> The best translation of *dianoia* is, perhaps, 'theme', and literature with this
> ideal or conceptual interest may be called thematic. When a reader of a
> novel asks, 'How is this story going to turn out?' he is asking a question
> about the plot, specifically about that crucial aspect of the plot which
> Aristotle calls discovery or *anagnorisis*. But he is equally likely to ask,
> 'What's the *point* of this story?' This question relates to *dianoia*, and
> indicates that themes have their elements of discovery just as plots do.[10]

Taking up this line of thought, and applying it to the Fourth
Gospel, one might observe that revelation is surely the paradigm
example of themes that contain what Frye calls 'an element of
discovery'.

Elsewhere[11] Frye speaks of διάνοια as 'the structure of imagery',
and glosses theme as 'the sense of the unity of mood which makes
certain images appropriate and others not'.[12] All this is a long way
from Aristotle's διάνοια; yet even if we return to something closer
to what Aristotle is saying, we should be able to see that the
thoughts of the leading characters and their coming-to-expression
in words must have some bearing on the plot. Unlike narrative,

---

[8] For an outstanding example of a study of just one of Aristotle's key terms,
ἀναγνώρισις, see Terence Cave, *Recognitions*.

[9] 'Under the head of διάνοια come all the effects to be produced by language
(λόγος)' (*Poetics*, 19. 3).

[10] *Anatomy*, 52.

[11] Ibid. 140.

[12] Ibid. 246.

which gives the author unlimited scope both to describe the events of the story and to reflect upon them, the words of a drama are mostly uttered by the characters, and devices like the Greek chorus or, in Shakespeare's case, voices off like Gower, Rumour, and what he still sometimes calls the Chorus, can only be employed sparingly unless (most obviously in Aeschylus' *Eumenides*) the commentators also join in the action. In practice, of course, the key ideas in narrative too must also be expressed somehow by the characters; otherwise the story risks losing immediacy and power.

If this happens on the stage, and if what Aristotle calls διάνοια has only marginal relevance to the plot of the drama, then the result is a ramshackle piece of writing, of little artistic merit. Even the sublimely far-reaching soliloquies of Shakespeare's great characters could not be transferred from one play to another without enormous loss. Hamlet talks, often dreamingly, of revenge; Macbeth reflects upon ambition; Othello gives vent to his jealousy. Similarly, the Jesus of the Fourth Gospel often speaks of revelation, though he never uses the word. Of all the Gospels, this is the one in which διάνοια is most intimately linked with μῦθος.[13]

In the Fourth Gospel, unlike the other three, Jesus is, notoriously, the object of his own message: what he reveals is himself. Revelation, ἀποκάλυψις, is the drawing back of the veil, the disclosure of something—some truth—that has previously been concealed.[14] In its simplest form it implies a movement, a passage, a plot—the transition, that is to say, from a state of hiddenness or obscurity to a state of openness and clarity. But another movement, or shall we say moment, is involved here also: the moment when viewers or listeners (for the revelation can be either visual or aural) reach understanding. No doubt it is theoretically possible for a light to shine without being seen: we know that if it shines in the darkness the darkness will not comprehend it. And it is possible also for words to be uttered without being heard—or understood. But light does not achieve its purpose until it is seen, nor words until their import is properly grasped. The Gospel story, a story

[13] Note, though, Tolbert's interesting contention, in *Sowing the Gospel*, that the key to the understanding of Mark's Gospel is to be found in the two central parables of the Sower and the Wicked Husbandmen.

[14] One may compare here Heidegger's extended discussion of the nature of truth in *Being and Time*, 256-69. Heidegger makes great play with the etymology of the Greek ἀλήθεια, which he derives, probably correctly, from the root of λανθάνειν ('to escape detection', 'to lie hidden'), preceded by alpha-privative. For him, truth is to be equated with uncovering (*Entdecken*) and uncoveredness (*Entdecktheit*).

already sketched or adumbrated in the Prologue, is played out within the framework of these various possibilities, possibilities of incomprehension as well as of acceptance. All that happens and all that is said, is contained in this framework, and accounts of repeated misunderstanding, of partial comprehension, and of deferred revelation exhibit a variety of options all of which are integral to the very concept of revelation, and to the story it enfolds.

Just how these options are exercised by the evangelist can be seen by all his readers. Elsewhere I have argued that for a proper appreciation of the Gospel it must be understood on two levels,[15] and this is most importantly true of the evangelist's conception of Jesus both as a historical personage and as the object of Christian faith. The relationship between these two figures, revealed and proclaimed by Jesus himself, is one of *identity-in-difference*. On the first level of understanding, that is to say the story level, his revelation met with incomprehension and rejection, with the result that his career was punctuated by a series of confrontations with his enemies, called in this Gospel 'the Jews'. These were scandalized by his revelatory claims and sought his death. Set over against Jesus' enemies are his friends—the disciples. They too, with the possible exception of the beloved disciple, failed to understand him during his lifetime, and any full comprehension of his message ('the truth') is deferred until he has returned to where he really belongs, his true home in heaven. Then and only then can his followers, who include the readers of the Gospel at all its successive stages, come to grasp, under the prompting of the Paraclete, the meaning of all Jesus has said and done whilst on earth. Then and only then can they 'enter into the truth': this is the second level of understanding.

In his short but eventful career as a teacher and prophet Jesus was (*a*) tracked down by his adversaries, and forced to go into hiding from time to time if he was to survive long enough to get his message across; and (*b*) listened to uncomprehendingly by his friends, who sought him for other reasons, knowing that he had the words of eternal life. Yet they had no clear idea of what they were looking for because the secret of Jesus' identity, the revelation that he embodied, was not—could not be—disclosed to them whilst he was still physically present to them. This, as we shall see,

---

[15] Cf. *Understanding*, 412–20.

is largely because much of the content of that revelation is centred upon his departure—for which the Gospel's most important term is ὑπάγειν, to withdraw.

Consequently—and this is the main burden of my argument—Jesus is portrayed throughout the Gospel as hiding in two different ways. He hides from his enemies because they plan to kill him, and he will not die until he is ready; he hides from his friends, not literally and physically, but spiritually and metaphorically because what he has to say is something they cannot yet grasp: 'I have still many things to say to you, but you are not yet able to take them in (βαστάζειν)' (John 16: 12). To these two modes of hiding correspond two modes of searching, and also two modes of discovery: although, as I have pointed out, discovery in the second of these modes is postponed until after his 'departure', it is suggested symbolically in the resurrection narrative. (One could also point to a third kind of search, though it is not one that needs to occupy our attention here: this is to be found in the well-meaning but misguided attempt on the part of some of Jesus' hearers to hunt him down so as to make him king (John 6: 15).)

The fairly straightforward distinction between the literal and the allegorical, or, if one prefers, between the historical and the spiritual (a distinction which was to have a long and eventful history in patristic and medieval exegesis) is not the end of the story, for the hide-and-seek metaphor crosses the boundary between the historical and the spiritual in a way that will be investigated later. But in the next section of this chapter we may consider how it is deployed in the first half of the Gospel in what J. L. Martyn calls the 'einmalig' and I call the first level of understanding, namely that which makes sense in terms of the story itself and the interaction between the different characters of the Gospel.

2. THE STORY LEVEL

The best place to begin might be the Prologue, which summarizes and foreshadows the bitter hostility Jesus will encounter from his own people; but the Prologue's dominant metaphor for revelation is light, and when light comes up against darkness it certainly does not react by attempting to hide. The darkness, however, fails to overcome the light, and the translation that best conveys the nuances of the word κατέλαβεν is arguably 'master', which means to understand as well as to defeat or control. There is an echo of this use in the last words uttered by Jesus in the first half of the Gospel, the Book of Signs: 'walk while you have the light, lest the darkness overcome you' (or possibly: 'overtake you': ἵνα μὴ σκοτία ὑμᾶς καταλάβῃ (12: 35)).

The story of Jesus' confrontation with the Jews really begins with the first angry flare-up that follows the healing of the cripple in chapter 5. But even as early as the beginning of chapter 4 Jesus is portrayed as anxious to evade the Pharisees: 'When Jesus (v.l.: the Lord) heard that the Pharisees had heard that Jesus was making and baptizing more disciples than John . . . he left Judaea and departed again to Galilee' (4: 1–3).[16]

The great series of confrontations between Jesus and the Jews in chs. 5–10 is often thought of as a gigantic trial scene. Anthony Harvey argues that the verb ἐδίωκον in 5: 16 should be translated 'they sought to bring a charge against him'.[17] But I notice that Jeffrey Staley prefers the translation 'stalk',[18] which I like. Throughout this long section we see Jesus eluding the grasp of his persecutors, both literally and symbolically, in spite of the fact that the story would be ruined and the history falsified unless they caught up with him from time to time. Chapter 7, for instance, opens with the statement that Jesus would not go about in Judaea because the Jews (Judaeans?) were seeking his death. But only a few verses later we read that he did go up to the feast (of Tabernacles) 'not openly (φανερῶς) but in secret (ἐν κρυπτῷ)' (7: 10). If he had remained in hiding in Galilee an important series of episodes would have been left untold.

---

[16] Viewed from the perspective of a continuous narrative this anxiety is puzzling. Nicodemus, it is true, 'a man of the Pharisees' and 'a ruler of the Jews' had come to Jesus 'by night' (3: 2), presumably because he did not want to be seen by day, but the Gospel does not in fact record any conflict with the Pharisees in the first four chapters; and the evangelist appears to be relying upon the foreknowledge of his readers that Jesus was at loggerheads with the Pharisees from the outset: this information must be included in any account of what modern jargon calls 'the implied readers' of the Gospel. An interpreter operating on the diachronic level is best advised to regard the opening of chapter 4 as a kind of *captatio benevolentiae* designed to reassure *Samaritan* readers that Jesus himself, although a Jew, had himself suffered the opprobrium of the party they themselves regarded as their most vehement adversaries.

[17] A. E. Harvey, *Jesus on Trial*, 51.

[18] J. L. Staley, 'Stumbling', 62; cf. *Understanding*, 138 n. 23, where I suggested 'they started to track him down'.

The confrontations at the feast build up to a climax at the end of chapter 8, when the Jews take up stones to throw at Jesus. His response is to leave the Temple and go into hiding (8: 59); but *the very next verse* (9: 1) introduces the episode of the encounter with the man born blind, an encounter which leads, inevitably, to yet another confrontation. The narrative then proceeds without a break to the last of the attempts to stone Jesus and the last of his challenging claims to equality with God: 'the Father is in me, and I in the Father' (10: 38). The consequence is another attempt to arrest him, 'but he slipped from their grasp' (ἐξῆλθεν ἐκ τῆς χειρὸς αὐτῶν) (10: 39).

There follows the story of the resurrection of Lazarus and the narrator's observations on the final (and only effective) decision to put Jesus to death. But once again, we are informed, 'he no longer went about openly (παρρησίᾳ)[19] among the Jews, but moved to Ephraim, where he stayed with his disciples' (11: 54). Meanwhile the hunt went on (the imperfect of ζητεῖν is used here) and the Jews said to one another, 'What do you think? That he will not come to the feast?' (11: 56). The reader knows that he will come to the feast, but this tiny question is just one of many devices employed by the narrator to convey the sense that Jesus was being continually hunted, even though he seems to have been able to come and go as he pleased, every appearance provoking a renewed outburst of hostility and another attempt to seize or stone him, which in turn leads to yet another disappearance, another hiding: the conclusion of the *story* of the Book of Signs states explicitly that 'he went and hid from them': ἀπελθὼν ἐκρύβη ἀπ' αὐτῶν (12: 36). On the first level of understanding (as John's first readers will certainly have known) the outcome of this literally deadly game of hide-and-seek was predetermined. Jesus' warning to his disciples not to allow the darkness to catch up with them (12: 35) was uttered in the full realization that in one important sense it was about to catch up with *him*.

When it does, there is a single pregnant allusion to the symbolism of darkness: 'and it was night' (13: 30), but then the

---

[19] The word παρρησία is used here almost as a technical term, contrasted with riddling discourse (παροιμίαι). It may also refer to plain speaking in a more general sense (7: 12, 26; 10: 24; 11: 14; 18: 20). Lastly, it can have a purely physical meaning, unconcealment, and be set against hiding (ἐν κρυπτῷ) (7: 4; 11: 54). This ambiguity assists the evangelist in his attempts to bind the two levels of understanding together.

story takes over and the symbolism is replaced by a characteristic irony. The forces that come to arrest Jesus in the garden are huge: the servants (ὑπηρέται) of the high priests and Pharisees, last seen as the temple proctors in chapter 7, arrive backed up by a whole Roman cohort (σπεῖρα), 600 men (or at the very least a maniple, 200 men) (18: 3). The irony in the question with which Jesus greets them ('Whom do you seek?') is readily detected by the reader—though not by the arresting-officers. The really crucial irony, however, emphasized by the narrator, who includes it in an authorial aside and allows Jesus to repeat it, is to be found in his answer to their response: Ἐγώ εἰμι (18: 6–8).

The irony here is twofold. To appreciate it fully we must recall Jesus' last encounter with the temple proctors, in chapter 7, when their attempt to arrest him came to nothing. He addresses them on that occasion in language that is intentionally mystifying: 'you will seek me and you will not find me; where I am you cannot come' (7: 34). The wording is important: ὅπου εἰμί ἐγώ—where I am. (When Jesus repeats and refers to this answer later, speaking to the disciples, he alters it to the more usual ὅπου ἐγὼ ὑπάγω (13: 33).) In 7: 35 the response to Jesus' assertion is made by 'the Jews', who take it literally and do not disguise their bewilderment: 'Where is he about to go that we cannot find him?' But if we read what Jesus says as a reply to the temple proctors who have been sent to arrest him, then the irony is manifest. For at their next appearance they have actually found him (though not, of course, on the second level of understanding), and the reader is aware that this discovery is a necessary preliminary to Jesus' final departure; his reply to the temple proctors is accurate in a way that they cannot appreciate: he is indeed about to go where they cannot follow.

This passage is central to my argument, and I shall return to it; but first a final comment on an additional irony in Jesus' reply to those come to arrest him. The claim underlying Jesus' apparently straightforward answer, 'I am the one you are looking for', is stressed by all commentators: that there is at least a hint of the claim to divinity associated earlier with the phrase Ἐγώ εἰμι seems to be confirmed by the extraordinary reaction of the arresting party (seemingly all of them): 'When he said to them Ἐγώ εἰμι, they drew back and fell to the ground' (18: 6).

3. THE SPIRITUAL LEVEL

So much then for the story level: the hide-and-seek culminates in a discovery and arrest which together make up the first scene of the last act of the drama. What I have called the spiritual level is more complex and more paradoxical. When children play the game of hide-and-seek they often do so in the virtual certainty that they will be discovered. (This is true of the somewhat macabre game Jesus plays with the Jews.) More often still they play in the unacknowledged hope that they *will* be discovered. Similarly, behind Jesus' concealment of his own identity (at best only partial) within the confines of the gospel narrative there lies the clear prospect of a revelation that will take place outside a story framed by his entry into and departure from the world.

Elsewhere I have argued extensively that the strangely paradoxical message inherent in the gospel genre is best served by an adaptation, amounting to a reversal, of the structure of the contemporary genre of apocalypse.[20] This involves a period of hiddenness or obscurity followed by a disclosure or discovery. In the nature of the case Jesus' identity as the Risen Lord who is the object of Christian worship cannot be fully affirmed until he has stepped over and outwith the framework of the gospel narrative, which is ostensibly (necessarily so) concerned with his public career, his life on earth.

Although the Jesus of the Gospel says virtually the same thing to his enemies and to his friends (and actually tells the latter (13: 33) that he is saying the same thing), the response they make is very different. His enemies exhibit total confusion; and when he repeats his prophecy of departure in 8: 21 they betray their perplexity by saying, 'Will he kill himself, since he says, "Where I am going, you cannot come"?' (8: 22). Simon Peter, in the conversation that introduces the farewell discourse, asks Jesus directly, 'Where are you going?' ($\pi o\hat{u}\ \dot{u}\pi\dot{a}\gamma\epsilon\iota s;$), and is told, 'Where I am going you cannot follow me now; but you shall follow afterwards' (13: 36).

None of this is plain speaking, but when the motif recurs for the last time Jesus is much more direct: 'I came from the Father and have come into the world; now I am leaving the world and going to the Father' (16: 28). To which his disciples reply in relief: 'Ah,

---

[20] *Understanding*, ch. 10.

now you are speaking plainly (παρρησίᾳ), not in any figure (καὶ παροιμίαν οὐδεμίαν λέγεις)' (16: 29).

The contrast between open speech and figures or riddles (behind which Jesus hides anew) is no doubt the most important of the ways in which the evangelist indicates the gulf between the incomprehension (real, if relative) of the disciples during Jesus' lifetime and the full understanding that will be available to them after his death. Once again, having developed this point fully elsewhere,[21] I do not need to elaborate it here.

The moment of full comprehension does not, indeed cannot, belong to narrative since the final disclosure has to be deferred until Jesus' departure. Neither Jesus' origins nor his destiny, the whence and the whither, which constitute the heart and essence of his revelation, can be properly contained within the narrative structure. This is best thought of as commencing *after* the Prologue. The repeated reference to Jesus' coming into the world implies that he had a previous existence elsewhere; but this is not part of the gospel story. In the narrative there is not even a mention of the childhood or upbringing of the protagonist; and he does not return, in the words of the Prologue, εἰς τὸν κόλπον τοῦ πατρός (1: 18) until the Gospel has come to an end and the account of the resurrection appearances is over. Thus Jesus' origin is indicated before the Gospel has begun and his destiny is not realized until after it has finished.

Although in its first aspect the hide-and-seek motif is worked out in the story and is an essential element of the plot, its true significance is unavailable to anyone whose reading is confined to following the plot. Admittedly, Jesus' words ('You will seek me and you will not find me') are uttered in the course of one of Jesus' dialogues with 'the Jews', but neither the reference nor the meaning of these words is part of the story. As far as the story goes, Jesus' attempt to go where he cannot be followed is eventually frustrated. Nor does the actual placing of this little dialogue make much difference.[22] It could equally well have occurred on any of the other occasions when an attempt is made to seize hold of Jesus.

All this means that in this Gospel διάνοια, in Frye's sense, is more important than μῦθος. We can grasp the point of the Gospel

---

[21] Ibid. 398–400.

[22] In its actual context this dialogue is out of place, for it interrupts the story of the attempted arrest of Jesus by the temple proctors; cf. *Understanding*, 142, 537. Part of my argument here is that *this does not matter.*

without a detailed knowledge of the plot. In saying this I do not wish to discount the narrative element altogether. John is a story-teller, and a good one; and without the story there would be no Gospel. But so much of the argument of the Gospel is to be found in discourse and in the asides of the author or narrator that with-out these the meaning of the story would be totally imperspicuous. Lastly, the story level is only the first, and the lower, of the two levels of understanding found in the Gospel. To confine oneself to it, or to enclose oneself within it, is to close the door and—dare I say it?—to close one's eyes to the Gospel's most important message.

So far I have argued that the hide-and-seek motif operates in the Gospel along two axes: Jesus is sought—stalked—by his enemies; he reveals himself to his friends, though in figures only, so that his revelation is concealed. These two axes intersect in the saying concerning Jesus' departure, which occurs in two series of texts: (*a*) in chs. 7–8, where Jesus is addressing the Jews; (*b*) in chs. 13–16, where he is addressing his disciples. In both of these the key-word is ὑπάγειν, 'withdraw'. Used in its special sense, as part of the community's private language, the meaning is plain to the reader but obscure to all the actors in the drama, friend and foe alike.[23] Especially noteworthy is the fact that Jesus' withdrawal, his departure to a place where those who seek will not find, is at the same time what he is disclosing: the riddle is the revelation, and Jesus' very inaccessibility is at the same time the clue to his identity. Thus the hide-and-seek motif, prominent on the story level as a way of illustrating Jesus' dealing with 'the Jews', both informs and controls the second level of understanding as well. Countering Bultmann's assertion that Jesus' revelation is confined to the sheer fact that he is the revealer, Wayne Meeks asserts: 'He reveals rather that he is an enigma.'[24] But the enigma is not devoid of content, and its content is largely summed up in the word ὑπάγειν. Jesus' departure, however mysterious, is not a hidden truth with no relation to the gospel story. Moreover, the part of the story to which it alludes is found in all four Gospels: it is the episode of Jesus' passion and resurrection, the visible fulfilment of Jesus' predictions of his imminent departure. Not that the inner reality of this departure can be read off directly from the narrative: the passion and death of Jesus, if not his revelation, are there for

---

[23] *Understanding*, 191–2.   [24] Cf. ibid. 551–2.

all to see, but *understanding* is reserved for those who accept Jesus' message, his hidden revelation. For the rest, however hard they seek, there is no revelation, only hiddenness. In the game of hide-and-seek the discovery, the ἀναγνώρισις, is restricted to those who have faith: all the others, like Pilate, who fails to recognize the truth when it is staring him in the face, may have their eyes wide open, but they are really blind.

The game is played on until the last possible moment. Mary Magdalene, waiting disconsolately by the tomb, is accosted by Jesus with the same question that he had put to the arresting officers in the garden three days earlier: 'Whom do you seek?' (20: 14; cf. 18: 4). And as if to underline the incapacity of all, friend and foe alike, to grasp his message while he is still on earth, he detaches himself, in a last symbolic gesture, from Mary's clutching fingers: 'Why do you cling to me, for I have not yet ascended to the Father' (20: 17).

4. WISDOM AND THE FOURTH GOSPEL

I shall be with you a little longer; and then I go (ὑπάγω) to him who sent me; you will seek me and you will not find me; where I am you cannot come (7: 33–4; cf. 13: 33).

These words, on which I have already commented extensively in this chapter, constitute what may be the only direct quotation from the Jewish wisdom literature in the Gospel.[25] Bultmann, notoriously reluctant to admit any direct use of the Old Testament by what he conceives to be the thoroughly Gnostic document upon which the evangelist drew, is slow to concede even that much. 'This', he observes, 'is without doubt a quotation from the revelation-discourses. . . . The Evangelist uses it again in 13: 33. The idea goes back to *myth* and was applied in Judaism to "Wisdom" (Prov. 1: 23–31).'[26] At the heart of the passage to which Bultmann refers are the following words, spoken by Wisdom herself: 'They will call upon me, but I will not answer; they will seek me diligently but will not find me' (Prov. 1: 28). Direct quotation or not, the reference to the figure of hidden

---

[25] Günter Reim is not prepared to allow that this is a direct quotation, and includes it in a list of 'formal parallels' (*Studien*, 162).

[26] *Gospel*, 307 n. 2.

Wisdom, the ultimate origin of the hide-and-seek motif that is the main subject of this paper, is unmistakable, and prompts the intriguing but difficult question whether John's debt to the whole wisdom tradition may be greater than has commonly been assumed.

One might argue this by stressing the links between wisdom speculation and the apocalyptic tradition that succeeded it, or rather branched out from it. The idea of remote or inaccessible wisdom, found at least as early as Job 28, can be traced through a series of sapiential texts, biblical and apocryphal, and eventually surfaces, if that is the right word, in apocalyptic. The closest analogue to the Johannine Logos, as his story is rapidly sketched out in the Prologue, occurs in a well-known passage from the Parables section of *1 Enoch*: 'Wisdom went out in order to dwell among the sons of men, but did not find a dwelling; wisdom returned to her place and took her seat in the midst of the angels' (42: 1–2).[27]

The idea of hidden wisdom is a paradoxical one, for unless wisdom is somehow made available it is like a book without a reader or, in the words of the Gospel, a light shining in the darkness, with no one to observe its radiance. Hence the persistent tension, evident wherever the motif is drawn upon by various writers up to and beyond the fourth evangelist, and manifesting itself in a variety of ways. A particularly interesting example comes from the Book of Wisdom itself:

> We can hardly guess at what is on earth,
>   and what is at hand we find with labour;
> But who has traced out what is in the heavens
> Who has learned thy counsel, unless thou hast given wisdom
>   and sent ($\H{\epsilon}\pi\epsilon\mu\psi\alpha\varsigma$) thy holy spirit from on high.

(Wisd. 9: 16–17)

There is no way of knowing if the fourth evangelist was acquainted with the Book of Wisdom: if he was, he must have been struck by the suggestion that only the holy spirit could ensure that the lessons of God would be learnt, and by the intimate association between wisdom (soon—chapter 10—to be identified as the providential guide of Israel's history) and the spirit.

[27] See above, p. 15.

The passages in the Gospel that give us direct access to the evangelist's reflections on the hide-and-seek motif can thus be seen to derive from Jewish wisdom speculation. Perhaps this is as far as we can go. The manifest differences between the Gospel, a story rooted in the particular, both temporal and geographical, and the wisdom books, collections of sayings or groups of discourses that have a timeless and universal quality, may discourage us from looking further. But I am struck by the thought that if one were asked to summarize, in a single phrase, the lessons of these books, one would be hard put to it to find a more accurate or comprehensive answer than the words of Jesus in the farewell discourse: 'I am the way, the truth, and the life' (14: 6). The sayings of the sages are offered as a way, a path of behaviour to follow which is true and right and leads to life. In the Book of Proverbs we have mostly to do with what may be called accessible wisdom, available to all and sundry, but only in a fragmented form, in an indefinite number of wise sayings. Most of these are in fact quite banal, and none is properly wise, for true wisdom is what informs the whole and cannot be reduced to a series of aphorisms or maxims. Wisdom steps outside to issue her invitation, but it is inside that she is to be found, as all true initiates will know. The Book of Wisdom, which, like the Gospel of John, has absorbed and reflected upon an earlier tradition, offers revelation in the form of a riddle (again like John). The answer to the riddle, as the Jews of the diaspora for which it was written will have realized, is the Hebrew Bible, for without this there is a surface text, and nothing more. The fourth evangelist replaces wisdom by the Logos and replaces the Hebrew Bible by the person of Jesus: 'You search the scriptures, because you think that in them you have eternal life; and yet I am the one to whom they bear witness' (John 5: 40).

Here is the Christian myth *par excellence*. Plunging deep into the vast reservoir of Jewish tradition (for without this nourishment the new myth would have wilted rapidly, leaving few traces), John's signal achievement is to have fortified the young, tender, delicate plant of Christianity with the mysterious power of a figure who, close to God but never fully identified with him, had long been present to the consciousness of Israel as the source of truth and life. Of Wisdom it could be said, more truly than of the Revealer of the Fourth Gospel, that she revealed nothing more than the fact of revelation. Israel, as we know, eventually identified her with the

Law, and in doing so, perhaps, deprived her of some of her power and mystery. But not entirely; for the Law has been the heart and strength of Judaism ever since. Christianity, however, under the guidance of John the evangelist, took a different tack, with the result that the story of Jesus, recorded in varying hues and shades in all four Gospels, became the dominant myth of the Western world. Had the revelation been divorced from the story, as Bultmann would have us believe, and forced to 'go it alone', then it would have faded away quietly, too frail and bloodless to survive. In fact, as we know, the myth lives on, sustained (but also, unfortunately, impoverished) by organized religion, and remarkably resistant to the incessant assaults of an ever-growing rationalism.

It may well be asked why the survival of the Christian myth, to all appearances, seems to have been guaranteed by its success in disguising itself as history. The world has had innumerable myths, and in their day they have lent significance to a vast array of human cultures and societies. But the survivors are those few which, however improbably, have been mistaken for faithful, even accurate records of the lives of individual human beings: Buddhism, Christianity, possibly Islam. The most interesting question is this: if the disguise fails and the façade falls, will the myths live on?

8

Studying John

I. HISTORICAL CRITICISM

As we near the end of the twentieth century, the study of the Bible, especially of its narratives, has a new look and a new feel. Books published only a few years ago, including my own *Understanding the Fourth Gospel* (1991), appear to many modern-minded critics dated and outmoded. Up to a point this is inevitable: biblical scholarship does not stand still (how could it?) and much of its enduring interest arises from the happy unpredictability it shares with all other branches of learning in the arts and sciences.

There is a clear difference, however, between new methods and new conclusions. In the case of the Fourth Gospel, the discovery of the Dead Sea Scrolls has helped scholars to see that it is a thoroughly Jewish document, and this realization has yet to be fully exploited. The fresh understanding that is then reached will have to be accredited to the time-honoured methods of historical criticism.

Historical criticism as such is not a method but an approach, or even an attitude—adopted in the conviction that the path to understanding the past lies in the attempt to place all human achievements, social, political, and religious structures as well as writings and works of art, in their original context: the term 'historical' is all-embracing. The roots of historical criticism go very far back, at least as far as Thucydides; but in biblical studies the two main landmarks are the European Enlightenment and the founding of the history-of-religions school in Göttingen little more than a century ago. The Bible, declared a small group of like-minded German scholars, must be studied with the same care and impartiality as any other work of literature. Anyone wishing to understand it properly must not only know the relevant languages but also have a sound grasp of the literary and social conventions that governed its composition.

When we are dealing with ancient texts, or indeed with any writing that has emerged from a society earlier than our own, historical and literary studies are inextricably intertwined; but they can be distinguished by what the scholastics would call their formal object. The attempt to understand the *meaning* of a literary text is called exegesis; accounting for its genesis, which is a rather different question, is the business of history.[1] Like all students of the writings of the past biblical scholars must be both exegetes and historians.

It must be stressed that for anyone anxious to *understand* the past there is no substitute for historical criticism. This may seem obvious, but in the past decade or so we have seen a proliferation of new methods (most of them, without irony, including the term 'criticism' in their self-description) which have questioned the necessity of any formal historical inquiry in the study of the Bible. Thus it has become necessary to defend not only history as such but also any exegetical practice that marches under the banner of historical criticism. What is required is a discussion of principles: we find ourselves for good or ill in the realm of philosophy, searching for some methodological justification of the historical and exegetical principles of traditional biblical scholarship. Second-order reflection upon history is philosophy of history (what might be called, adopting a coinage of Hayden White, 'metahistory'), which stands to history itself in the same relation as hermeneutics stands to exegesis or interpretation, and as Aristotle's *Metaphysics* stands to his *Physics*.

We must begin then with some reflections first upon the philosophy of history and then upon literary criticism, in the sense in which this term is currently employed in biblical studies. These will be followed by some brief remarks upon one currently popular mode of approaching the Bible, reader-response criticism. The fourth section is a critique of what is perhaps the most notorious of modern literary-critical styles, that of deconstruction; and the chapter will conclude with a few observations upon what is sometimes called committed exegesis.

On the question of historical method I will be brief, partly because it appears to me to be less contentious, partly because this is not the place to expatiate at length upon an exceedingly

---

[1] See *Understanding*, 121–3, where, taking up a suggestion of Lucien Goldmann, I discuss this distinction more fully.

complex topic. The first point to make is that historians are also, in the nature of the case, rhetoricians. They are condemned to present their conclusions more strongly than the evidence may warrant, if only because it is tedious for the writer and irritating for the reader for the argument to be constantly interrupted with all the qualifications that, in strict logic, might be required: 'probably', 'possibly', 'one may suggest with some hesitation', or, more strongly, 'it may be asserted with reasonable confidence'. A forcible presentation of a historical thesis is imposed, it may fairly be said, by the very nature of the discipline. Historians are out to persuade, and they may do themselves a disservice by understating their case.

In the second place it must be confessed that in periods for which the evidence is sparse (as is true of the history and society of first-century Palestine), historians experience a besetting temptation to overvalue it simply because it is the only evidence there is. So besides instances of what may appear, because of the rhetoric of the discipline, to be exaggerated claims, there will be occasions when individual scholars become over-confident. At certain points in my book, *Understanding the Fourth Gospel*, I attempted to indicate my own reservations,[2] but no doubt there are many other places where I should have done so and did not. Cases of excessive claims may reasonably be highlighted by other scholars, especially if they occur in an argumentative chain which, like any other chain, can be no stronger than its weakest link. But these are examples of the misuse or ineffective application of historical methods: it is the workman who is to blame, not his tools.

This point can be illustrated with reference to the Fourth Gospel. If the book had a history, as we can be almost certain (!) that it did, this cannot be reconstituted with any assurance: the traces are always faint and seldom point unambiguously in a single direction. Some scholars (Marinus de Jonge is a good example) are convinced that no theory built on such slight and slender evidence can be anything more than guesswork.[3] This is a

---

[2] e.g. pp. 159 ('somewhat tenuous . . . far from conclusive'), 237 ('may appear improbable . . . cannot be proved'), 293 (of chapter 8: 'the most tentative in the book').

[3] Notably in *Stranger from Heaven*, p. viii: 'The present author is very skeptical about the possibility of delineating the literary sources in the Fourth Gospel and does not share the optimism displayed by some of his colleagues when they try to

respectable opinion, but it is founded not upon a disagreement concerning principles and methods but upon a different assessment of the nature of the evidence. De Jonge remains one of the finest exponents of the historical critical method that is the butt of modern theoreticians.

What happens when scholars disagree? Sometimes, especially when they are confident of having something fresh and interesting to say, they may plough their own furrow with no more than the occasional sidelong glance at their fellow-workers toiling alongside them. C. H. Dodd, perhaps the most influential British scholar of his generation, generally worked in this fashion. But the majority of scholars do engage with one another's work, and consequently it is hard to see how they can refrain from evaluating it. In doing so, of course, they should not base their assessment simply upon the degree to which earlier scholarship approximates to their own interpretation. They should obviously proceed on the basis of evidence and argument. Here too one simple example will suffice. Some Johannine scholars (the latest, to my knowledge, being Kenneth Grayston) hold that the Letters were composed before the Gospel;[4] others, probably the majority, take the opposite view. However finely balanced the arguments, both sides cannot be right. Reading Grayston, one may be less confident that the writer of the First Letter was commenting, in his exordium, upon the Prologue of the Gospel. But those who disagree with Grayston do so not because his view does not accord with their own but because they evaluate the evidence differently.[5] Were scholars investigating the same texts to stop arguing with one another biblical criticism would look very strange indeed: it would have come to resemble a diners' club whose members meet regularly in one another's homes, cooking delicious meals which they can all

distinguish between sources and redaction.' For further comments on this problem see Chapter 4.

[4] 'Passages in the [First] Epistle often look like first attempts at material which later appears in the Gospel, where its presence can be justified if it began from the situation for which the Epistle was the earlier written response' (*Johannine Epistles*, 14).
[5] The weakness of this suggestion is that the evangelist betrays little of the explicit anti-docetism of the Epistle (esp. 1: 1; 4: 1–3; cf. 2 John 7). But this objection depends on the view that the two authors belong to the same party, a view called into question by Ernst Käsemann ('Ketzer und Zeuge'). Moreover some scholars, notably Udo Schnelle (*Antidoketische Christologie*), detect more anti-docetic elements in the Gospel than I do. The evidence is clearly not compelling enough to allow certainty on one side or the other.

enjoy peacefully together, knowing that there is no likelihood that anyone will make invidious comparisons. But that is not scholarship.

The fact that scholars frequently disagree points to another problem. It may cause some people to wonder whether there is any way of arbitrating between them. For if there is to be arbitration the only person competent to act in this capacity is another scholar, and so the difficulty, far from being resolved, is exacerbated. (The same is true of legal disputes.) Are we therefore to conclude that all three must be allowed to have their say whilst everybody not involved in the debate is condemned to watch helplessly from the sidelines? This would certainly be so if the issues were simply matters of taste or preference, for then there would obviously be no rational way of deciding between them.

Here we must be careful. Most people, I think, would be prepared to admit that opting for one side or the other of a historical debate is not like choosing a hat or admitting to a preference for strawberries over raspberries. Matters of taste such as these are not open to rational argument: they are properly subjective. Historical judgements are of a different order. Most reasonably intelligent people are well aware that they cannot engage in discussions of any kind, on history, politics, or religion, without bringing to them some sort of prior opinion or prejudice. But the generally acknowledged impossibility of 'presuppositionless exegesis' (Bultmann's phrase) should not be taken as an excuse for equating disagreements about serious subjects with statements of taste or preference. To regard the existence of prejudices as a reason for abandoning argument would be like saying that if you have a squint there is no point trying to see straight. Of course we all have prejudices; of course we all have prior interests; of course both our preliminary expectations and our eventual conclusions are going to be coloured by these. But true scholarship must depend upon a readiness to adjust our own views according to the evidence available; and this, unlike an addiction to strawberries, can always be rationally assessed. It is in this sense that historical judgements may be said to differ from personal tastes and preferences in being based on arguments that aim for objectivity. The objectivity I have in mind depends upon the possibility of reaching conclusions concerning the past by weighing up the available evidence in a rational manner: it does *not* involve the claim either that one person's responses and attitudes must be the same as those of everybody else or that historians approach their subject without bias.

Nor does it involve the claim (and this is a further point) that when studying history we can achieve the *kind* of certainty that pertains to the physical sciences. Our certainty that Caesar crossed the Rubicon is different from our certainty that light travels faster than sound because it is based on different kinds of evidence. (There is no room to pursue this point here.) In many cases, moreover, the available evidence may well be too skimpy for *any* certainty, so that any pretence of certainty is ill-founded. But any judgement of this sort is a posteriori, based not on principle but, to repeat, on a reasoned assessment of the evidence.

This brings us to one final point. Because historians draw upon evidence of different kinds, whose reliability may vary, their judgements remain theoretically corrigible and provisional: they are not to be inscribed on stone. Not only must we be ready to confront new evidence, we must also be ready to review existing evidence organized in new ways in the service of fresh proposals. This does not mean that evidence is to be thought of as an assembly of a finite number of smallish building-blocks (data) like pieces of a Lego set; as if, once constructed, it could then be dismantled into constituent uninterpreted parts. Like the testimony of witnesses in, say, a murder trial, the sources or data are themselves always pre-interpreted.[6] (Collingwood, making a similar point in *The Idea of History*, actually uses the word 'testimony'.)[7] And of course the evidence for the prosecution is going to look different from the evidence for the defence. None the less, when the jury reaches its verdict it will have been persuaded by one version of the same testimony given by the same witnesses; and that version may reasonably be described as a particular way of assembling both the 'material' evidence and the sworn testimony of the witnesses. Judgements, both historical and forensic, are generally fallible because one can seldom if ever be sure that new evidence will not turn up to force a reassessment of one's original conclusions. But judgements have to be reached on the basis of what evidence is currently available; and the theoretical possibility that fresh

---

[6] I am indebted for this comparison to an unpublished paper by James Bradley, 'Belief, Reasoning and Interpretation'.

[7] In his Epilegomena, §3: 'Historical Evidence' (249–82).

evidence may come to light does not constitute a reason for supposing that it will.

To conclude, then, if absolute certainty is unobtainable, this does not mean that we should not be striving for ever greater objectivity, any more than we should abandon the search for truth because we know that ultimately truth will always elude us. Lessing's famous option (not truth, but the search for truth) remains as valid today as when he made it. Few, surely, would wish to advise the guild of biblical scholars to refrain altogether from making historical judgements; and fewer still would maintain that one judgement is as good as another. But meaning is a different matter.

2. LITERARY CRITICISM

Where does meaning come from? One currently popular answer to this question is that it comes from the reader, responding to a text that can have no meaning until it is read. This answer, I suggest, rests on two mistakes: first, upon a confusion over the meaning of meaning, and secondly, upon an over-exalted view of the contribution of the reader.

In one sense of the word 'meaning', it might be argued, there is no meaning until there is communication. According to this view an utterance is meaningless until it is heard and a text meaningless until it is read. This is analogous to the view that there is no sound that is not heard and no colour that is not seen, for our conception of a sound is of something heard and the very idea of colour is associated with sight. But this too is mistaken. If it be urged that a tree falling in the forest makes no sound unless it is heard, or that an Alpine plant has no colour until it is seen, the answer is that this is simply wrong. In both cases there are already, in principle, measurable waves; monkeys may have heard the crash of the falling tree; and some intrepid climber may have caught a glimpse of the flower. Perhaps not; but even the unperceived is in principle perceivable. What is more, though every individual perception of sights and sounds may always be subtly different, the source of the perception is none the less determinate in a sense that we can all understand.

Before turning to the question that concerns us here, that of written texts, we may introduce a further analogy, which may help us to see in what sense readers may be held to contribute to the meaning of what they read. This is the analogy of the musical score.[8] Traditionally, musical notations—the 'languages' of musical composition—are devised to determine such matters as melody, rhythm, tempo, and key. Performances may differ widely, but most people will be able to say when a piece is out of tune, and any competent musician will be able to say if and at what points a particular rendering diverges from what the composer has written in other respects also. But if the notation alone is insufficient, and a composer feels obliged to resort to other directives (*piano* or *forte*, *andante* or *allegro*, *accelerando* or *ritardando*), then this puts a limit on the determinacy of the piece in question, and in any case critics will disagree on which 'interpretation' is most faithful to the composer's intentions. But although the notation is not the music and even the most obsessively meticulous composer (Stravinsky?) can never altogether eliminate the possibility of differing interpretations, the room for disagreement will always be limited. If the line between *piano* and *pianissimo* can never be determined with any exactitude, it will still be possible, to take a couple of obvious examples, to distinguish between *piano* and *forte*, *staccato* and *legato*.

One major difference, however, has to be acknowledged between the score and the text. A musical score, as any linguist will be quick to point out, employs a code: written texts, with few exceptions, are composed in one or (occasionally) more *languages*; and a

---

[8] The source of this comparison is Umberto Eco's *Opera Aperta*. Eco's first examples of 'open works' are of aleatory music: named scores of Berio, Boulez, Pousseur, and Stockhausen. A classical composition, says Eco, supposes 'an assembly of sound units which are arranged by the composer in a fixed and finished manner (*in modo definito e conchiuso*) before presenting it to the listener'. He converted his idea into conventional signs which oblige the performer, whoever it may be (*il eventuale esecutore*), to reproduce the music more or less as the composer himself imagined it (*sostanzialmente la forma immaginata dal compositore*). As opposed to this, aleatory compositions have no fixed message but depend upon a whole variety of possibilities left to the discretion of the performer: 'consistono . . . in una possibilità di varie organizzazioni affidata all'initiative dell'interprete' (pp. 26–7). For Eco the paradigm examples of open works in the field of literature are Mallarmé's *Le Livre*, with all its blanks, and Joyce's *Finnegans Wake*, both of them leaving much more to the reader's imagination than any classical, 'closed' writing. Another 'open' work is Jacques Derrida's *Glas*, in which a seemingly rather random series of comments on various texts by Hegel are aligned with, on the opposite page, some equally random comments on Jean Genet. Readers of *Glas* are left to make what sense they may of the conjunction.

code has a greater fixity and determinacy than a language can ever have. To understand a code all one has to do is to decipher it: the comprehension of a language is an altogether more complex affair.

Nevertheless, in the most important sense a written text is determinate in the same way as a musical score. Texts, like scores, can be *read*, and some texts (plays) can be performed also. Until this happens, some will want to say, such texts, like musical scores, are unrealized. (One could also use the example of an algebraic equation, which is similarly determinate, but not 'realized' until values are filled in.) It could also be said that all texts (not just plays) are designed to be read, and that readings, like performances, are bound to differ to some degree. Nevertheless, the extent to which differences are perceived as tolerable will depend on the nature of the text in question. A complex piece of writing like a play or a poem will permit a wider variety of interpretations than a weather report: it will be less determinate.

This is not to say, however, that any play or poem is completely indeterminate, or that it may not be misinterpreted or misread in much the same way that a musician may, whether from wilfulness or incompetence, disregard the instructions of a written score. To take an objectivist view of meaning is simply to maintain that readers of texts, like musicians, can make mistakes; for texts, like musical scores, are predetermined in a way that may permit us to say of one interpretation or another that it is clearly wrong. And while there is always the possibility that authors and composers too may make mistakes, by writing something that they did not intend to write, most texts will reflect the intentions of their authors, and in this sense it is legitimate to say that the meaning of texts is bestowed by their authors.[9] Because written languages, like musical notations, involve conventions that are in principle accessible to non-native speakers, those acquainted with the relevant conventions are able to understand them. Such an 'objectivist' view of meaning, far from being reactionary and outmoded, is surely the only view that is rationally defensible.

At this point it may be objected that the meaning of a text is

[9] This is not to confuse authorial intention with textual meaning, which will generally be determined from context and usage—of words, idioms, genres, etc. Yet if authors have something informative to say about what they meant, why should we not listen to them? On this subject see Eco's lecture, 'Between Author and Text', *Interpretation*, 67–88.

determined by the context in which it is read (Stanley Fish). This is surely wrong. One may concede to Fish that no text has a determinable meaning unless there is a context to allow a determination to be made, but not that the meaning is actually determined by the context (which would be like saying that a composer's music is determined by the circumstances in which it is written and performed). Part of the process of establishing the meaning of any document, ancient or modern, lies in discovering its original context. But this will be different, unavoidably so, from any subsequent context in which the text is read. Fish is no doubt right to assert that arguments concerning meaning must be conducted within what he calls 'interpretive communities' and that the boundaries of these may change. But none of this entails a collapse into what he calls 'a total and debilitating relativism', which, as he says, is unavoidable without 'a shared basis of agreement at once guiding interpretation and providing a mechanism for deciding between interpretations'.[10]

This comment of Fish is interesting, for he is widely and rightly regarded as one of the staunchest champions of the theory that all texts are essentially and ineluctably indeterminate. This position, however, is not for him tantamount to relativism; and he expressly allows for the possibility of rational discussion from within a shared basis of agreement. Where such agreement is lacking, anything goes; and Fish relishes the challenge of inventing wildly improbable sets of conditions that will promote completely outrageous readings of this or that well-known novel or poem: how to read Blake's *Tyger* poem, for instance, as an allegory of the digestive process; or see Mr Collins as the unsung hero of *Pride and Prejudice*.[11]

These examples, I would wish to argue, far from demonstrating the essential indeterminacy of texts, exhibit instead the polymorphous perversity of the human imagination. The fact that ancient texts (and modern texts too, for that matter) are susceptible of an indefinite number of different readings is of no more significance than the fact that you can use a wine crater as a chamber pot. One must, I think, concede to Fish that with sufficient ingenuity it is possible to devise scenarios that are likely

[10] *Is There a Text in This Class?*, 317.
[11] Both examples are drawn from a lecture entitled 'What Makes an Interpretation Acceptable?' (*Text*, 338–53).

to encourage what are prima facie profoundly implausible interpretations of any text one cares to name. But these are marginal cases, and the circumstances in which they have been concocted take them outside the normal framework of exegesis and interpretation.[12] Moreover, as we have seen, Fish himself is far from drawing the relativistic conclusions that one might expect. So even if we accept his arguments we can continue to debate the merits of one interpretation over another.

It may be helpful in conclusion to isolate and summarize a number of very different presuppositions which may lie behind both the disparagement of the critical study of the Bible and the ready support given to alternative approaches. Only rarely are these presuppositions spelled out:

1. All opinions are subjective, which is why people disagree. Arguments may be used to persuade, but ultimately one opinion is as good as another.

2. (Fish). Texts are essentially indeterminate. What meaning they have is bestowed upon them by their readers. These always work from within a particular set of conventions (which may change), and these permit arguments to be conducted with some hope of resolution. In such a context (within a specified interpretive community) one opinion may be adjudged better (or at any rate stronger) than another.

3. It is not always possible to determine the circumstances in which any particular text has been produced. The evidence may be insufficient. In such cases it is best to acknowledge ignorance and refrain from advancing extravagant hypotheses.

4. All texts of any complexity lend themselves to a variety of interpretations and what these will turn out to be can never be predicted in advance.

5. We should interpret all texts, especially the canonical writings of the Bible, in the form in which they have been transmitted, without probing into their prehistory.

6. The newer literary approaches, having now fully established

---

[12] No doubt Fish would have some sardonic comments to make on this use of the word 'normal', and there will always be literary critics who, like some theatrical directors, attach more value in their interpretations to novelty than fidelity. I am thinking of a recent production of *The Marriage of Figaro* at Covent Garden in which the Countess appeared as a drunken slut. Although there is nothing either in the music or in the libretto to justify this portrayal, the fact that the opera was actually performed like this proves that the 'interpretive community' allowed it.

themselves, are rightly assumed to be superior to the traditional methods they have superseded.

It would be wrong to suggest that any of these principles are defended precisely as stated here. Once removed from their protective surroundings, some of them (most obviously the first and the last) look especially vulnerable and exposed. Yet they or their ghosts still hover influentially around. Of the other principles, (4) is a truism, but one which need not be allowed to interfere with attempts to recover the original meaning. There is some problem with (2), which summarizes one side of a debate likely to rumble on for a long time to come; but it too is consonant with traditional exegetical methods; (5) has already been dealt with in Chapter 6. This leaves (3), which must be given due weight. Yet it differs from the rest: it is not an a priori principle but a practical conclusion based on the nature of the texts in question. As such it may indeed affect any decision about how to proceed in individual cases but should not be allowed to inhibit judgement or to banish hypotheses altogether from the realm of history.

When many or all of these propositions are jumbled up, as happens frequently, then the inference is likely to be drawn that the labours of the historian or exegete as traditionally conceived are futile. There is a wonderful image in John Donne's third satire where Truth is pictured as towering above her human devotees, remote yet not totally inaccessible, challenging any brave enough to attempt the climb:

> On a huge hill
> Cragged and steep, Truth stands, and hee that will
> Reach her, about must, and about must goe;
> And what the hills suddennes resists, winne so.

In their own small sphere and modest way scholars have in the past joined philosophers and artists in essaying the ascent, albeit with less confidence than Donne that they will ever reach the summit. Should they abandon the struggle altogether, either in response to the specious arguments of self-appointed theorists or simply out of confusion and muddle, society would be that much poorer. The thought brings sadness, and anger too. Yet confusion is one thing, deliberate destructiveness another. Before turning to this (it goes by the name of deconstruction) one more approach, akin to narrative criticism, requires some discussion.

3. READER-RESPONSE CRITICISM

'Reader-response theories', stresses Anthony C. Thiselton, in a recent compendium of biblical hermeneutics, 'call attention to the active role of communities of readers in constructing what counts for them "what the text means".'[11] The truth is that some do but others do not. Thistleton's description emphasizes the interest of such theories in *application* (meaning for) as opposed to *understanding* (meaning) (a distinction that will be developed in the final section of this chapter); but not all reader-response theorists allow this distinction. Nor do all direct their attention to what Thistleton calls 'communities of readers', as if the members of Christian communities all over the world were deliberately putting their heads together to 'construct' meanings.

Thistleton's use of the present tense ('what counts for them') might give the impression that reader-response theorists are interested in inquiring how Christians in the modern world do in fact respond to the Bible: what they make of it. If this were so, then it would not be hard to find opportunities for individuals or groups to shut themselves up for whatever time they needed to read with due care and attention a passage or text selected for their perusal. Precisely who would be eager to study their findings, and for what purpose, is less clear—certainly not professional exegetes, who make use of analytical tools unavailable to ordinary readers (one difference being that they study the text in the language it was written in). To invite particular groups to respond to something resembling an organized questionnaire is in any case a procedure more suited to sociology than to exegesis.

Perhaps this is why the typical readers envisaged by such theories are not present-day Christians, either old or young; for only professional scholars are likely to have a working knowledge of Hebrew or Greek, and these are certainly not the people reader-response theorists have in mind. (They would be far too likely to come up with unexpected and disconcerting answers.) Willy-nilly, then, they are forced to imagine readers who belong, not to their own world or ours, but to the world of the sacred writers themselves. This being so, the obvious move, one would think, would

---

[11] *New Horizons*, 515.

be to reconstruct as far as possible the situation of the original readers of the text in question, the people the author had in mind as he wrote. That is in fact a traditional ploy of historical critics, who are unlikely to quibble with any suggestion that anyone anxious, for instance, to understand Paul's letters, must enter imaginatively into the world of the Thessalonians, the Corinthians, and all the rest. But there is a difference. Historical critics, as we know, are not actually averse to looking for information about these groups from other sources; whereas for reader-response critics intratextuality is the name of the game. In Chapter 6 we saw how Jeffrey Lloyd Staley refused to allow the 'implied reader' of the Fourth Gospel access to anything except the text of the Gospel itself, and that in doing so he was constructing for himself a surrogate exegete, responding to every hint and inflection of the implied author and grasping, unlike any reader before or since, the total meaning of the text.

One way of injecting a little novelty into the exegetical project is to postulate that the implied reader (the only one, for the moment, that we are concerned with) has only just come across the text of the Gospel, and is reading it *for the first time*. This procedure, however, is both strange and problematic. It is strange because we are dealing *ex hypothesi* with sacred writings, texts that are going to be read again and again, often aloud, by or in the hearing of people who are already familiar with them. So the typical reader, the person one might suppose reader-response theorists to be chiefly interested in, is someone who already knows the text and is continuing to find in it hitherto unexpected riches (very much in the manner of his or her twentieth-century successors). No first-time reader, surely, could be expected to plumb these riches at a sitting; and a moment's reflection should suffice to convince us that this is true of any work of art of any complexity, be it a poem, a painting, or a piece of music. 'Often,' remarks Proust's narrator apropos of Vinteuil's sonata, 'one hears nothing when one listens for the first time to a piece of music that is at all complicated.' On any reasonable projection such a hearer or reader's response is likely to be severely limited (and thus leave the exegete with a lot of work to do).

The problems inherent in this procedure may be seen from a single example, a study of the story of the Samaritan woman specifically intended to illustrate this approach. Lyle Eslinger, attempting to chart 'the course of a reader through the Gospel', presumes, he declares:

to follow a first-time reader, not already well-versed in the story or Christian theology. If one might allow, for a moment, that the gospel of John was not written with a specifically Christian audience in mind, this first-time reader would not be such an implausible intended audience for 'the good news'. Nevertheless, it is possible for even a jaded Christian reader with a modicum of self-awareness to follow the logic of such a reading and to receive a similar impress from it as I am suggesting for the first-time reader.[14]

An astute first-time reader of Eslinger's article might be able to guess at its theme from the title: 'The Wooing of the Woman at the Well'; and Eslinger does in fact argue that the episode acquires most of its force and piquancy by misleading the reader into supposing that the encounter of Jesus and the Samaritan woman will turn out to be a betrothal scene in the manner of similar episodes in the Old Testament, all taking place in the proximity of wells: Eliezer and Rebekah (Genesis 24), Jacob and Rachel (Genesis 29), Moses and Zipporah (Exodus 2). The suggestion is reinforced, continues Eslinger, by a series of *doubles entendres*, all with sexual overtones, which leads the reader to believe 'that both characters are engaging in a bit of covert verbal coquetry'.[15] When, for instance, the woman 'coyly points out that Jesus has no bucket to draw water out of the deep well . . . she is really talking about her own "well" but conceals her lasciviousness under the guise of an innocent reference to Jacob's well'.[16]

Surely no Christian reader, however jaded, would have the remotest suspicion that an encounter between Jesus and any woman, Jew or Samaritan, married or single, would turn out to be

---

[14] 'Wooing of the Woman', 181 n. 16. Introducing his article, which was published in the second issue of a new periodical, *Literature and Theology*, in 1987, Eslinger comments that 'in biblical studies we are beginning to see a shift from historical concerns to those of the New Critics' (p. 167). Extraordinary, when one reflects that in secular literary studies the New Criticism had been out of fashion for the best part of thirty years.

[15] Ibid. 177.

[16] Ibid. 175. Eslinger had shown earlier in his article the extent of what he calls the 'euphemistic' use of words such as $\pi\eta\gamma\acute{\eta}$ and $\kappa\rho\acute{\epsilon}\alpha\rho$ in the LXX, especially Prov. 5: 15–18 and Cant. 4: 12, 15 (pp. 170–1). This justifies his further comment concerning the woman's provocative question: 'she has just "exposed" her "well" by mentioning it, now she wants Jesus to reveal the source of his "living water"' (p. 175).

a seduction scene; still less would he or she reflect concerning Jesus that, in Eslinger's words, 'perhaps all his treasures are not in heaven after all'. This is the world of *Jesus Christ, Superstar*. But Eslinger's non-Christian reader, though no theologian, is far from being an illiterate lout; on the contrary, he is something of a biblical scholar. Here is someone who has read Genesis and Exodus with some care, and on learning that Jesus sat down at Jacob's well at the sixth hour (ὥρα ἦν ὡς ἕκτη), he finds his memory jolted into the reflection that it was still before sundown (ἔτι ἐστὶν ἡμέρα πολλή, Gen. 29: 7) when Jacob saw Rachel approaching the well. It is surely most improbable that anyone with such a combination of ignorance and awareness, archness and insensibility, would have actually stumbled upon John's Gospel and started reading at Chapter 4.

No doubt this is an extreme example. But it well illustrates the methodological difficulties inherent in this type of exegesis. Reader-response theorists do their best to guard their first-time readers from any knowledge that might sully the purity of their responses and prevent them from reacting to the text in the way that they (the theorists) have imagined. But ignorant as they are, they must know *something*, and *what* they know, aside, presumably, from the ability to read Koine Greek, will be prescribed by the theorists who are their only-begetters. It is hard to see this procedure as anything other than aleatory exegesis of the worst kind. Doubtless anyone who reads and engages with a rich and rewarding text of any kind (not just a laundry list or a weather report) will at the same time be searching and probing, filling in the gaps (Iser's term) and drawing upon his or her individual stock of knowledge and experience to *interpret* the text in question. This is something that we all do instinctively for ourselves without being told by imper-tinent critics what our responses should be. Why not face the fact that implied readers, as they are called, are simply doing the exegetes' job for them, but with one hand tied behind their back? Undo the knot and they are transformed into real readers, free to use whatever tools are lying to hand. These are the tools of historical criticism.

4. THE THREAT OF DECONSTRUCTION

The founder father of deconstruction, Jacques Derrida, is first and foremost a philosopher, albeit a philosopher deeply interested in literature. His first published works, in the late 1960s and early 1970s, employed rigorous literary analyses to demonstrate the essential incoherence of what Derrida regarded as key philosophical writings, paradigm cases of the ultimately untenable 'logocentrism' of Western philosophy from Plato right up to Husserl and Heidegger. Derrida is anxious not to be seen to be replacing one metaphysical system with another. His work is critical in the strongest and most negative sense of the word. He writes with extreme care and subtlety, and it is quite hard (though perhaps not impossible)[17] to detect in him the kinds of inconsistency which he loves to expose in others. Yet despite its expressly anti-metaphysical aims his work has a curiously metaphysical ring, because words coined for purely technical purposes, *déconstruction* itself,[18] *archi-écriture* ('primal writing' or *Urschrift*),[19] and the now notorious *différance*[20] have come to be thought of, against his express wishes, as designating *concepts*.

[17] See e.g. Seán Burke, *Death and Return*; John M. Ellis, *Against Deconstruction*.

[18] During a round-table discussion following a lecture on Nietzsche, Derrida revealed in response to a questioner that when he coined the word 'déconstruction' he was thinking of two words (*Destruktion*—destructuration rather than destruction—and *Abbau*) used by Heidegger to suggest the dismantling of an edifice 'to see how it is constituted or deconstituted'. Heidegger had operated an *Abbau* in this sense upon 'the whole of classical ontology, the whole history of Western philosophy'. Derrida insisted nevertheless that he did not see this operation as a negative one, and continued: 'Je ne me sens pas en situation de *choisir* entre une opération disons négative, nihiliste, qui viendrait s'acharner pour démonter des systèmes et l'autre opération. J'aime beaucoup tout ce que je déconstruis à ma manière . . .' (*L'Oreille de l'autre*, 118-19). 'The other operation', presumably, is the theoretical dismantling ascribed to Heidegger. Perhaps Derrida's evasive response entitles us to distinguish between his philosophy and his literary criticism.

[19] The idea of a vast network of primal writing (the English term fails to capture the clever allusion to *architecture*) replaces the key category of experience, as employed by Hjelmslev, which Derrida says can only be used *sous rature* (the Derridean equivalent of very heavy scare-quotes), thus disowning any responsibility for using the term himself. By putting Husserlian brackets round the whole of experience he claims to reveal a transcendental field of experience which, being the condition of every conceivable linguistic system, 'ne peut pas faire partie du système linguistique lui-même' (*De la grammatologie*, 88-9). Is not this metaphysics, only lightly disguised?

[20] As has been repeatedly pointed out, the word combines the two senses of the French word *différer*, to differ and to defer. Derrida himself has defined the word as 'l'opération du différer qui, à la fois, fissure et retarde la présence, la soumettant du

Taken, then, as the metaphysic Derrida did not intend it to be, deconstruction is a kind of purposely emasculated Hegelianism. Hegel's characteristic ploy was to set two contrary ideas off against one another, the negative force arising from this opposition being enough to generate a whole series of further concepts, in a movement to which Hegel gave the general name of *Aufhebung*, a term that combines the ideas of suppression of the opposition and its resumption at a higher level. When two ideas are put together in the deconstructive mode, however, they lie motionless side by side, impotent and inert, deprived of all generative power. Neither the meaning presumably intended by the author whose work is being subjected to this process nor the subversive subtext disclosed by it has any authority on its own. For Hegel's *Aufhebung* Derrida has substituted his own term, *différance*, whose effect is not to generate a new meaning, but to frustrate indefinitely all attempts to assign *any* stable meaning.[21] George Steiner speaks of *différance* as an echo of Hegel's *Aufhebung*;[22] but I think of it more as a shadow, a kind of sinister *Doppelgänger*.

Procedures of this kind soon began to be applied to literary texts, first by Derrida's American epigones, then by the master himself. This, needless to say, was not good news for traditional biblical criticism, even though many of the actual techniques employed by Derrida had long been fruitfully applied to detect aporias and hidden meanings in a variety of biblical texts.[23] Frankly, however,

---

même coup à la division et au délai originaires. La différance est à penser avant la séparation entre le différer comme délai et le différer comme travail actif de la différence' (*La Voix et le phénomène*, 98).

[21] Both the hint of castration and the suggestion that *différance* is intended to replace *Aufhebung* come from Derrida himself. Like Kierkegaard he cannot leave Hegel alone: 'La *différance*—qui n'est donc pas la contradiction dialectique en ce sens hegelian—marque la limite critique des pouvoirs idéalisants de la relève [= *Aufhebung*] partout où ils peuvent, directement ou indirectement, opérer. Elle *inscrit* la contradiction ou plutôt, la différance restant irréductiblement différentiante et disséminante, *les* contradictions' (*La Dissémination*, 12 n. 5). In the same essay (entitled 'Hors Livre') he speaks of the Hegelian dialectic as 'la dialectique phallo-centrique', and of 'la relève' as constituting the 'truth' of logocentrism (p. 56 n. 32). Again, moving beyond dyads and triads, he opts for the figure of the square: 'Bien qu'il ne soit qu'un triangle ouvert en sa face quatrième, le carré écarté desserre l'obsidionalité du triangle et du cercle qui de leur rhythme ternaire (Œdipe, Trinité, Dialectique) ont gouverné la métaphysique.' One reason he likes the square is because it is 'regularly and explicitly' linked with castration (p. 32; cf. pp. 47–8 n. 24)! [22] *Real Presences*, 122.

[23] Ellis argues that the great weakness of deconstruction as a method of literary criticism lies in the fact that instead of searching out a new interpretation it puts all

it brings no joy to the newcomers either: after a round in the ring with deconstruction, narrative and reader-response criticism reel back to their corners looking decidedly groggy.[24]

No one has seen this more clearly or argued it more cogently than Stephen D. Moore. After a masterly analysis of the aims and methods of a variety of literary criticisms, he eventually turns to deconstruction, fully aware that in doing so he is tilting at traditional modes of exegesis as well as at the more recent fashions. With a tentativeness that verges on the apologetic he raises his lance in the direction of some well-known interpreters of the Fourth Gospel ('recklessly no doubt, for I am not a licensed Johannine scholar, much less a licensed deconstructor').[25] Despite his demurrers he is fully conversant with all the evangelist's strategies of irony, and in a brief analysis of the story of the Samaritan woman (very different from that of Eslinger, considered above) he offers a neat summary of the water symbol in the Gospel, with its interplay of literal and figural meanings. But this short section is entitled 'The *Failure* of Johannine Irony' (my italics): the whole *raison d'être* of deconstruction is to subvert the text as it stands, and Moore avows himself 'as interested in what might be out of the control of the Johannine writers at this point as in anything that has traditionally been said to be within their control'.[26] He finds what he is looking for in the flow of water from Jesus' side after his death, arguing that the water here is neither simply literal nor yet fully figural, and that 'two levels of meaning are collapsed that should have been kept apart'.[27]

Whatever we may think of Moore's attempt at deconstructive exegesis (for he is arguably being *too* clever here), it cannot, and is not intended to satisfy his readers' thirst for understanding. There is no living water here, but a brackish substance which is all that deconstructionists have to offer in return. From a sheerly literary point of view Stephen Moore, like many of his predecessors in

the emphasis on debunking the old (*Against Deconstruction*, 80). This is not entirely fair. Performances (and performers) differ greatly.

[24] Such at any rate must be one's conclusion after reading Stephen D. Moore's brilliant analysis of a succession of literary approaches to the Gospels in *Literary Criticism*. Treating deconstruction, as he does, as the last in the line, he exposes the theoretical weaknesses of the rest.

[25] *Literary Criticism*, 159.

[26] Ibid. 162.

[27] Ibid. 163. A note of disapproval has crept in here. But why should not the evangelist manipulate his meanings as he chooses?

the field of secular literature, is capable of verbal feats of great dexterity. But leap and cavort as they will, taking off from the text in a fascinating variety of convoluted turns and twists, the value of their performance, in the last analysis, lies in its capacity to dazzle an admiring audience. What it cannot do without frustrating its own declared ends (and that would be a deconstruction indeed) is to guide them into a fuller understanding of the text itself. Like a brilliant cadenza, it finds a starting-point in the text; but unlike any true cadenza it cannot lead us back into it. Dancing away from the substance, the shadow enjoys a life of its own, but the end is what Moore himself calls 'a kind of cognitive paralysis'.[28]

Dissatisfied, as well he might be, with his dispiritingly negative conclusions, Moore makes some attempt to escape from them by offering to revise his deconstructive reading in a positive sense. John's reader, he claims, who resembles some of his characters (Nicodemus, the Samaritan woman) in being unable to separate the literal from the figural, is simply a forerunner to a second reader, 'able to smile superciliously at the straight man (or dupe), as the dupe once smiled at the Samaritan woman, and able to comprehend the instability of the literal/figural dichotomy, while the dupe reels helplessly in the throes of the reversal'. But this second reader (the ideal reader) is not destined to occupy the throne for long, since another usurper is waiting in the wings, 'the role-player reader-critic that I have become'.[29] Moore betrays his uneasiness by refusing to come down firmly on the side of either of his hypothetical readers. With obvious reluctance he remains sitting on the fence—which is where all true deconstructionists belong.

The term 'deconstruction' is often employed as a shibboleth or a bogy-word with the intention of discouraging the uninitiated from asking too many awkward questions. But the real thing is no bogy; it is rather a demon or a jinnee, and one suspects that few of those who invoke its aid—at any rate from within the ranks of biblical scholarship—are likely to be genuine votaries or prepared to watch its ravages undismayed. A hardy handful may be tough

---

[28] Ibid.
[29] Ibid. 169. In a subsequent article, 'Are there Impurities?', Moore refines and redefines his argument along Lacanian lines, offering a deep psychoanalytical interpretation of the hidden motives of both partners in the dialogue at the well. He aims to show that deconstruction 'can enable us to read against the grain of the biblical authors' intention in ways that affirm women' (p. 215).

enough to look on unruffled as the Word is displaced from the centre and God, along with his fellow-authors, is expelled from his pre-eminent place in the human cosmos. For that is what deconstruction is really about; it is certainly no ally of narrative and reader-response criticism, any more than Nietzsche (to whom Derrida acknowledges some debt) would have been. Much more congenial, to their way of thinking, would be the contemporary movement of committed exegesis that calls into question the distinction, fundamental in earlier hermeneutical theory, between understanding and application.

5. UNDERSTANDING AND APPLICATION

'Our best-laid political theories have been staggered by Nazi Germany.' This is the opening, not of a patriotic tract or diatribe, but of a work of literary criticism, composed during the months of May–June 1941 and published the following year. G. Wilson Knight's *The Chariot of Wrath* has as its subtitle *The Message of John Milton to Democracy at War*, and as its epigraph a sentence from Churchill's speech to the United States Congress in December 1941. It is shot through with what, to one Englishman reading it half a century later, seems an embarrassingly crude nationalism, justified only, if at all, by the appalling dangers that were looming over the United Kingdom at the time it was written. Of continuing interest, however, is Knight's own justification of his project; for he insists upon the relevance to his own times of Milton's prose and poetry.[30] The opposition (which he takes to be eternal) between Satan and Messiah is reflected, he says, in the civil conflict of Milton's own day and 'even more directly [in] our own World War'.[31] Milton's Messiah he sees 'by a somewhat daring equation' as Great Britain[32] and Satan as Nazi Germany:[33] 'Satan's legions attend their leader like hordes of black-uniformed Nazis gathered . . . to hear Hitler speak at Nuremberg. The cries of "Sieg Heil!" thundering heroic resolution have their counterpart in *Paradise Lost*.'[34] Knight even finds the aerial warfare that took place the preceding year to have been anticipated by Milton (*Paradise*

---

[30] Respectively, pp. 22 and 83. There is a good discussion of Knight's work by Stanley Fish, 'Transmuting the Lump', 257-60.

[31] p. 126.   [32] p. 140.   [33] p. 147.   [34] pp. 143-4.

Lost, 2. 533ff.);[35] and suggests that 'Messiah's God-empowered chariot' (derived ultimately from the great vision of the prophet Ezekiel) is 'at once a super-tank and a super-bomber', appearing as it does 'with a rushing sound, like some gigantic, more than human airplane, an almighty thing of blazing and supernal fabrication',[36] and he quotes *Paradise Lost*, 6. 746–76 to prove it.

Knight contends that in refusing to dissociate Milton's project from his own he is guilty of 'no arbitrary act of interpretation',[37] and similar assertions occur throughout his book. Here is his fullest account:

My usual method of neglecting considerations outside the statement of the art-form itself breaks down [in regard to *Paradise Lost*]. That method I pushed as far as might be in *The Burning Oracle*, and its comparative failure argues the necessity of bringing to bear on our interpretation knowledge of Milton's life and work as a whole. Nor does the greatness of the conception, almost too great to be contained and therefore breaking its artistic bounds, stop, properly among the problems of Milton's day: it speaks even more insistently to our own.[38]

Thus Knight combines an explicit renunciation of the tenets of the New Criticism (championed in a book of that name by John Crowe Ransom published about the time he was writing) with a defence of the legitimacy of extending the application of Milton's work, composed in the seventeenth century, to the crisis facing Great Britain in the Second World War.

What may strike a literary critic as the boldest and most unusual feature of Knight's work is a commonplace in biblical criticism,[39] where liberation and feminist theologies and others besides have, in the course of the last couple of decades, carved out for themselves significant niches in faculties of theology and departments of religious studies. In doing so they may be seen, from the perspective of the history of the discipline, to be giving contemporary expression to the second of the two central aims of biblical study: understanding and application.

Some influential voices resist the suggestion that the meaning of an ancient text can be adequately distinguished from its

---

[35] p. 123.   [36] pp. 158–9.   [37] p. 166.   [38] p. 121.

[39] That *Paradise Lost* itself stands directly in the biblical tradition is a far from irrelevant datum, for this is what enables it to assume something of the authority of a sacred text. The example is none the less a useful one, for the canon to which the poem belongs is not biblical but literary.

significance for the present day.[40] But the example of Milton tells
in favour of the distinction. However justified Knight may be
in applying the lessons of *Paradise Lost* to the circumstances of
the Second World War, no one would wish to argue that Milton
had Hitler in mind as he wrote, or that the meaning of the poem
as it emerged from the presses in any of its seventeenth-century
editions included allusions to events that were to transpire nearly
three centuries later. The attempt to recover the original meaning
of the poem (which requires, as Knight reluctantly concedes,
'knowledge of Milton's life and work as a whole') is not the same
as declaring and demonstrating its relevance for the interpreter's
own contemporaries. Any legitimate application must build upon
historical criticism; otherwise it will be nothing more than a
bombastic *ferverino*, what Knight calls 'an arbitrary act of interpretation'; its power to persuade, divorced from any reference to the
original meaning of the text, must reside solely in the rhetorical
skills of the preacher, playing upon the prejudices of audience or
readers.

Just how arbitrariness is to be avoided, and how legitimacy in
interpretation is to be proved are tricky questions of philosophical
hermeneutics. One solution is to deny the theoretical legitimacy of
instituting any comparison between different levels of meaning.
Since my concern in the present book is with understanding rather
than application I may leave these questions to others. Whatever
answers may be given, the old distinction between meaning and
meaning for must be upheld. Feminists and liberationists, and any
whose programme is based on or prompted by current ethical
concerns—whether or not these have a direct biblical input—may
be perfectly entitled to seek for further inspiration and encouragement in the Bible itself. They will have their own agenda and will
usually, no doubt, focus their attention upon texts they think likely
to yield some dividends, by way of inspiration or argument, to the
cause they are eager to promote. But in doing so they should not
pretend that they are attempting to *understand* the biblical text.
Provided that they declare their interest openly, having already

[40] The most determined champion of the distinction between meaning and
significance is E. D. Hirsch, Jr. In his book *Aims* he says he gets it from Husserl
(p. 2), but it is quite close to the old distinction advanced by Ernesti between *facultas intelligendi* and *facultas explicandi*. The most uncompromising opponent of the distinction is Stanley Fish, who says that it comes from Frege (*What Comes Naturally*,
71).

decided what they wish to find in the text (resembling in this respect the majority of Christian readers in the pre-critical era), then they may go their own way without fear of being disturbed by any of the findings of traditional exegesis. The two tracks may be parallel but they will never converge.

If the distinction between understanding and application is ignored[41] and the two tracks are confused, there is the risk, I fear, of a quasi-fundamentalism setting in. The freedom of critical exegesis, rightly lauded by James Barr and recently reaffirmed by John Barton,[42] is, more than anything else, freedom from the shackles of fundamentalism, from the conviction that the true meaning of the text is already given (how?) and that critical exegesis, the product of merely human reasoning, has nothing of importance to add. We must be on our guard against those who would wish, for similar reasons to the old-fashioned fundamentalists, to shoulder aside objective exegesis, either in the mistaken conviction that it is not possible or because it appears to them to have no value. Mark C. Brett has recently suggested that the only alternative to what he calls committed exegesis 'seems to be a retreat into scholarship as pure contemplation [*an ivory tower?*], and such a retreat is probably illusory'.[43] But why should

[41] Richard Rorty, who agrees with Hirsch that we have to distinguish between finding meaning (roughly, how an author would explain his own work) and finding significance (the relation of the text to 'the nature of man, the purpose of life, the politics of our day and so forth'), disagrees with him about the possibility of comparing the two. For Hirsch 'valid criticism [= the discovery of significance] is dependent upon valid interpretation [= the discovery of meaning]' (*Validity*, 162). This Rorty denies, since he regards what he calls the different levels of meaning as self-contained and incommensurate (*Objectivity*, 78–92). It would certainly be hard to find *rules* for discriminating between a good application (discovery of significance) and a bad one.

[42] In his inaugural lecture as Oriel and Laing Professor of the Interpretation of Holy Scripture, entitled *The Future of Old Testament Study*, Barton argues that the crucial term is biblical *criticism*: 'Despite the fact that the term "the historical critical method" has more or less replaced it in many contexts, it is not a method or even a series of methods; nor is it a mode of study which regards history as all-important. It is a particular attitude towards the study of the biblical text, which . . . until recently was widely regarded as normal in most university faculties of theology' (p. 8). He goes on to cite James Barr's suggestion that 'freedom is the central content of the idea of criticism when it is applied to the Bible' (ibid.; cf. J. Barr, *Holy Scripture*, 33).

[43] 'At the very least,' he adds, 'scholarship is often driven by motives like the advancement of a career, and in such cases the ethical choice seems to be between personal advancement and broad emancipatory commitments' ('Reader Criticisms', 27). This remark, which comes at the end of an excellent discussion of a variety of

historical criticism be dismissed as pure contemplation or the decision to practise it be called a retreat, as if it were mainly characterized by a timid reluctance to face up to the challenges of the real world?

6. CONCLUSION

If the foregoing discussion of narrative criticism and its allies has been largely negative, this is not because I see no value in it. No reasonable person could object to a consistent determination to study the stories of the Bible with due regard for the characteristics these share with other stories, however dissimilar. But such study needs to be accompanied by the awareness that, unlike most stories and novels, most biblical narratives, and certainly the gospels, build upon already existing traditions and sources that to a greater or less extent limit as well as stimulate the creative freedom of their authors. It is much to be regretted that the limitations are seldom if ever acknowledged by narrative criticism.

More serious is the neglect, amounting sometimes to disdain, of the well-tried methods of historical criticism.[44] There is no obvious reason why the two approaches should not be combined, and it may be argued that the best practitioners of the historical critical method (the names of Bultmann and Dodd as well as the lesser-known name of Hans Windisch spring to mind) showed a keen sense of the literary qualities of the Fourth Gospel. It would be wrong to maintain that narrative criticism has contributed nothing new to the understanding of the gospels. But honesty compels me to say that in my opinion its contribution has been small, and that like the New Criticism in secular literature, which was lost from view some time in the 1960s, it contains within itself the seeds of its own de(con)struction, and is unlikely to survive beyond the turn of the millennium.

[44] Introducing a collection of narrative-critical studies, Mark Stibbe comments on what he calls the 'loss of historical consciousness' among current literary critics of John: 'First of all, and most obviously, they have rejected historical criticism. Nearly all the books which study the final form of John's Gospel begin with at least some brief and iconoclastic rejection of former, more historical methods' (M. W. G. Stibbe (ed.), *The Gospel of John as Literature*, 1).

BIBLIOGRAPHY

This bibliography is restricted to books or articles cited in the text or notes. Commentaries are generally referred to in the notes by the name of the commentator alone.

COMMENTARIES

BARRETT, C. K., *The Gospel according to St. John*, 2nd edn. (London, 1978).

BAUER, W., *Das Johannesevangelium erklärt*, 3rd edn. (Tübingen, 1933).

BECKER, J., *Das Evangelium des Johannes*, 2 vols. (Gütersloh, 1979/81).

BERNARD, J. H., *The Gospel according to St. John*, 2 vols., ed. A. H. McNeile (Edinburgh, 1928).

BROWN, R. E., *The Gospel according to John*, 2 vols. (New York, 1966/70).

BULTMANN, R., *The Gospel of John* (Oxford, 1971) (= *Das Evangelium des Johannes* (Göttingen, 1941), with the Supplement of 1966).

ELLIS, P. F., *The Genius of John: A Composition-Critical Commentary on the Fourth Gospel* (Collegeville, Minn., 1984).

HAENCHEN, E., *Das Johannesevangelium* (Tübingen, 1980).

HIRSCH, E., *Das vierte Evangelium in seiner ursprünglichen Gestalt verdeutscht und erklärt* (Tübingen, 1936).

LIGHTFOOT, R. H., *St. John's Gospel* (Oxford, 1956).

LINDARS, B., *The Gospel of John* (London, 1972).

LOISY, A., *Le Quatrième Évangile*, 2nd edn. (Paris, 1921).

ODEBERG, H., *The Fourth Gospel: Interpreted in its Relation to Contemporaneous Religious Currents in Palestine and the Hellenistic-Oriental World* (Uppsala, 1929).

SCHNACKENBURG, R., *The Gospel according to St. John*, 3 vols. (London, 1968/80/82).

WELLHAUSEN, J., *Das Evangelium Johannis* (Berlin, 1908).

BOOKS AND ARTICLES

ABERLE, M. VON, 'Über den Zweck des Johannesevangelium', *Theologische Quartalschrift*, 42 (1861), 37-94.

ABRAMS, M. H., *The Mirror and the Lamp* (Oxford, 1953).

ALAND, K., 'Eine Untersuchung zu Joh I 3, 4: Über die Bedeutung eines Punktes', *ZNW* 59 (1968), 174-209.

ARISTOTLE, *The Poetics*, ed. W. H. Fyfe, 2nd edn. (Cambridge, Mass., 1932).

ASHTON, J. 'The Identity and Function of the Ἰουδαῖοι in the Fourth Gospel', *NT* 27 (1985), 40–74.

——'The Transformation of Wisdom: A Study of the Prologue of John's Gospel', *NTS* 27 (1986), 40–75.

——*Understanding the Fourth Gospel* (Oxford, 1991).

——(ed.), *The Interpretation of John* (London, 1986).

ATTRIDGE, H. W., 'Thematic Development and Source Elaboration in John 7: 1–36', *CBQ* 42 (1980), 160–70.

BACON, B. W., *The Fourth Gospel in Research and Debate*, 2nd edn. (New-haven, 1918).

BAKKER, A., 'Christ an Angel?', *ZNW* 32 (1933), 255–65.

BAMMEL, E., '"John did no miracle": John 10: 41', in C. F. D. Moule (ed.), *Miracles: Cambridge Studies in their Philosophy and History* (London, 1965), 175–202.

BARKER, M., *The Older Testament: The Survival of Themes from the Ancient Royal Cult in Sectarian Judaism and Early Christianity* (London, 1987).

BARR, J., *Holy Scripture: Canon, Authority, Criticism* (Oxford, 1983).

BARRETT, C. K., *Essays on John* (London, 1982).

BARTON, J., *The Future of Old Testament Study* (Oxford, 1993).

BAUMGARTNER, W., 'Zum Problem des "Jahwe-Engels"', *Zum Alten Testament und seiner Umwelt* (Leiden, 1959), 240–6.

BECKER, J., 'Das Johannesevangelium im Streit der Methoden (1980–1984)', *TRu.* 51 (1986), 1–78.

BELLE, G. VAN, *De Semeia-Bron in het vierde evangelie: Onstaan en groei van een hypothese* (Leuven, 1975).

BENTON, J., '778: Entering the Date', in D. Hollier (ed.), *A New History of French Literature* (Cambridge, Mass., 1989), 1–6.

BERGER, K., 'Zu "das Wort ward Fleisch": Joh 1, 14a', *NT* 16 (1974), 161–6.

BEUTLER, J., 'Der alttestamentlich-judische Hintergrund der Hirtenrede in Johannes 10', in J. Beutler and R. T. Fortna (eds.), *The Shepherd Discourse*, 18–32.

——and FORTNA, R. T. (eds.), *The Shepherd Discourse of John 10 and its Context* (Cambridge, 1991).

BOER, M. C. DE, 'Narrative Criticism, Historical Criticism, and the Gospel of John', *JSNT* 47 (1992), 35–48.

BOISMARD, M.-É., *Moïse ou Jésus: Essai de christologie johannique* (Louvain, 1988).

BORGEN, P., 'God's Agent in the Fourth Gospel', in J. Ashton (ed.), *The Interpretation of John*, 67–78.

BORNHÄUSER, K., *Das Johannesevangelium: Eine Missionsschrift für Israel* (Gütersloh, 1928).

BOWKER, J. W., 'The Origin and Purpose of St. John's Gospel', *NTS* 11 (1964/5), 398-408.

BRETSCHNEIDER, C. T., *Probabilia de evangelii et epistularum Johannis, apostoli, indole et origine* (Leipzig, 1820).

BRETT, M. G., 'The Future of Reader Criticisms?', in F. Watson (ed.), *The Open Text: New Directions for Biblical Studies* (London, 1993), 13-31.

BROWN, R. E., *The Community of the Beloved Disciple: The Life, Loves and Hates of an Individual Church in New Testament Times* (New York and London, 1979).

——'Johannine Ecclesiology—The Community's Origins', *Int.* 31 (1977), 379-93.

——'"Other Sheep Not of this Fold": The Johannine Perspective on Christian Diversity in the Late First Century', *JBL* (1978), 5-22.

BÜHNER, J.-A., *Der Gesandte und sein Weg im vierten Evangelium: Die kultur- und religionsgeschichtliche Grundlagen der johanneischen Sendungs- christologie sowie ihre traditionsgeschichtliche Entwicklung* (Tübingen, 1977).

BULTMANN, R., 'The History of Religions Background of the Prologue of the Gospel of John', in J. Ashton (ed.), *The Interpretation of John*, 18-35.

BURKE, S., *The Death and Return of the Author: Criticism and Subjectivity in Barthes, Foucault and Derrida* (Edinburgh, 1992).

BURKITT, F. C. (ed.), *Evangelion da-Mepharreshe*, i (Cambridge, 1904).

BUSSE, U., 'Open Questions on John 10', in J. Beutler and R. T. Fortna (eds.), *The Shepherd Discourse*, 6-17.

CARSON, D. A., 'Current Source Criticism of the Fourth Gospel: Some Methodological Questions', *JBL* 97 (1978), 411-29.

CAVE, T., *Recognitions* (Oxford, 1988).

CHARLES, R. H. (ed.), *The Book of Enoch*, 2nd edn. (Oxford, 1912).

CHATMAN, S., *Story and Discourse: Narrative Structure in Fiction and Film* (Ithaca, NY, 1978).

CHIESA, B., and LOCKWOOD, W. (eds.), *Ya'qūb al-Qirqisānī on Jewish Sects and Christianity: A Translation of 'Kitab al-anwar', Book 1, with Two Intro- ductory Essays*, Judentum und Umwelt, 10 (1984).

COGGINS, R. J., *Samaritans and Jews* (Oxford, 1975).

COLLINGWOOD, R. G., *The Idea of History* (Oxford, 1946).

COLPE, C., 'Heidnische, jüdische und christliche Überlieferung in den Schriften aus Nag Hammadi III', *JAC* 17 (1974), 106-26.

COMPTON-BURNETT, I., *The Novelist Today: Contemporary Writers on Modern Fiction*, ed. Malcolm Bradbury, 2nd edn. (London, 1990).

CONZELMANN, H., 'The Mother of Wisdom', in J. M. Robinson (ed.), *The Future of Our Religious Past: Essays in Honour of Rudolf Bultmann* (London, 1971), 230-43.

COPE, L., 'The Earliest Gospel was the "Signs Gospel"', in E. P. Sanders (ed.), *Jesus, the Gospels and the Church: Essays in Honor of William R. Farmer* (Mason, Ga., 1987), 17–24.

COWLEY, A. (ed.), *Aramic Papyri of the 5th Century B. C.* (Oxford, 1923).

CULPEPPER, R. A., *The Anatomy of the Fourth Gospel: A Study in Literary Design* (Philadelphia, 1983).

—— 'The Pivot of John's Prologue', *NTS* 27 (1981), 1–31.

—— and SEGOVIA, F. F. (eds.), *Semeia 53: The Fourth Gospel from a Literary Perspective* (Atlanta, 1991).

CUMING, C. J., '"The Jews" in the Fourth Gospel', *ExpT* 60 (1948/9), 290–2.

DAHL, N. A., 'The Johannine Church and History', in J. Ashton (ed.), *The Interpretation of John*, 122–40.

DAY, J., *God's Conflict with the Dragon and the Sea* (Cambridge, 1985).

DERRIDA, J., *La Dissémination* (Paris, 1972).

—— *De la grammatologie* (Paris, 1967).

—— *L'Oreille de l'autre* (Montreal, 1982).

—— *La Voix et le phénomène* (Paris, 1967).

DODD, C. H., 'The Appearances of the Risen Christ: An Essay in Form-Criticism of the Gospels', in *More NT Studies*, 102–33.

—— 'A Hidden Parable in the Fourth Gospel', in *More NT Studies*, 30–40.

—— *Historical Tradition in the Fourth Gospel* (Cambridge, 1963).

—— *The Interpretation of the Fourth Gospel* (Cambridge, 1953).

—— *More New Testament Studies* (Manchester, 1968).

—— 'The Prologue to the Fourth Gospel and Christian Worship', in F. L. Cross (ed.), *Studies in the Fourth Gospel* (London, 1957), 9–22.

DU RAND, J. A., 'A Syntactical and Narratological Reading of John 10 in Coherence with Chapter 9', in J. Beutler and R. T. Fortna (eds.), *The Shepherd Discourse*, 94–115.

ECKERMANN, J. C. R., *Über die eigentlich sicheren Gründe des Glaubens an die Haupttatsachen der Geschichte Jesu, und über die wahrscheinliche Entstehung der Evangelien und der Apostelgeschichte* (Altona, 1796).

ECO, U., *Interpretation and Overinterpretation* (Cambridge, 1992).

—— *Opera Aperta* (Milan, 1962).

ELLIS, J. M., *Against Deconstruction* (Princeton, NJ, 1989).

ESLINGER, L., 'The Wooing of the Woman at the Well: Jesus, the Reader and Reader-Response Criticism', *Literature and Theology*, 1 (1987), 167–83. Also in M. W. G. Stibbe (ed.), *The Gospel of John as Literature*, 165–82.

FAURE, A., 'Die alttestamentlichen Zitate im viertem Evangelium und die Quellenscheidungshypothese', *ZNW* 21 (1922), 99–121.

FEUILLET, A., 'Prologue du Quatrième Évangile', *DB Sup.* viii (Paris, 1972), 623–88.

FISH, S., *Doing What Comes Naturally: Change, Rhetoric and the Practice of*

Theory in Literary and Legal Studies (Oxford, 1989).

—— *Is There a Text in This Class: The Authority of Interpretive Communities* (Cambridge, Mass. and London, 1989).

—— 'Transmuting the Lump: *Paradise Lost* 1942-1979', *Doing What Comes Naturally*, 247-93.

FORTNA, R. T., 'Christology in the Fourth Gospel: Redaction-Critical Perspectives', *NTS* 21 (1974/5), 489-504.

—— *The Fourth Gospel and its Predecessor: From Narrative Source to Present Gospel* (Edinburgh, 1988).

—— *The Gospel of Signs: A Reconstruction of the Narrative Source Underlying the Fourth Gospel* (Cambridge, 1970).

—— 'Source and Redaction in the Fourth Gospel's Portrayal of Jesus' Signs', *JBL* 89 (1970), 151-66.

FOSSUM, J., 'The Magharians: A Pre-Christian Jewish Sect and its Significance for the Study of Gnosticism and Christianity', *Henoch*, 9 (1987), 303-44.

FREGE, G., 'Über Sinn und Bedeutung', *Zeitschrift für Philosophie und philosophische Kritik*, 100 (1892), 25-50.

FREI, H. W., *The Eclipse of Biblical Narrative: A Study in Eighteenth and Nineteenth Century Hermeneutics* (New Haven, Conn. and London, 1974).

FREYNE, S., *Galilee from Alexander the Great to Hadrian, 323 B.C.E. to 135 C.E.* (Notre Dame, Ind., 1980).

FRYE, H. N., *Anatomy of Criticism* (Princeton, NJ, 1957).

GIBLIN, C. H., 'The Tripartite Narrative Structure of John's Gospel', *Bib.* 71 (1990), 449-67.

GOLB, N., 'Who were the Maġārīya?', *JAOS* 80 (1960), 347-59.

GOLDIN, J., '"Not by Means of an Angel and not by Means of a Messenger"', in J. Neusner (ed.), *Religions in Antiquity: Essays in Memory of E. R. Goodenough* (Leiden, 1968), 412-24.

GRAYSTON, K., *The Johannine Epistles* (London, 1984).

GUILDING, A., *The Fourth Gospel and Jewish Worship* (Oxford, 1960).

HAACKER, K., 'Gottesdienst ohne Gotteserkenntnis. Joh 4, 22 vor dem Hintergrund der jüdisch-samaritanischen Auseinandersetzung', in B. Benzing *et al.* (eds.), *Wort und Wortlichkeit: Fs. E. Rapp*, i (Meisenheim am Glan, 1976), 110-26.

—— *Die Stiftung des Heils: Untersuchungen zur Struktur der johanneischen Christologie* (Stuttgart, 1972).

HARRIS, J. R., 'The Origin of the Prologue to St. John's Gospel', *Exp.* 12 (1916), 147-70; 314-20; 388-400; 415-26.

HARTMAN, L., 'Johannine Jesus-Belief and Monotheism', in L. Hartman and B. Olsson (eds.), *Aspects on the Johannine Literature* (Coniectanea Biblica, NT Series, 18; Uppsala, 1987), 85-99.

HARVEY, A. E., *Jesus on Trial: A Study in the Fourth Gospel* (London, 1976).

HEEKERENS, H.-P., *Die Zeichen-Quelle der johanneischen Redaktion: Ein Beitrag zur Entstehungsgeschichte des vierten Evangeliums* (Stuttgart, 1984).

HEIDEGGER, M., *Being and Time* (Oxford, 1973).

HICKLING, C. J. A., 'Attitudes to Judaism in the Fourth Gospel', in M. de Jonge (ed.), *L'Évangile de Jean* (Leuven, 1977), 347-54.

HIRSCH, E. D., *The Aims of Interpretation* (Chicago and London, 1976).

——*Validity in Interpretation* (Chicago and London, 1977).

HURTADO, L. W., *One God, One Lord* (London, 1988).

INGARDEN, R., *The Cognition of the Literary Work of Art* (Evanston, Ill., 1973).

ISER, W., *The Implied Reader: Patterns of Communication in Prose Fiction from Bunyan to Beckett* (Baltimore and London, 1974).

JONGE, M. DE, *Jesus: Stranger from Heaven and Son of God* (Missoula, Mont., 1977).

——'The Use of the Word "Anointed" in the Time of Jesus', *NT* 8 (1966), 132-48.

KÄSEMANN, E., 'Ketzer und Zeuge: Zum johanneischen Verfasserproblem', *ZTK* 48 (1951), 292-311.

——*New Testament Questions of Today* (London, 1969).

——'The Structure and Purpose of the Prologue to John's Gospel', *NT Questions of Today*, 138-67.

——*The Testament of Jesus: A Study of the Gospel of John in the Light of Chapter 17* (London, 1968) (= *Jesu Letzter Wille nach Johannes 17* (1st edn., Tübingen, 1966; 3rd edn., 1971)).

KNIGHT, G. R. W., *The Chariot of Wrath: The Message of John Milton to Democracy at War* (London, 1942).

KNOX, R., *Absolute and Abitofhell* (London, 1915).

KRAABEL, A. J., 'The Roman Diaspora: Six Questionable Assumptions', *JJS* 33 (1982), 445-64.

KRAFT, E., 'Die Personen des Johannesevangeliums', *EvT* 16 (1956), 18-32.

KRIEGER, M., *A Window to Criticism: Shakespeare's Sonnets and Modern Poetics* (Princeton, NJ, 1964).

KYSAR, R., 'Johannine Metaphor—Meaning and Function: A Literary Case-Study of John 10: 1-8', *Semeia*, 53 (1991), 81-111.

——'The Source Analysis of the Fourth Gospel: A Growing Consensus?', *NT* 15 (1973), 134-52.

LAMARCHE, P., 'The Prologue of John', in J. Ashton (ed.), *The Interpretation of John*, 36-52.

LEROY, H., *Rätsel und Missverständnis: Ein Beitrag zur Formgeschichte des Johannesevangeliums* (Bonn, 1968).

LINDARS, B., *Behind the Fourth Gospel* (London, 1971).

—— *Essays on John* (Louvain, 1992).

—— 'John and the Synoptic Gospels: A Test Case', *NTS* 27 (1980/1), 287-92.

—— 'The Persecution of Christians in John 15: 18-16: 4a', in W. Horbury and B. McNeil (eds.), *Suffering and Martyrdom in the New Testament: Studies presented to G. M. Styler by the Cambridge NT Seminar* (Cambridge, 1981), 48-69.

LOWE, M., 'Ιουδαῖοι of the Apocrypha', *NT* 23 (1981), 56-90.

—— 'Who were the Ιουδαῖοι?', *NT* 18 (1976), 101-30.

MACH, M., *Entwicklungsstadien des jüdischen Engelglaubens in vorrabbinischer Zeit* (Tübingen, 1992).

McKANE, W. (ed.), *Proverbs* (London, 1970).

McNAMARA, M., *Targum and Testament* (Shannon, 1972).

MARTYN, J. L., 'Glimpses into the History of the Johannine Community', *Gospel of John*, 90-121.

—— *The Gospel of John in Christian History* (New York, Ramsay, and Toronto, 1978).

—— *History and Theology in the Fourth Gospel*, 1st edn. (New York, 1968); 2nd edn. (Nashville, 1979).

—— 'Source Criticism and *Religionsgeschichte* in the Fourth Gospel', in J. Ashton (ed.), *The Interpretation of John*, 99-121.

MEEKS, W., '"Am I a Jew?" Johannine Christianity and Judaism', in J. Neusner (ed.), *Christianity, Judaism and Other Greco-Roman Cults: Studies for Morton Smith at Sixty* (Leiden, 1975), 163-86.

—— 'Equal to God', in R. T. Fortna and B. T. Gaventa (eds.), *The Conversation Continues: Studies in Paul and John in Honor of J. Louis Martyn* (Nashville, 1990), 309-22.

—— 'Galilee and Judea in the Fourth Gospel', *JBL* 85 (1966), 159-69.

—— 'The Man from Heaven in Johannine Sectarianism', in J. Ashton (ed.), *The Interpretation of John*, 141-73 (=*JBL* 91 (1972), 44-72).

—— *The Prophet-King: Moses Traditions and the Johannine Christology* (Leiden, 1967).

MLAKUZHYIL, G., *The Christocentric Literary Structure of the Fourth Gospel* (Rome, 1987).

MOORE, S. D., 'Are there Impurities in the Living Water that the Johannine Jesus Dispenses? Deconstruction, Feminism, and the Samaritan Woman', *Biblical Interpretation*, 1 (1993), 207-27.

—— *Literary Criticism and the Gospels: The Theoretical Challenge* (New Haven, Conn. and London, 1989).

MOULTON, J. H., and MILLIGAN, G., *The Vocabulary of the Greek Testament* (London, 1930).

NAVEH, J., and SHAKED, S., *Amulets and Magic Bowls* (Jerusalem and Leiden, 1985).

NEIRYNCK, F., *et al.*, *Jean et les Synoptiques: Examen critique de l'exégèse de M.-E. Boismard* (Leuven, 1979).

NEUSNER, J., GREEN, W. S., and FRERICHS, E. (eds.), *Judaisms and Their Messiahs at the Turn of the Christian Era* (Cambridge, 1987).

NICHOLSON, G. C., *Death as Departure* (Chico, Calif., 1983).

NICOL, W., *The Sēmeia in the Fourth Gospel* (Leiden, 1972).

NORDEN, E., *Agnostos Theos* (Leipzig and Berlin, 1913).

OLSSON, B., *Structure and Meaning in the Fourth Gospel: A Text-Linguistic Analysis of John 2: 1-11 and 4: 1-42* (Lund, 1974).

ØSTENSTAD, G., 'The Structure of the Fourth Gospel: Can it be Defined Objectively?', *ST* 45 (1991), 33-55.

PAINTER, J., *The Quest for the Messiah: The History, Literature and Theology of the Johannine Community* (Edinburgh, 1991).

——'Tradition, History and Interpretation in John 10', in J. Beutler and R. T. Fortna (eds.), *The Shepherd Discourse*, 53-74.

PETERSON, N. R., *Rediscovering Paul* (Philadelphia, 1985).

POLLARD, T. E., 'Cosmology and the Prologue of the Fourth Gospel', *Vig. Chr.* 12 (1958), 147-53.

POTTERIE, I. DE LA, 'Le Bon Pasteur', in H. Cazelles *et al.* (eds.), *Populus Dei: Studi in honore del Cardinale Alfredo Ottaviani per il cinquantesimo del sacerdozio, 18 marzo 1966*, ii. *Ecclesia* (Rome, 1969), 927-68.

——'"Nous adorons, nous, ce que nous connaissons, car le salut vient des Juifs": Histoire de l'exégèse et interprétation de Jn 4, 22', *Bib.* 64 (1983), 74-115.

——*La Vérité dans Saint Jean*, i. *Le Christ et la vérité: L'Esprit et la vérité*; ii. *Le Croyant et la vérité* (Rome, 1977).

POWELL, M. A., *What is Narrative Criticism: A New Approach to the Bible* (London, 1993).

RAD, G. VON, *Wisdom in Israel* (London, 1970).

REIM, G., *Studien zum alttestamentlichen Hintergrund des Johannesevangeliums* (Cambridge, 1974).

RICHTER, G., 'Die Fleischwerdung des Logos im Johannesevangelium', *NT* 13 (1971), 81-126; 14 (1972), 257-76.

RISSI, M. 'Der Aufbau des vierten Evangeliums', *NTS* 29 (1983), 48-53.

——'Die Hochzeit in Kana (Joh 2: 1-11)', in F. Christ (ed.), *Oikonomia: Heilsgeschichte als Thema der Theologie. Oscar Cullman zum 65. Geburtstag gewidmet* (Hamburg and Bergstedt, 1967), 76-92.

ROBINSON, J. A. T., 'The Destination and Purpose of St John's Gospel', *NTS* 6 (1959/60), 117-31.

RORTY, R., 'Texts and Lumps', *Objectivity, Relativism, and Truth* (Cambridge, 1989).

ROWLAND, C., *The Open Heaven* (London, 1982).

SABBE, M., 'John 10 and its Relationship to the Synoptic Gospels', in

J. Beutler and R. T. Fortna (eds.), *The Shepherd Discourse*, 75–93.

SANDAY, W., *The Criticism of the Fourth Gospel* (Oxford, 1905).

SCHÄFER, P., *Rivalität zwischen Engeln und Menschen* (Berlin and New York, 1975).

SCHMITHALS, W., 'Der Prolog des Johannesevangeliums', ZNW 70 (1979), 16–43.

SCHNACKENBURG, R., 'Die Hirtenrede Joh 10, 1–18', *Das Johannesevangelium*, iv. *Ergänzende Auslegungen und Exkurse* (Freiburg im Breisgau, Basle, and Vienna, 1984), 131–43.

—— 'Zur Traditionsgeschichte von Joh 4, 46–54', BZ 8 (1964), 58–88.

SCHNELLE, U., *Antidoketische Christologie im Johannesevangelium: Eine Untersuchung zur Stellung des vierten Evangeliums in der johanneischen Schule* (Göttingen, 1987).

SCHULZ, S., *Untersuchungen zur Menschensohn-Christologie im Johannesevangelium* (Göttingen, 1957).

SCHÜSSLER FIORENZA, E., 'Wisdom Mythology and the Christological Hymns of the New Testament', in R. L. Wilken (ed.), *Aspects of Wisdom in Judaism and Early Christianity* (Notre Dame, Ind., 1975), 17–41.

SCHWARTZ, E., 'Aporien im vierten Evangelium', *Nachrichten vor der Königlichen Gesellschaft der Wissenschaft zu Göttingen: Philologisch-historische Klasse* (1907), 342–72; (1908), 115–48; 149–88; 497–650.

SCHWEIZER, A., *Das Evangelium Johannis nach seinem innern Werthe und seiner Bedeutung für das Leben Jesu kritisch untersucht* (Leipzig, 1841).

SEGAL, A. F., *Two Powers in Heaven* (Leiden, 1977).

SEGOVIA, F. F., 'The Journey(s) of the Word of God: A Reading of the Plot of the Fourth Gospel', *Semeia*, 53 (1991), 23–54.

SIMONIS, A. J., *Die Hirtenrede im Johannes-Evangelium: Versuch einer Analyse von Johannes 10, 1–18 nach Entstehung, Hintergrund und Inhalt* (Rome, 1967).

SKARSAUNE, O., *The Proof from Prophecy: A Study in Justin's Martyr's Proof-Text Tradition* (Leiden, 1987).

SMEND, R. (ed.), *Die Weisheit des Jesus Sirach* (Berlin, 1906).

SPITTA, F., *Das Johannes-Evangelium als Quelle der Geschichte Jesu* (Göttingen, 1910).

—— *Zur Geschichte und Litteratur des Urchristentums*, i (Göttingen, 1893).

STALEY, J. L., *The Print's First Kiss: A Rhetorical Investigation of the Implied Reader in the Fourth Gospel* (Atlanta, 1988).

—— 'Stumbling in the Dark, Reaching for the Light: Reading Character in John 5 and 9', *Semeia*, 53 (1991), 55–80.

STEINER, G., *Real Presences: Is there anything in what we say?* (London, 1989).

STIBBE, M. W. G., 'The Elusive Christ: A New Reading of the Fourth Gospel', JSNT 44 (1991), 19–38.

——(ed.), *The Gospel of John as Literature: An Anthology of Twentieth-Century Perspectives* (Leiden, 1993).

STRACK, H. L., and BILLERBECK, P., *Kommentar zum neuen Testament aus Talmud und Midrasch*, 7th edn., 6 vols. (Munich, 1978).

THISELTON, A. C., *New Horizons in Hermeneutics* (London, 1992).

THOMPSON, J. M., 'Accidental Disarrangement in the Fourth Gospel', *Exp.* 9 (1915), 421–37.

——'The Composition of the Fourth Gospel', *Exp.* 11 (1916), 34–46.

——'Is John xxi. an Appendix?', *Exp.* 10 (1915), 139–47.

——'Some Editorial Elements in the Fourth Gospel', *Exp.* 14 (1917), 214–31.

——'The Structure of the Fourth Gospel', *Exp.* 10 (1915), 512–26.

THYEN, H., '"Das Heil Kommt von den Juden"', in D. Lührmann and G. Strecker (eds.), *Kirche: Festschrift für Günther Bornkamm zum 75. Geburtstag* (Tübingen, 1980), 163–84.

——'Johannes 10 im Kontext des vierten Evangeliums', in J. Beutler and R. T. Fortna (eds.), *The Shepherd Discourse*, 116–34.

TOLBERT, M. A., 'A Response from a Literary Perspective', *Semeia*, 53 (1991), 203–12.

——*Sowing the Gospel: Mark's World in Literary-Historical Perspective* (Minneapolis, 1989).

TOMSON, P. J., 'The Names Israel and Jew in Ancient Judaism and the New Testament', *Bijdragen, tijdschrift voor filosofie en theologie*, 47 (1986), 120–40; 266–89.

TURNER, J. D., 'The history of religions background of John 10', in J. Beutler and R. T. Fortna (eds.), *The Shepherd Discourse*, 33–52.

UNNIK, W. C. VAN, 'The Purpose of St. John's Gospel', *Studia Evangelica*, i (Texte und Untersuchungen, 73; Berlin, 1959), 382–411.

VANCIL, J. W., 'Sheep, Shepherd', *The Anchor Bible Dictionary*, ed. D. N. Freedman *et al.*, v (New York, 1992), 1187–90.

VAWTER, B., 'Prov 8: 22: Wisdom and Creation', *JBL* 99 (1980), 205–16.

VERMES, G., *The Dead Sea Scrolls in English*, 2nd edn. (Harmondsworth, 1975).

WAHLDE, U. C. VON, *The Earliest Version of John's Gospel: Recovering the Gospel of Signs* (Wilmington, Del., 1989).

——'The Johannine "Jews": A Critical Survey', *NTS* 28 (1981/2), 33–60.

——'The Terms for Religious Authorities in the Fourth Gospel: A Key to Literary-Strata?', *JBL* 98 (1979), 231–53.

WEAD, D. W., *The Literary Devices in the Fourth Gospel* (Basle, 1970).

WEISS, H., 'The Sabbath in the Fourth Gospel', *JBL* 110 (1991), 311–21.

WEIZSÄCKER, C. VON, *Untersuchung über die evangelische Geschichte*, 2nd edn. (Tübingen and Leipzig, 1901).

WENDT, H. H., *Die Schichten im vierten Evangelium* (Göttingen, 1911).

WENGST, K., *Bedrängte Gemeinde und verherrlichter Christus: Der historische Ort des Johannesevangeliums als Schlüssel zu seiner Interpretation* (Neukirchen-Vluyn, 1981).

WERNER, M., *Die Entstehung des christlichen Dogmas* (Berne, 1941).

WEVERS, J. W., *Notes on the Greek Text of Exodus* (Atlanta, 1990).

WINDISCH, H., 'Der johanneische Erzählungsstil', in H. Schmidt (ed.), *EYXAPIΣTHPION Festschrift für H. Gunkel*, ii (Göttingen, 1923), 174–213. ET in M. W. G. Stibbe (ed.), *The Gospel of John as Literature*, 25–64.

WOLFSON, H. A., 'The Pre-Existent Angel of the Magharians and Al-Nahāwandī', *JQR* 91 (1960–1), 89–106.

WYLLER, E. A., 'In Solomon's Porch: A Henological Analysis of the Architectonic of the Fourth Gospel', *ST* 42 (1988), 151–67.

INDEX OF BIBLICAL REFERENCES

INDEX OF MODERN AUTHORS

INDEX OF SUBJECTS